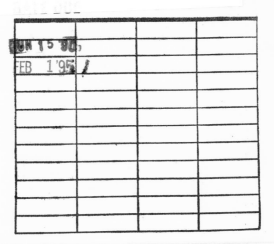

AUG 29 '88

LIVING
BLACK
AMERICAN
AUTHORS

LIVING BLACK AMERICAN AUTHORS

A BIOGRAPHICAL DIRECTORY

Ann Allen Shockley and Sue P. Chandler

R.R. BOWKER COMPANY
New York & London, 1973
A Xerox Education Company

XEROX

Published by R.R. Bowker Co. (A Xerox Education Company)
1180 Avenue of the Americas, New York, N.Y. 10036
Copyright © 1973 by Xerox Corporation
All rights reserved
International Standard Book Number: 0-8352-0662-9
Library of Congress Catalog Card Number 73-17005
Printed and bound in the United States of America

Library of Congress Cataloging in Publication Data
Shockley, Ann Allen.
    Living Black American authors: a biographical
directory.
    1. American literature—Negro authors—Bio-bibliog-
raphy.   2. American literature—20th century—Bio-
bibliography.   I. Chandler, Sue P., 1933-   joint
author.   II. Title.
PS153.N5S5   810′.9′896073   73-17005
ISBN 0-8352-0662-9

Contents

Foreword

When black writers' workshops were held at Fisk University in 1965 and 1966, there assembled a sizeable number of persons. Some were budding writers, others seasoned; some angry, others complacent; some producers, others consumers; some young, others mature, yet all linked by a common bond of deep devotion to the works of the black literary artists. They sat in awe as the new black poets such as Don L. Lee and Sonia Sanchez read their brutally frank and vibrant lines in defiance of "the system" and "the Man." They listened in silence and with a kind of reverence when such forerunners as the late Arna Bontemps, Margaret Walker, and Gwendolyn Brooks spoke to them in that carefully constructed, yet penetrating manner manifested in many of their works.

With the appearance of students from John Oliver Killens' Fisk Writers Workshop, there emerged a powerful, angry, and promising set of young, black, literary revolutionaries such as Nikki Giovanni and the late Donald L. Graham, each of whom has subsequently received acclaim in his or her own right. Each had a story to tell, a battle to fight in his own right and in his own way. Each rode the tides of a sea that is rough for all budding authors, but especially so for blacks.

Some may ask immediately if black writers' conferences are necessary. The answer is emphatically, "Yes." Most black writers belong to a unique fraternal order, comprised of persons who have natural insights into the feelings and experiences of black people. They feel a need to recognize and appreciate their own diverse and independent thought. They also feel a need to determine their role and to assess their impact on American scholarship.

Countless black writers have long believed that interpretation of the black experience must be subjective, as is possible only when it comes from authors who are themselves black. Throughout the history of American literature white authors have attempted to portray black life and character in both fiction and nonfiction. Early writers such as Whittier, Melville, and Longfellow were among the pioneers of this tradition. Late in the nineteenth century, Joel Chandler Harris, Thomas Nelson Page, George Washington Cable, and others continued in this vein. During the twentieth century, exploitation of black folkways and characters by such authors as Lillian Smith, Erskine Caldwell, and Gunnar Myrdal extended this tradition.

The majority of white writers stereotyped the black figures in their writings, reducing them to happy slaves or comic freedmen. Dialect was not uncommon. The American public also saw these stereotyped figures on the screen. It has required half of the present century to erase the traditional stereotyped black figure, while other myths propagated by many white writers, such as the intellectual inferiority of blacks, are yet to be dismissed.

As early as the eighteenth century, however, black poets Phillis Wheatley and Jupiter Hammon caught a vision that was to remain characteristic of many black writers during the next two centuries. In different tones and in a different manner, they reflected an element of race-consciousness so powerful as to significantly enhance the beauty of their poetry. As black writers continued to emerge, some regarded themselves simply as writers, while others insisted on being regarded as black writers, or even as members of particular schools of writers. Many, though not all of these writers, have dealt with black themes, some attempting to erase past stereotypes, others not.

The task of identifying black writers bibliographically is a monumental one. Such publications as *Negro Caravan* by Sterling Brown, *The Negro Author* by Vernon Loggins, and *The Negro Novel in America* by Robert Bone represent earlier, limited attempts at bibliographic identification. More recently, Darwin Turner's *Afro-American Writers,* and Howard University's *Dictionary Catalog of the Arthur B. Spingarn Collection of Negro Authors* have extended these efforts. Together, these publications take inventory of black essayists, poets, novelists, folklorists, and other authors, and their works, affording us an historical perspective of their literary contributions. Attention must be focused also, however, on contemporary black writers, whose intellectual ferment is keenly noticeable.

The nation now has before it a group of persons, linked by accident of birth and often by the themes upon which they write, who are producing a body of literature which is vital to the study of the black aspect of American history and culture. They constitute a new black Renaissance, an era of new vigor, pride, creativity, and self-expression. Their works portray a new independence. Whether these authors are writers of protest, overt or subtle, or have other messages to convey, they must be identified and acknowledged as living contributors to scholarship.

This pioneer work, through its emphasis on the biographical treatment of living authors, adds a new dimension to the range of biographical publications available on the black author in America.

JESSIE CARNEY SMITH
University Librarian
Fisk University

Preface

The paucity of information about living black American authors led to the compilation of this work. Many of our less familiar as well as famous black authors are tragically omitted from standard biographical reference books about contemporary authors. With more books by black writers being published now than ever before, it is of the utmost importance to have a work that will identify these writers and provide information about their backgrounds and work.

There were unique obstacles to the compilation of this book. At the outset, the need was to identify black authors and to locate them. News releases describing the project and requesting black authors to contact us were issued to such leading black publications as *Black World, Black Scholar Sepia,* and to the trade publication, *Publishers Weekly.*

Covering letters and questionnaires were sent to publishers requesting them to forward the questionnaires to their black authors. Several of the publishers did not know if their authors were black or otherwise. It is a known fact that many books written about the black experience have been and are being written by white writers. A few publishers, surmising that books about blacks were by blacks, mistakenly mailed the questionnaires to white authors. The venerable Earl Conrad, who has written prolifically on black and white subjects for almost thirty-five years, and who is of Jewish extraction, was one of those misidentified and forwarded a questionnaire by his publisher. He responded with a very kind letter stating: "I truly wish I could be in a dictionary of black authors."

Some black authors desired inclusion, but left some or all questions unanswered, and simply listed the titles of their publications. Despite the lack of biographical information on these people, they were included for the purpose of recognizing them as black writers.

The word "author," as used in this work, includes those who have written books, who have works in progress, or who have published in anthologies, newspapers, journals, or periodicals. Quite a few of those listed are editors of works, and in the cases where they have stated this, it has been indicated. Authors of plays, television scripts, and filmstrips are included.

Questions for the biographical sketches are keyed: (1) Name and occupation; (2) Place and date of birth; (3) Education; (4) Family; (5) Professional experience;

(6) Memberships; (7) Awards; (8) Publications; (9) Mailing address.

Information about some authors whom we were unable to contact, but who, because of their importance, should definitely be included, was secured through various printed sources. Celebrity authors whose stories were ghost-written or "as told to" are omitted. A limited number of authors, who failed to respond to the questionnaires and could not be located in any sources, are also included, with listings of their works.

The List of Black Publishers following the Biographies section brings together the names and addresses of some of the most active firms specializing in publishing or reprinting the works of black authors. It is hoped that this list will call readers' attention to these sources, many of which are difficult to locate through other sources. The title Index lists alphabetically all books mentioned in the Biographies section, giving for each the author's name, and, when available, the date and place of publication, and the publisher's name although in some cases, not the original publisher of the work.

The book was completed on weekends and at times that could be effectively sandwiched in between, with the assistance of Mrs. Sue P. Chandler, Assistant Librarian, Special Collections and Assistant Professor, Library Science. Clerical assistance was provided through a faculty research grant by Dr. James R. Lawson, President of Fisk University. The encouragement and backing of Dr. Lawson was most gratifying.

Grateful acknowledgment is extended to my former secretary, Mrs. Alice Mason, who painstakingly typed all drafts of the manuscript during her spare off-duty hours. A warm expression of gratitude goes to Miss Clarencetta Jelks, Assistant Archivist for Special Collections, who completed the final draft of the manuscript.

Because of the aforementioned difficulties in locating and identifying living black American authors, this work is not all-inclusive. It is hoped that at a later date, a larger and more comprehensive book will be available. However, this can be done only with the cooperation of the authors themselves.

This compilation is a pioneer venture, and as such, is subject to error. But in the final analysis, it is what is attempted and accomplished that breathes spirit and life into such an effort. We hope this book will serve as a useful reference tool for librarians, researchers, students, scholars, and laymen.

We believe the work is a meaningful and important landmark to those black writers who are making a niche in the publishing world which has neglected black writers for too long. The attainments listed in these entries give testament to an awakening response to black authors and their work.

Writing takes a certain amount of self-confidence and a deep interest and concern for scholarship and humanity. Some say that black writers are no different from white ones. But to be a black writer takes a great deal of guts and spirit, for black writers in America face an inequitable society and the insensitivity of a predominantly white publishing world. The writing of black authors is a response to American society, a vehicle for expression and illumination of the black experience through personal revelations, ideas, thoughts, and reactions.

For those black authors who are currently contributing their talent and scholarship to the field of letters, we dedicate this book as a small monument to their faith in themselves and in the vocation of writing.

ANN ALLEN SHOCKLEY
Associate Librarian,
and Head, Special Collections
Fisk University
Nashville, Tennessee 37203

List of Abbreviations

The abbreviations used in this compilation are arranged in alphabetical order. Conjunctions, prepositions, and the ampersand are ignored.

A.A.—Associate in Arts
AAAS—American Association for the Advancement of Science
AAHPER—American Association for Health, Physical Education, and Recreation
AAU—Association of American Universities; Amateur Athletic Union of the United States
AAUP—American Association of University Professors
AAUW—American Association of University Women
ACLS—American Council of Learned Societies
ACLU—American Civil Liberties Union
ACRL—Association of College and Research Libraries
ACS—American Chemical Society
adminstr.—administrator
adminstrn.—administration
adminstrv.—administrative
adv.—advisory
AETA—American Educational Theatre Association
AFD—Doctor of Fine Arts
AFT—American Federation of Teachers
agr.—agriculture
AKA—Alpha Kappa Alpha
ALA—American Library Association
Am.—American
A & M—Agricultural and Mechanical
A.M.E.—African Methodist Episcopal
AM & N—Agricultural, Mechanical, and Normal
ANP—Associated Negro Press
ASCAP—American Society of Composers, Authors and Publishers

ASHA—American School Health Association; American Social Health Association; American Social Hygiene Association; American Speech and Hearing Association
ASNLH—Association for the Study of Negro Life and History
assn.—association
assoc.—associate
asst.—assistant
A & T—Agricultural and Technical
AUS—Army of the United States
aux.—auxiliary

B.A.—Bachelor of Arts
B.D.—Bachelor of Divinity
B.E.—Bachelor of Education
B.J.—Bachelor of Journalism
bldg.—building
B.Mus.—Bachelor of Music
B.S.—Bachelor of Science
B.S.J.—Bachelor of Science in Journalism
B.S.L.S.—Bachelor of Science-Library Science
B.Th.—Bachelor of Theology
bull.—bulletin

CARE—Cooperative for American Relief Everywhere
CCC—Civil Conservation Corps
CCCC—Conference of College Composition and Communication
chmn.—chairman
Cin.—Cincinnati
CIO—Congress of Industrial Organizations
CLA—College Language Association
Co.—Company
C & O—Chesapeake & Ohio Railway

coll.—college
com.—committee
commn.—commission
commr.—commissioner
conf.—conference
cons.—consultant
coop.—cooperative
CORE—Congress of Racial Equality
corp.—corporation
corr.—correspondent
cpl.—corporal
CTA—California Teachers Association

d.—daughter
D.C.L.—Doctor of Civil Law
D.D.—Doctor of Divinity
D.Ed.—Doctor of Education
dept.—department
dir.—director
dist.—district
div.—division
D.Lit.—Doctor of Literature
Dr.—Drive
D.Sc.—Doctor of Science

ed.—education; educational
Ed.D.—Doctor of Education
Eng.—England
ESEA—Elementary and Secondary Education Act of 1965

fed.—federal
FEPC—Fair Employment Practices Commission

gen.—general
Ger.—Germany
govt.—government

HARYOU—Harlem Youth Opportunities Unlimited
HEW—Health, Education and Welfare
H.H.D.—Doctor of Humanities
hon.—honorary
hosp.—hospital

ICC—Interstate Commerce Commission
inst.—institute
instr.—instructor
internat.—international
Internat. Assn.—International Association
IRA—International Reading Association
is.—island

J.C.D.—Doctor of Civil Law
J.D.—Doctor of Jurisprudence
j.g.—junior grade
jr.—junior

Jur.D.—Doctor of Law

K. of P.—Knights of Pythias

LA—Los Angeles
Lab.—Laboratory
LACC—Los Angeles City College
LAL—Langley Aeronautical Laboratory
lang.—language
lectr.—lecturer, lectureships
L.H.D.—Doctor of Humane Letters; Doctor of Humanities
lib.—library
libn.—librarian
lit.—literature
Litt.D.—Doctor of Letters
Litt.M.—Master of Letters
LL.B.—Bachelor of Laws
LL.D.—Doctor of Laws
LSUNO—Louisiana State University New Orleans
lt.—lieutenant

m.—married, marriage
M.A.—Master of Arts
M.Ed.—Master of Education
M.F.A.—Master of Fine Arts
M.L.A.—Master of Liberal Arts
MLA—Modern Language Association
M.L.S.—Master of Library Science
M.Phil.—Master of Philosophy
M.S.—Master of Science
MSC—Morgan State College
M.S.L.S.—Master of Science-Library Science
MSTA—Maryland State Teachers Association
M.S.W.—Master of Social Work
mus.—music
Mus. B.—Bachelor of Music

NAACP—National Association for the Advancement of Colored People
NACA—National Advisory Committee for Aeronautics
NADSA—National Association of Dramatic and Speech Arts
NAIRO—National Association of Intergroup Relation Official
NAPSAE—National Association for Public School Adult Education
NASA—National Aeronautics and Space Administration
nat.—national
NCCJ—National Conference of Christians and Jews
NCHC—National Collegiate Honors Council
NCJW—National Council of Jewish Women
NCTE—National Council of Teachers of English

NDEA—National Defense Educational Act
NEA—National Educational Association
NNPA—National Newspaper Publishers
Association
NPI—Negro Press International
NSF—National Science Foundation
NYC—New York City
NYS—New York State

OBAC—Organization of Black American
Culture
OEO—Office of Economic Opportunity
OWI—Office of War Information

P.E.N.—Poets, Playwrights, Editors, Essayists and Novelists
Ph.B.—Bachelor of Philosophy
Ph.D.—Doctor of Philosophy
Phila.—Philadelphia
pl.—place
pres.—president
prin.—principal
prof.—professor
PSEA—Pennsylvania State Education
Association
PTA—Parent Teacher Association
pub.—public; publisher; publishing
publ.—publication (s)
PUSH—People United to Save Humanity

QM—quartermaster

RCA—Radio Corporation of America
rep.—representative
ret.—retired

SAA—Society of American Archivists
schs.—schools

SCLC—Southern Christian Leadership
Conference
sec.—secretary
SEEK—Search for Education, Elevation and
Knowledge
sgt.—sergeant
SNCC—Student Nonviolent Coordinating
Committee
soc.—society
sociol.—sociological
spl.—special
S.T.D.—Doctor of Sacred Theology
S.T.M.—Master of Sacred Theology
S.U.N.Y.—State University of New York
supr.—supervisor, supervisory
supt.—superintendent

tchr.—teacher
tech.—technical, technology
Th.D.—Doctor of Theology
treas.—treasurer

U.A.W.—United Automobile, Aerospace
and Agricultural Implement Workers
of America
UN—United Nations
USAID—United States Agency for Internat-
ional Development
USIA—United States Information Agency
USIS—United States Information Service

VEA—Virginia Education Association
vis.—visiting
VISTA—Volunteers in Service to America
v.p—vice president

YMCA—Young Men's Christian Association
YWCA—Young Women's Christian
Association

Biographies

ADAMS, RUSSELL, Educator
Born: Baltimore, Md., August 13, 1930.
Education: B.A., Morehouse Coll., 1948-52; M.A., Univ. of
    Chicago, 1952-58; Ph.D., ibid., 1956-58.
Family: m. Eleanor McCurine; children, Sabrina Vanessa,
    Russell Lowell.
Professional Experience: Research dir., American Negro
    Emancipation Centennial Authority, 1961-63; asst. prof.,
    North Carolina Coll., 1965-69; assoc. prof., Federal City
    Coll., 1969-71; chmn., Afro-American Studies Dept.,
    Howard Univ., 1971-.
Memberships: Am. Pol. Science Assn.; Am. Historical Soc.;
    NAACP.
Awards: Education Board Awardee; Dovella Mills Foundation
    Grantee; Danforth Assn.
Publications: Contributed to journals. Editor, Great Negroes
    Past and Present, 1963, 1964, 1970.
Mailing Address: Afro-American Studies Dept., Howard Uni-
    versity, Washington, D.C. 20001.

ADDISON, LLOYD
Publications: The Aura and the Umbra, 1970.

AKHNATON, ASKIA, see ECKELS, JON

ALHAMISI, AHMED AKINWOLE
Publications: Editor, Black Arts: An Anthology of Black
    Creations (with Harum Kofi Wangara), 1969; Guerilla
    Warfare, 1970; Holy Ghosts, 1972.

ALLEN, JAMES EGERT, Educator
Born: Greenwood, S.C., Oct. 11, 1896.
Education: A.B., Johnson C. Smith Univ., 1912-16; A.M.,
    New York Univ., 1945-50; Oxford Univ., 1953; Ed.D.,
    New York Univ., 1952-54.

Family: m. Ethel Starke.
Professional Experience: Tchr., Presbyterian Academy, Ark.,
    1916-17; tchr., Brainerd Inst., Chester, S.C., 1917-18;
    head, Academic Dept., Okoloma Inst., Okoloma, Miss.,
    1919-22; fed. postal service, 1922-25; tchr. and ed. coor-
    dinator, N.Y., 1926-67; assoc. editor, Kappa Alpha Psi
    Journal, 1937-67.
Memberships: Phi Delta Kappa; Kappa Alpha Psi; NAACP.
Awards: International Dictionary of Biography (London) Certifi-
    cate of Merit; Man of the Year, YMCA, N.Y.
Publications: Contributed to journals. Author, The Negro in
    New York, 1964.
Mailing Address: 16 St. Nicholas Pl., New York, N.Y. 10031.

ALLEN, ROBERT L., Educator
Born: Atlanta, Ga., May 29, 1942.
Education: B.S., Morehouse Coll., 1958-63; Univ. of Vienna,
    1961-62; Columbia Univ., 1963-64; M.A., New School for
    Social Research, 1965-67.
Family: m. Pamela.
Professional Experience: Caseworker, welfare dept., N.Y.C.,
    1964-65; reporter, National Guardian, 1967-69; assoc.
    prof., San Jose State Coll., 1969-.
Memberships: Am. Sociol. Assn.; Bay Area Black Journalists.
Awards: Merrill Travel-Study Grant, 1961-62; Woodrow Wil-
    son Fellowship, 1963-64.
Publications: Contributed to journals. Author, Black Awaken-
    ing in Capitalist America, 1969.
Mailing Address: 327 Pestana Ave., South Cruz, Calif. 95060.

ALLEN, SAMUEL (Paul Vesey), Poet, Attorney
Born: Columbus, Ohio, 1917.
Education: A.B., Fisk Univ., 1938; J.D., Harvard Law School;
    New School for Social Research; Sorbonne, Paris.
Professional Experience: General practice and service as
    Deputy Asst. Dist. Attorney, N.Y.C.; assoc. prof. law,
    Tex. Southern Univ.; attorney, U.S. govt.; Chief Counsel,
    Community Relations Service; poet-in-residence, Tuske-
    gee Inst., Feb.-Mar. 1968; Avalon Professor (Endowed
    Chair for Creative Work in Arts), Tuskegee Inst., 1968-
    70; vis. poet, Annapolis Fine Arts Festival, Annapolis,
    Md., June 1968; vis. prof. English, Wesleyan Univ., Sept.
    1970 - Jan. 1971; prof. English, African and Afro-Ameri-
    can Lit., 1971-; lectr., including Virginia State Coll.,
    American Univ., Northwestern Univ., Antioch Coll.,
    Shrine of Black Madonna; cons., scholastic magazine on
    development of black lit. anthologies for Los Angeles
    Unified Sch. Dist.; editorial bd., Afro-American Studies,
    Brooklyn Coll., N.Y.; advisory com., "Black Orpheus,"
    Lagos, Nigeria.

Publications: Contributed book reviews and articles to numerous journals and poetry to over fifty anthologies in America and abroad; translator, Orphée Noir by Jean Paul Sartre, Présence Africaine, 1960. Author (Paul Vesey) Elfenbein Zähne (Ivory Tusks), a bilingual volume of poetry, Heidelberg, Ger., 1956; Ivory Tusks and Other Poems, 1968; co-editor, Pan Africanism Reconsidered, 1962; Poems from Africa, 1972.
Mailing Address: English Dept., Boston University, Boston, Mass. 02215.

AMAN, MOHAMMED M., Educator, Librarian
Born: Cairo, Egypt, January 3, 1940.
Education: B.A., Cairo Univ., Egypt; M.S., Columbia Univ.; Ph.D., Univ. of Pittsburgh.
Family: m. Mary Jo.
Professional Experience: Reference libn. and bibliographer, National Library, Cairo, Egypt, 1961-63; cataloger (part-time), Inst. of Higher Management, Cairo, Egypt, 1961-62; head libn., Arab Information Center, N.Y.C., 1964-65; researcher, Knowledge Availability System Center, Univ. of Pittsburgh, 1965-66; reference and govt. documents libn., Duquesne Univ. Lib., Pittsburgh, 1966-68; evening libn., Alleghany Community Coll. Lib., Pittsburgh, 1967-68; asst. prof. lib. sci., St. John's Univ., 1969-71; assoc. prof. lib. sci., St. John's Univ., 1971-; cons., Child Welfare League of America; internat. correspondent, International Library Reviews, London and New York; Advisory Board, St. John's Univ. Centennial Congress for Librarians.
Publications: Contributed to books and professional journals.
Author, A Guide to African Reference Books (in press).
Mailing Address: 104-17 192 St., Hollis, N.Y. 11412.

AMINI, JOHARI, see LATIMORE, JEWEL

AMIS, LOLA ELIZABETH JONES, Educator
Born: Norfolk, Va., Feb. 26, 1930.
Education: B.S., Hampton Inst., 1950; Univ. of Rhode Island, 1958; Univ. of Maryland, 1965; M.L.A., Johns Hopkins Univ., 1967.
Family: Children, Brenda Cheryl, Regina Dorise, Sharon Denise.
Professional Experience: Tchr. English, Norfolk City Pub. High Schs., 1954-62; Charlottesville Pub. High Schs., 1962-63; Baltimore Pub. High Schs., 1963-67; asst. prof. English, Morgan State Coll. and Community Coll. of Baltimore, 1967-.
Memberships: AFT; MSTA; CLA.

Awards: Arena Players Citation in Drama, 1967.
Publications: Three Plays, 1965.
Mailing Address: 1578 Pentwood Rd., Baltimore, Md. 21212.

ANDERSON, ODIE, Broker
Born: Chicago, Ill., Oct. 25, 1943.
Education: A.A., DePaul Univ., 1964-66; B.A., ibid., 1966-70;
    J.D., ibid., 1970.
Family: m. Regina Elizabeth; children, April Lucinda, Casimir,
    Courtenay, Odie, Jr.
Professional Experience: Broker, Williams and Associates,
    1967-.
Memberships: Urban League; Council on Foreign Relations;
    World Federalist Organization; Pi Gamma Mu; vice
    pres., Phi Rho Pi.
Awards: Forty-three public speaking awards; twenty-five sale
    achievement awards.
Publications: Trial of God, 1970.
Mailing Address: 3550 South Rhodes, Chicago, Ill. 60653.

ANDERSON, WILLIAM A., Educator
Born: Akron, Ohio, May 28, 1927.
Education: B.A., Univ. of Akron, 1956-60; M.A., Kent State
    Univ., 1960-61; Ph.D., Ohio State Univ., 1962-66.
Family: m. Norma.
Professional Experience: Instr., Kent State Univ., 1961-62; re-
    search assoc., Ohio State Univ., 1962-69; assoc. prof.,
    Arizona State Univ., 1969-.
Memberships: Am. Sociol. Assn.; Alpha Kappa Delta; Alpha Phi
    Alpha; Pi Gamma Mu.
Awards: Fellow, Univ. of Akron, 1957; Ohio State Univ., 1963.
Publications: Contributed to journals. Author, Disaster and
    Organizational Changes, 1969.
Mailing Address: 322 West LaGuna Dr., Tempe, Ariz. 85281.

ANGELOU, MAYA, Author
Born: St. Louis, Mo., April 4, 1928.
Education: George Washington High Sch., 1945; studied music
    seven years, dance with Martha Graham, Pearl Primus,
    Ann Halprin, and drama with Frank Silvera, Gene Frankel.
Family: s. Guy Johnson.
Professional Experience: Assoc. editor, Arab Observer,
    Cairo, Egypt, 1962-63; free-lance writer, Ghanaian
    Times, Accra, Ghana, 1963-65; free-lance writer, Ghana-
    ian Broadcasting Corporation, Accra, Ghana, 1963-65;
    asst. adminstr., Inst. of African Studies, Sch. of Music
    and Drama, Univ. of Ghana, Legon-Accra, Ghana, 1963-
    65; feature editor, African Review, Accra, Ghana, 1965-

66; professional performer on stage and screen for fifteen years, appearing in such productions as Porgy and Bess European Tour Company (sponsored by the U.S. Dept. of State), 1954-55, film, 1958; Calypso Heatwave, 1957; Cabaret for Freedom, 1960; The Blacks, 1961-64; lectr., Univ. of California, fall, 1966.
Publications: Contributed to journals. Author, plays, The Best of These, 1966; The Clawing Within, 1966-67; Adjoa Amissah, 1967; screenplay, Georgia, Georgia, 1972; book, I Know Why the Caged Bird Sings,1969.
Mailing Address: Random House, 201 East 15 St., New York, N.Y. 10022.

ANTHONY, EARL
Publications: Picking up the Gun, 1970; Time of the Furnaces: A Case Study of Black Student Revolt, 1971; editor, Black Poets and Prophets (with Woodie King).

ARKHURST, JOYCE COOPER, Librarian
Born: Seattle, Wash., Oct. 20, 1921.
Education: B.A., Univ. of Washington, 1940-44; Columbia Univ. Lib. Sch., 1948-49.
Family: m. Frederick; d., Cecile Nanaba.
Professional Experience: Libn. I., N.Y. Pub. Lib., 1949-56; libn., New Lincoln Sch., N.Y., 1957-58; childrens' libn. and community coordinator, Chicago Pub. Lib., 1968-70; developed program of new Childrens' Neighborhood Center.
Memberships: Delta Sigma Theta; Nat. Urban League Guild; Jack and Jill of Am.
Publications: The Adventures of Spider, 1964.
Mailing Address: 2500 Johnson Ave., Riverdale, N.Y. 10463.

ARNEZ, NANCY L.
Publications: The Rocks Cry Out, 1968.

ATKINS, RUSSELL, Author, Composer, Editor
Born: Cleveland, Ohio, Feb. 25, 1926.
Education: Cleveland Sch. of Art; Cleveland Music Sch. Settlement; Cleveland Inst. of Music, 1945.
Professional Experience: Publicity manager and asst. dir., The Sutphen Sch. of Music, (Nat. Guild of Community Music Schools), 1957-60; cons., writers workshops and conferences, including Opportunities Industrialization Center, Muntu Poets Workshop, Free Lance Poets Workshop, Karamu Poetry Workshop, Cosmep. Writer's Conf., Calif., Karamu Writers Conf., Cleveland, WIVZ-TV, Cleveland;

editor and founder, Free Lance magazine, Cleveland,
1950; lectr., readings, including Ohio Writers Conf.,
Cleveland State Univ., Western Reserve Univ. "Poets-
in-the Schools," Cleveland Summer Arts Festival, 1968;
works presented by Langston Hughes on radio; Marianne
Moore, WEVD, "The World of Books," N.Y.C., 1951;
musical works include pieces for piano, cello, violin;
composition, "The Theory of Psychovisualism" intro-
duced with music, Darmstadt Festival of Avant-Garde
Music, Germany, 1956, by Stefan Wolpe; performances
of chamber work by Cleveland Orchestra; collaborated
with Robert Shaw and the Kulas Choir on "In Memoriam."
Memberships: Poet Lecturers' Alliance; Poetry Seminar,
WCLV; Ohio Poets Assn.; Com. of Small Magazines,
Editors and Pubs., Calif., N.Y.; Coordinating Council of
Literary Magazines, Nat. Endowment for the Arts; Am.
Biographical Inst.
Publications: Contributed poetry to magazines and numerous
anthologies. Author, Phenomena, 1961; Objects, 1963;
Objects 2, 1963; Heretofore, 1968; Presentations, 1969;
Psychovisualism, 1956, 1958; The Nail and Maefictum,
1971.
Mailing Address: Free Lance, 6005 Grand Ave., Cleveland,
Ohio 44104.

ATTAWAY, WILLIAM
Publications: Let Me Breathe Thunder, 1939; Blood on the
Forge, 1941; Calypso Song Book, 1957.

AUSTIN, LETTIE J. (Mrs. Lewis H. Fenderson), Educator
Born: Joplin, Mo., March 21, 1925.
Education: B.A., Lincoln Univ., 1946; M.A., Kansas State Univ.,
1947; M.A., Univ. of Nottingham, 1954; M.S., Howard
Univ., 1963; Ed.D., Stanford Univ., 1952.
Professional Experience: New York Univ., 1949-50; instr.,
Howard Univ., 1947-50; vis. lectr. Am. lit., Univ. of
Maryland overseas program, 1952-53; asst. prof. Eng-
lish, Howard Univ., 1954-57; assoc. dir., Inst. for Tchrs.
of English, Tex. Southern Univ., summer sessions, 1961-
64; cons., diagnostic test committee, 1955-56; dir., read-
ing program, Howard Univ., 1954; curriculum prepara-
tion specialist, Educational Services, Inc., Watertown,
Mass., 1964-65; assoc. prof. English, Howard Univ.,
1958-67; asst. dir., NDEA Inst. Tchrs. of English, Tex.
Southern Univ., summers 1965-66; reader, Educational
Testing Service, Princeton, N.J., 1966-; prof. English,
Howard Univ., 1968-.
Awards: Fulbright recipient, 1952-54.

Publications: Contributed to journals. Author, College Reading Skills, 1966; The Black Man and the Promise of America (with L. H. Fenderson and S. P. Nelson), 1970.
Mailing Address: Box 920, Howard University, Washington, D.C. 20001.

BAILEY, PEARL MAE, Singer
Born: Newport News, Va., Mar. 19, 1918.
Education: William Penn High Sch., Philadelphia, Pa.
Family: 2nd m. Louis Bellson; children, Tony, DeeDee.
Professional Experience: Singer, 1933-; stage debut, St. Louis Woman, N.Y.C., 1946; actress, House of Flowers, Broadway musical; night club singer; guest, TV programs; "Pearl Bailey Show."
Awards: Donaldson award, 1936; Spl. Tony Award, Hello Dolly, 1967-68.
Publications: Raw Pearl, 1968; Talking to Myself, 1971; Pearl's Kitchen, 1973.
Mailing Address: Box 52, Northridge, Calif. 91324.

BAILEY, RONALD W.
Publications: Editor, Black Business Enterprise: Historical and Contemporary Perspectives, 1971.

BAKER, AUGUSTA, Librarian
Born: Baltimore, Md., April 1, 1911.
Education: A.B., State Univ. of N.Y., 1933; B.S., ibid., Library Science, 1934.
Family: m. Gordon Alexander; s. James III.
Professional Experience: Public libn., 1937-53; asst. coordinator, children's services and storytelling specialist, 1953-61; lectr., Columbia Univ., Sch. of Library Service, 1956-; Rutgers Univ., Graduate Library Sch., 1963-67; guest lectr. and workshop dir., including Syracuse Univ., Univ. of Southern Nevada; founder, James Weldon Johnson Memorial Collection of children's books about Negro life, Countee Cullen Regional Branch, N.Y. Pub. Lib., 1941; organizer, lib. work with children, Trinidad Pub. Lib., Trinidad, B.W.I., 1953.
Memberships: ALA: councillor, 1965-68, bd. of dir., Childrens' Services Division, 1967-68, exec. bd., 1968-72; chmn., Newbery-Caldecott Awards Com., 1966; N.Y. Lib. Assn.; N.Y. Lib. Club; Delta Sigma Theta; Women's Nat. Bk. Assn.
Awards: First Dutton-Macrae Award for advanced study in the field of library work with children, 1953; Parents' Magazine Medal for outstanding service to the nation's children, 1966; ALA Grolier Award for outstanding achieve-

ment in guiding and stimulating the reading of children and young people, 1968; Constance Lindsay Skinner Award, Women's Nat. Bk. Assn., 1971.
Publications: Contributed numerous articles to professional magazines and press. Author, The Talking Tree, 1955; The Golden Lynx, 1960; The Black Experience in Children's Books, 1971; editor-in-chief, Young Years: Anthology of Children's Literature, 1960; editor, Once Upon a Time, 1964; editor, Recordings for Children, 1964.
Mailing Address: 115-33 174 St., St. Albans, N.Y. 11434.

BAKER, HOUSTON A., JR., Educator
Born: Louisville, Ky., March 22, 1943.
Education: B.A., Howard Univ., 1961-65; M.A., Univ. of Calif., Los Angeles, 1965-67; Univ. of Edinburgh, 1967-68; Ph.D., Univ. of Calif., Los Angeles, 1968.
Family: m. Charlotte P.
Professional Experience: Instr., summer school, Howard Univ.; instr. English, Yale Univ., 1968-69; asst. prof. English, Yale Univ., 1969; assoc. prof., Dept. of English, Univ. of Virginia, 1970-.
Memberships: MLA; Phi Beta Kappa; Kappa Delta Pi.
Awards: John Hay Whitney Fellow, 1965-66; NDEA Fellow, Univ. of Calif., Los Angeles.
Publications: Contributed to journals and anthologies. Author, Long Black Song: Essays in Black Literature and Culture, 1972; Twentieth Century Interpretations of Native Son, 1972.
Mailing Address: Dept. of English, University of Virginia, Charlottesville, Va. 22901.

BALDWIN, JAMES, Author
Born: New York, N.Y., Aug. 2, 1924.
Education: DeWitt Clinton High Sch., N.Y.C.; D.Litt. (hon.), Univ. of British Columbia, 1963.
Professional Experience: Nonliterary jobs, 1942-45; moved to Paris, 1948-56; active in civil rights movement, U.S.A.
Awards: Saxton Fellow, 1945; Rosenwald Fellow, 1948; Guggenheim Fellow, 1954; Partison Review Fellow, 1956; Nat. Inst. of Arts and Letters, 1956.
Publications: Fiction: Go Tell It on the Mountain, 1953; Giovanni's Room, 1956; Another Country, 1962; Going to Meet the Man, 1965; Tell Me How Long the Train's Been Gone, 1968; essays: Notes of a Native Son, 1955; The Fire Next Time, 1963; Nothing Personal (with Richard Avedon), 1964; plays: The Amen Corner, 1955; Blues for Mr. Charlie, 1964; nonfiction: A Rap on Race (with Margaret Mead), 1971; No Name in the Street, 1972; A Dialogue (with Nikki Giovanni), 1972.
Mailing Address: 137 West 71 St., New York, N.Y. 10023.

BAMBARA, TONI CADE, Educator, Author
Born: New York, N.Y.
Education: B.A., Queens Coll., 1959; M.A., City Coll. of N.Y.,
1963.
Professional Experience: Community organizer, health and
youth worker, 1959-61; free-lance writer, 1961; dir. psy-
chiatry, Metropolitan Hospital Recreation, 1961; program
dir., Settlement Houses, Brooklyn, Manhattan, Bronx,
N.Y., 1961-65; tchr., City Coll., Rutgers Univ., 1965-.
Publications: The Black Woman, 1970; Tales and Short Stories
for Black Folks, 1971; Gorilla, My Love, 1972; Junior
Casebook on Racism, 1973.
Mailing Address: 232 East 124 St., New York, N.Y. 10035.

BARAKA, IMAMU AMIRI (LeRoi Jones), Author
Born: Newark, N.J., Oct. 7, 1934.
Education: Rutgers Univ., 1951-52; B.A., Howard Univ., 1952-
54.
Family: m. Amina (Sylvia Jones); children, 2nd m., Ras Jua
Al Aziz, Obalaji Malik Ali, Asia, Maisha; 1st m., Lisa,
Kellie.
Professional Experience: U.S. Air Force; editor, Yugen maga-
zine; founder, Black Arts Repertory Theater Sch., Har-
lem, N.Y., 1964; founder, Spirit House Movers and
Spirit House Theater, Newark, N.J.
Memberships: Committee for Unified Newark to bring black
self-determination to the city.
Awards: Whitney Fellowship, 1962-63; Obie Award, best play,
1964; Guggenheim Fellowship, 1965-66.
Publications: Numerous plays and books; latest include System
of Dante's Hell, 1965; Tales, 1967; Black Music, 1967;
Black Magic Poetry, 1969; Four Black Revolutionary
Plays, 1969; Poem for Black Hearts, 1970.
Mailing Address: 33 Stirling St., Newark, N.J. 07103.

BARBOUR, FLOYD
Publications: Compiler, Black Power Revolt: A Collection of
Essays, 1968; editor, Black Seventies, 1970.

BARKSDALE, RICHARD K., Educator
Born: Winchester, Mass., Oct. 31, 1915.
Education: A.B., Bowdin Coll., 1937; A.M., Syracuse Univ.,
1938; A.M., Howard Univ., 1947; Ph.D., Harvard Univ.,
1951; L.H.D. (hon.), Bowdin Coll., 1972.
Family: m. Mildred W.; children, Adrienne, James, Richard,
Calvin.
Professional Experience: Instr. English, Southern Univ., 1938-
39; chmn., Dept. of English, Tougaloo Coll., 1939-42; 2d
lt., FA, AUS, 1943-46; prof. English, 1949-53; dean of

graduate sch., North Carolina Central Univ., 1953-58; chmn., dept. of English, Morehouse Coll., 1958-62; prof. English,1962-67; dean of the graduate sch., Atlanta Univ., 1967-71; prof. English, 1971; dir., English Undergraduate Studies, dept. of English, Univ. of Illinois at Urbana-Champaign, Sept. 1972-; cons., National Endowment for the Humanities, Ford Foundation, Office of Education, Academic Administrn. for TACTICS.
Memberships: Bd. of dir., NCTE; vice pres., CLA; adminstrv. bd., Nat. Fellowships Fund for Black Americans, Atlanta, Ga.
Awards: Outstanding Educator of America, 1971.
Publications: Contributed articles to journals, anthologies, and a short story to Phylon. Edited Black Writers of America: A Comprehensive Anthology (with Kenneth Kinnamon), 1972; A Bibliographical Handbook on the Life and Literary Career of Langston Hughes (in process).
Mailing Address: University of Illinois at Champaign-Urbana, 100 English Building, Urbana, Ill. 61801.

BARRAX, GERALD WILLIAM, Educator
Born: Attalla, Ala., June 21, 1933.
Education: B.A., Duquesne Univ., 1959-63; M.A., Univ. of Pittsburgh, 1967-69.
Family: Children, Dennis Scott, Gerald William, Joshua Cameron.
Professional Experience: A/1c, U.S. Air Force, 1953-57; clerk and carrier, U.S. Post Office, 1958-67; instr., North Carolina Central Univ., 1969-70; special instr., N.C. State Univ., 1970-.
Publications: Poetry in anthologies. Author, Another Kind of Rain, 1970.
Mailing Address: 1813-B Gorman St., Raleigh, N.C. 27606.

BATES, DAISEY
Publications: Long Shadow of Little Rock, A Memoir, 1962.

BAXTER, ZENOBIA L., Educator
Born: Shelbyville, Tenn., Feb. 27, 1907.
Education: Mus.B., Chicago Coll. Music; M.A., Northwestern Univ.; Ph.B., Univ. of Chicago.
Family: s. Frank L. IV.
Professional Experience: Cons., pupil personnel, Chicago Bd. of Ed., 1962; ed. lectr., Loyola Univ., 1966-; 1st Negro tchr., piano, organ, harmony, Chicago Coll. of Music.
Memberships: Delta Kappa Gamma Internat. Honor Soc.; NAACP; Chicago Personnel and Guidance Assn.; Am. Personnel and Guidance Assn.; Ladies Aux. Fraternal Order of Police.

Awards: 1st prize Nat. Song Writing Contest; 2nd pl. Univ. of
Chicago Song Writing Contest; Phi Beta Sigma Nat. Frat.
Achievement Award, 1961; Woman of the Year Achieve-
ment Award; Nat. Assn. College Women, 1967; Woman of
the Year, Lola M. Parker Achievement Award, Iota Phi
Lambda Internat. Sorority, 1968.
Publications: Your Life in a Big City, 1967; Teachers Manual
for Your Life in a Big City, 1967.
Mailing Address: 5922 South King Dr., Chicago, Ill. 60637.

BAYTON, JAMES A., Educator
Born: Whitestone, Va., April 5, 1912.
Education: B.S., Howard Univ., 1931-35; M.S., ibid., 1935-36;
Ph.D., Univ. of Pennsylvania, 1938-43.
Family: m. Daisy A.
Professional Experience: Assoc. prof., Virginia State Coll.,
1939-43; social science analyst, U.S. Dept. of Agr., 1943-
45, 1948-54; assoc. prof., Southern Univ., 1945-46; assoc.
prof., Morgan State Coll., 1946-47; vice pres., Nat. Ana-
lysts, Inc., Phila., Pa., 1954-61; vice pres., Universal
Marketing Research, Inc., N.Y.C., 1962-65; Senior Fel-
low, Brookings Inst., 1966-67; prof., Howard Univ.,
1947-.
Memberships: Am. Psychological Assn.
Awards: Phi Beta Kappa.
Publications: Tension in the Cities, 1968.
Mailing Address: 5908 11 St., N.W., Washington, D.C. 20001.

BEASLEY, EDWARD, JR., Educator
Born: Omaha, Neb., June 3, 1932.
Education: B.A., Lincoln Univ., 1950-55; Univ. of Omaha, 1955-
56; Univ. of Kansas, 1960; M.A., Kansas State Coll.,
1963-64; certificate, NDEA Inst. on Black History, Spel-
man Coll., summer 1966.
Family: m. Bessie; children, Deborah, Edward, Delores,
Donna.
Professional Experience: 2nd lt., U.S. Army Reserves, 1952-
62; tchr. Am. history, Kansas City, Kans., 1956-68;
instr. history, Black Metropolitan Jr. Coll., Kansas
City, Mo., 1968-; chmn., Black Studies Com., Univ. of
Missouri.
Memberships: Pres., Social Studies Council, Kansas City,
Kans., 1968-69; NEA.
Awards: Village United Presbyterian Church $10,000 grant to
initiate a vocational and cultural program for the inner-
city community.
Publications: Professional articles and television script based
on KMBC's "The Negro in America."
Mailing Address: 4826 Sortor Dr., Kansas City, Kans. 66104.

BECK, ROBERT (Iceberg Slim)
Publications: Pimp: Story of My Life, 1968; Mama Black
    Widow, 1970; Naked Soul of Iceberg Slim, 1971; Trick
    Baby, 1971.

BECKHAM, BARRY EARL, Urban affairs associate
Born: Philadelphia, Pa., March 19, 1944.
Education: A.B., Brown Univ., 1962-66.
Family: m. Betty Louise Hope; children, Brian Elliott, Bonnie
    Lorine.
Professional Experience: Asst. editor, Chase Manhattan Bank,
    1966-67; pub. relations assoc., Western Electric Co.,
    1968-69; pub. relations assoc., Nat. Council YMCAs,
    Sept. 1967 - May 1968; urban affairs assoc., Chase Man-
    hattan Bank, 1969-70; vis. lectr., Brown Univ., 1970-.
Memberships: Exec. board, P.E.N. Am. Center; Author's
    Guild.
Publications: Contributed to magazines and newspapers.
    Author, My Main Mother.
Mailing Address: 22 Irving Ave., Providence, R.I. 02906.

BENNETT, GWENDOLYN B., Poet
Born: Giddings, Tex., 1902.
Education: Columbia Univ.; Pratt Institute; Académie Julian
    and Ecole du Panthéon, Paris, France.
Professional Experience: Instr. art, Howard Univ.; editorial
    staff, Opportunity magazine.
Publications: Poems including Heritage, Hatred, and Sonnets.

BENNETT, HAL, Author
Born: Buckingham, Va., April 21, 1930.
Professional Experience: Fiction editor, Afro-American news-
    paper, 1953-55.
Publications: A Wilderness of Vines, 1966; The Black Wine,
    1968; Lord of Dark Places, 1970.
Mailing address: Owen Laster, William Morris Agency, Inc.,
    1350 Ave. of the Americas, New York, N.Y. 10019.

BENNETT, LERONE, JR., Author, Historian
Born: Clarksdale, Miss., Oct. 17, 1928.
Education: B.A., Morehouse Coll., 1949; D. Litt. (hon.), More-
    house Coll., 1966.
Family: m. Gloria Sylvester; children, Alma Joy, Constance,
    Courtney, Lerone III.
Professional Experience: Reporter, Atlanta Daily World, 1949-
    51; city editor, Atlanta Daily World, 1952-53; assoc.
    editor, Ebony magazine, 1953-58; senior editor, Ebony

magazine, 1958-; vis. prof. history, Northwestern Univ.,
1969-71; chmn., Dept. of African-American Studies,
Northwestern Univ., Evanston, Ill., 1972-.
Memberships: Kappa Alpha Psi; bd. of dir., Parkway Com-
munity House.
Awards: Patron Saints Soc.; Midland Authors, 1965; Book of
the Year, Capital Press Club, 1963.
Publications: Contributed numerous articles to journals and
periodicals. Author, Before the Mayflower, 1962; The
Negro Mood, 1964; What Manner of Man, 1964; Confron-
tation: Black and White, 1965; Black Power U.S.A., 1968;
Pioneers in Protest, 1968; The Challenge of Blackness,
1972.
Mailing Address: 820 South Michigan Ave., Chicago, Ill. 60605.

BERKLEY, CONSTANCE E., Poet
Born: Washington, D.C., Nov. 12, 1931.
Education: Dunbar High Sch., 1946-49; Howard Univ., 1949-51;
Columbia Univ., 1968-71.
Family: m. Louis; children, Robert Clifford, Richard Andrew,
David A. (stepson).
Professional Experience: Prior to 1957: legal stenographer,
secretary, asst. pharmacist, buyer of electronic equip-
ment, jr. accountant; contributing editor, American
Dialog.
Memberships: Harlem Writers' Guild; Negro Ensemble Play-
wrights Group; Women's Strike for Peace; Cultural Com.
for CORE; Local Democratic Reform clubs; Nat. Council
Am. Soviet Friendship; PTA.
Publications: Poems included in People in Poetry: Poems by
Blacks; Freedomways; Penumbra; Black Sun.
Mailing Address: 19 Maple St., Brooklyn, N.Y. 11225.

BILLINGSLEY, ANDREW, Educator
Born: Marion, Ala., Mar. 20, 1926.
Education: A.B., Grinnell Coll., 1951; M.S., Boston Univ. Sch.
of Social Work, 1956; M.A., Univ. of Michigan, 1960;
Ph.D., Florence Heller Grad. Sch. for Advanced Studies
in Social Welfare, Brandeis Univ., 1964.
Family: m. Amy Loretta Tate; children, Angela Eleanor,
Bonita Rebecca.
Professional Experience: Personnel sergeant, AUS, Quarter-
master Corps, 1944-46; dir., Youth Services Projects,
Am. Friends Service Com., Chicago Regional Office,
1951-54; psychiatric social worker, Wisconsin Dept. of
Pub. Welfare, Mendota State Hospital, 1956-58; social
worker and research asst., Mass. Soc. for the Prevention
of Cruelty to Children, 1960-63; asst. dean of students,
1964-65, asst. prof., assoc. prof. social welfare,

1964-70, asst. chancellor, academic affairs, 1968-70,
Univ. of Calif., Berkeley; vice pres., academic affairs,
Howard Univ., Washington, D. C., 1970-; internat.
work camp, Ortona, Italy, summer 1949; dir., community
service project, Am. Friends Service Com., summer
1958; dir., Friends Internat. Student Center, Univ. of
Mich., 1959-60; cons., Nat. Urban League, N.Y.C., 1968;
editorial bd., The Black Scholar and Afro-American
Studies.
Memberships: Including Inst. of the Black World; Am. Sociol.
Assn.; Nat. Assn. of Social Workers; Nat. Assn. of Black
Social Workers; adv. com., Secretary of Health, Educa-
tion and Welfare on Health Protection and Disease Pre-
vention; bd. of dirs., Council on Social Work Ed.; Race
Relations Information Center; Nat. Assn. of Black Child
Development; adv. com., Family and Individual Services,
Nat. Urban League; Publications Adv. Com., Child Wel-
fare League of Am.
Awards: Biannual Nat. Assn. of Social Workers Research
Award for major research contribution of social work
knowledge, 1964; Univ. of Calif. Faculty Fellowship,
summer 1966; fellow, Metropolitan Applied Research
Center, N.Y.C., 1968; research grants, Children's
Bureau, U.S. Dept. HEW, for research on child welfare,
1966-70; Michael Schwerner Memorial Award, N.Y.C.,
1969.
Publications: Contributed numerous articles to books and
journals. Author, Black Families in White America,
1968; Children of the Storm (with Jeanne Giovannoni),
1972.
Mailing Address: Howard University, Washington, D.C. 20001.

BLACKWELL, DAVID, Educator, Statistician
Born: Centralia, Ill., Apr. 24, 1919.
Education: A.B., Univ. of Illinois, 1938; A.M., ibid., 1939; Ph.D.
ibid., 1941; D.Sc., ibid., 1966.
Family: m. Ann Madison; children, Ann, Julia, David, Ruth,
Grover, Vera, Hugo, Sara.
Professional Experience: Instr. mathematics, Southern Univ.,
1942-43; instr. mathematics, Clark Coll., 1943-44; asst.
prof., prof. mathematics, Howard Univ., 1944-54; prof.
statistics, Univ. of Calif., Berkeley, 1954-; fellow, Inst.
Math. Statistics, pres. 1955.
Memberships: Am. Math Soc.; Am. Statis. Assn.
Publications: Theory of Games and Statistical Decisions (with
M. A. Girshick), 1954; Basic Statistics, 1969.
Mailing Address: Basic Books, 404 Park Ave. S., New York,
N.Y. 10016.

BLASSINGAME, JOHN W., Educator, Author
Born: Covington, Ga., Mar. 23, 1940.
Education: B.A., Fort Valley State Coll., 1960; M.A., Howard
    Univ., 1961; M. Phil., Yale Univ., 1968; Ph.D., ibid, 1971.
Family: m. Teasie; children, John, Tia.
Professional Experience: Instr., Howard Univ., 1961-65;
    assoc., curriculum project in Am. History, Carnegie
    Mellon Univ., 1965-70; asst. editor, Booker T. Washing-
    ton Papers; lectr., Univ. of Maryland 1968-69; lectr.,
    1970-71, asst. prof. history 1971-, acting chmn. Afro-Am.
    Studies, Yale Univ., 1971-72; contributing editor, Black
    Scholar, 1971; editorial bd., Journal of Negro History,
    1973-; editorial bd., Reviews in Am. History, 1973;
    adv. bd., Afro-Am. Bicentennial Corp., 1971-; bd.,
    Centre Internationale de Recherches Africaines, 1971-.
Memberships: Assn. of Behavioral and Social Sciences; ASNLH;
    Southern Historical Assn.; advisory bd., Am. Historical
    Assn.
Awards: Howard Faculty Research Grant, 1963; Esso Faculty
    Fellowship, 1965; Ford Faculty Fellowship, 1969; Yale
    Univ. Study of the City Grant, 1970; National Endowment
    for the Humanities Fellowship, 1972-73.
Publications: Contributed numerous articles and book reviews
    to journals. Author, The Slave Community, 1972; Sambos
    and Rebels: The Character of the Southern Slave, 1972;
    Black New Orleans, 1860-1880 (in press); editor, New
    Perspectives on Black Studies, 1971; In Search of Amer-
    ica (with David Fowler, Eugene Levy, Jacqueline Hay-
    wood), 1972; The Autobiographical Writings of Booker
    T. Washington (with Louis Harlan), 1972.
Mailing Address: Dept. of History, Yale University, New Haven,
    Conn. 06520.

BODDIE, CHARLES E., Clergyman
Born: New Rochelle, N.Y., June 13, 1911.
Education: B.A., Syracuse Univ., 1933; M.A., Univ. of Roch-
    ester, 1949; B.D., Colgate Rochester Divinity Sch., 1936;
    D.D. (hon.), Keuka Coll., 1951.
Family: 2nd m. Mabel Bell Crooks; children, 1st m., Wilma,
    Richard; stepdaughters, Camara, Shauree.
Professional Experience: Theologue and asst. pastor, Mt.
    Olivet Baptist Church, Rochester, N.Y.; pastor, Monu-
    mental Baptist Church, Elmira, N.Y.; pastor, First
    Baptist Church, Huntington, W.Va.; missionary, personnel
    dept., Am. Baptist Foreign Mission Societies, 1956; in-
    spected Am. Baptist Mission stations for the Am. Baptist
    Convention on a world-wide tour, Sept. 21, 1961-Feb. 6,
    1962; spl. minister, Southern Baptist Convention Foreign
    Mission Soc. to preach in Africa, 1970; pres., Am.
    Baptist Coll. of the Bible and Am. Baptist Seminary,

Nashville, Tenn., Oct. 1, 1963-; lectr., including Coll.
chapel speaker, Bucknell Univ., and conferences at
Chautauqua, Iowa Falls, Lakeside, Williams Bay.
Memberships: Including Am. Guild of Organists; Omega Psi
Phi; Bd. of Ed. and Publication Bd., Am. Baptist Conven-
tion, eight yrs.; Internat. Platform Assn.
Award: Man of the Week, Huntington, W.Va.; Man of the Year,
Rochester, N.Y.
Publications: Contributed to journals. Author, Giant in the
Earth, 1944; God's Bad Boys, 1972.
Mailing Address: Box 8063, Nashville, Tenn. 37207.

BOGGS, JAMES, Author
Born: Marion Junction, Ala., May 28, 1919.
Education: Dunbar H. Sch., Bessmer, Ala., 1937.
Family: m. Grace Lee; children, six.
Professional Experience: Field hand, Washington; ice cutter,
Minnesota; WPA worker, Detroit; auto worker, Detroit,
1941-68.
Publications: The American Revolution: Pages from a Negro
Worker's Notebook, 1963; Racism and the Class Struggle:
Further Pages from a Black Worker's Notebook, 1970.
Mailing Address: 3061 Field St., Detroit, Mich. 48214.

BOLES, ROBERT
Publications: The People One Knows, 1964; Curling, 1968.

BOND, JULIAN, Legislator, Civil rights leader
Born: Nashville, Tenn., Jan. 14, 1940.
Education: B.A., Morehouse Coll., 1971; LL.D. (hon.), Dal-
housie Univ., 1969; LL.D. (hon.), Univ. Bridgeport, 1969;
LL.D. (hon.), Wesleyan Univ., Conn., 1969; LL.D. (hon.),
Univ. of Oregon, 1969; LL.D. (hon.), Syracuse Univ.,
1970; LL.D. (hon.), Eastern Mich. Univ., 1971; LL.D.
(hon.), Tuskegee Inst., 1971; LL.D. (hon.), Howard Univ.,
1971; LL.D. (hon.), Morgan State Univ., 1971; LL.D.
(hon.), Wilberforce Univ., 1971; D.C.L., Lincoln Univ.,
1970.
Family: m. Alice Louise Clopton; children, Phyllis Jane,
Horace Mann, Michael Jeffrey, Julia.
Professional Experience: Reporter, feature writer, Atlanta
Inquirer, 1960-61; managing editor, ibid., 1963; repre-
sentative, Georgia House of Representatives, 1965-;
Memberships: Bd. dir., Southern Conference Ed. Fund; Robert
F. Kennedy Memorial Fund; Southern Regional Council,
Highlander Research and Ed. Center; Nat. Sharecroppers
Fund; Southern Elections Fund; Delta Ministry project,
Nat. Council Churches; Voter Ed. Project; New Demo-
cratic Coalition; NAACP.

Publications: A Time to Speak, A Time to Act: The Movement
in Politics, 1972.
Mailing Address: 361 Westview Dr., S.W., Atlanta, Ga. 30310.

BOOKER, SIMEON SAUNDERS, Journalist
Born: Baltimore, Md., Aug. 27, 1918.
Education: A.B., Virginia Union Univ., 1942; Cleveland Coll.;
Harvard Univ.
Family: m. Thelma Cunningham; children, Theresa, Simeon,
James.
Professional Experience: Chief, Washington Bureau, Johnson
Publications.
Awards: Nieman Fellow, 1950-51.
Publications: Black Man's America, 1964.
Mailing Address: Johnson Publishing Co., 1750 Pennsylvania
Ave., N.W., Washington, D.C.

BOULWARE, MARCUS HANNA, Educator
Born: Chester, S.C., May 17, 1907.
Education: A.B., Johnson C. Smith Univ., 1927-31; M.A., Univ.
of Mich., 1935-36; Ph.D., Univ. of Wisconsin, 1945-51;
post-doctoral studies, Wayne State Univ., summer 1953;
Indiana Univ., summer 1962; Florida State Univ., 1963-
67.
Family: m. Bernice Allen; children, Marcus H., Jr., Marguerite, Philomena (Althea) Martin, James Musco (deceased).
Professional Experience: Instr. English, Prairie View Coll.,
1937-38; instr. English, AM & N Coll., Pine Bluff, Ark.,
1938-39; instr. English, Alabama State Coll., 1939-44;
instr. English, Albany State Coll., 1952-53; instr. English, St. Augustine's Coll., 1953-59; dir., speech and
hearing program, Florida A & M Univ., summers 1960-67;
coordinator, training program in speech, pathology and
audiology, Tenn. State Univ., 1967-68; dept. of speech,
Florida A & M Univ., 1960-.
Memberships: Am. Speech and Hearing Assn.; Florida Speech
and Hearing Assn.; Speech Assn. of Am.; Kappa Alpha
Psi.
Awards: Scholarships in ed. of exceptional children from
Audiology Foundation, Elks Foundation, and Florida Cere-
bral Palsy, Inc.
Publications: Contributed twelve articles on speech and nine
on snoring to professional journals. Author, The Riddle
of Snoring, 1969; The Oratory of Negro Leaders: 1900-
1968.
Mailing Address: Box 310-A, Florida A & M University,
Tallahassee, Fla. 32307.

BRACEY, JOHN H., JR., Lecturer
Born: Chicago, Ill., July 17, 1941.
Education: B.A., Roosevelt Univ., 1966-69.
Family: m. Jessica Swain.
Professional Experience: Mail clerk, U.S.A. Signal Engineer-
ing Agency, 1960-61; interviewer and cons., Inst. for Soc.
Research, Univ. of Mich.,1965; research asst., Chicago
Urban League, 1967-68; lectr. history, Northeastern Ill.
State Coll., spring 1969; lectr. Afro-Am. history,
Northern Ill. Univ., 1969-; Editorial Selection Com.,
Bobbs-Merrill Black Studies Reprints, 1969-.
Memberships: Phi Alpha Theta, Roosevelt Univ. chapter; Am.
Historical Assn.; Organization of Am. Historians; Assn.
for the Study of Negro Life and History; Southern Histori-
cal Assn.
Awards: NDEA fellowship in history, Northwestern Univ.
Publications: Black Nationalism in America (with August
Meier and Elliott Rudwick), 1969; The Afro-American:
Selected Documents (with August Meier and Elliott Rud-
wick), 1970.
Mailing Address: 1116 Foster Ave., Evanston, Ill. 60201.

BRADFORD, WALTER
Publications: T.C. Terry Callier, True Christian.

BRANCH, WILLIAM B., Author, Producer, Director
Born: New Haven, Conn., Sept. 11, 1929.
Education: B.S., Northwestern Univ., 1945-49; M.F.A., Colum-
bia Univ., 1956-58; resident fellow, Yale Univ., 1965-66.
Family: d. Rochelle Ellen.
Professional Experience: Free-lance writer, producer, direc-
tor, 1950-; staff producer-writer, Educational Broadcast-
ing Corp.,channel 13, N.Y.C., 1962-64; dir., "The Jackie
Robinson Show," NBC, 1959; writer, dir., "The Alma
John Show, " 1963-65; assoc. in film, Columbia Univ.
Sch. of Arts, 1968-69; vis. playwright, Smith Coll.,
Northhampton, Mass., summer 1970; North Carolina
Central Univ., Durham, N.C., spring 1971; ed. instr., U.S.
Army, Nuremburg, Ger., 1951-53; actor, theatre, films,
radio and television, 1946-55; field rep., Ebony magazine,
1949-50; producer, NBC-TV, N.Y.C.; lectr., including
Harvard, Univ. of Ghana, Fisk, UCLA.
Awards: John Simon Guggenheim Fellowship, 1959-60; Yale
Univ., ABC Fellowship, 1965-66; Am. Film Festival
Blue Ribbon Award for Still a Brother: Inside the Negro
Middle Class, 1969; Robert E. Sherwood Television
Award for NBC television drama, Light in the Southern
Sky; Nat. Academy of Television Arts and Sciences
Emmy award nomination for Still a Brother: Inside the
Negro Middle Class, 1969.

Publications: Contributed to newspapers and anthologies.
Plays produced include A Medal for Willie, off-Broadway,
Oct. 1951-Jan. 1952; In Splendid Error, Greenwich Mews
Theatre, N.Y.C., Oct. 1954-Jan. 1955; A Wreath for
Udomo, Lyric Hammersmith Theater, London, Nov. 1961.
Published plays: In Splendid Error, included in Black
Theatre, 1970; A Medal for Willie, in Black Drama An-
thology, 1971.
Mailing Address: 53 Cortlandt Ave., New Rochelle, N.Y. 10801.

BRAZIER, ARTHUR M.
Publications: Black Self-Determination: The Story of the
Woodlawn Organization, 1969.

BREWER, JOHN MASON, Author, Folklorist
Born: Goliad, Tex., Mar. 24, 1896.
Education: A.B., Wiley College, 1917; M.A., Indiana Univ., 1950;
D. Litt.
Family: m. Mae Thornton Hickman; 2nd m. Ruth Helen Brush;
s., 1st m., John Mason, Jr.
Professional Experience: Prof. English, Livingston Coll.,
Salisbury, N.C., 1959-69; A & T Univ. of North Carolina,
Greensboro; vis. prof. anthropology, 1967-69; distin-
guished vis. prof. English, 1969-, East Texas State Univ.,
Commerce; lectr., Yale Univ., Fisk Univ., Clark Coll.,
Tuskegee, Univ. of Toronto, Univ. of Texas, Duke Univ.,
Univ. of Colorado, Univ. of Arizona; International Folk
Festival, 1955; general editor, Negro Heritage.
Memberships: Am. Folklore Soc., 2nd v.p.; Texas Institute of
Letters; North Carolina Folklore Soc., 1st v.p.; bd of
dir., Nat. Folk Festival Assn.; chmn., Folklore Section,
South Central Modern Language Assn.; elected life mem.,
Louisiana Folklore Soc., 1970.
Awards: General Ed. Bd.; Am. Philosophical Soc.; Piedmont
Univ. Center for Study of Negro Folklore at the Library
of Congress; Nat. Library of Mexico, Nat. Univ. of
Mexico; television station, WTVI, Charlotte, N.C., to
do five series film based on anthology, American Negro
Folklore; Chicago Bk. Fair, American Negro Folklore,
one of 60 bestlooking books published in U.S., 1968; 21st
Annual Writers Roundup award for American Negro Folk-
lore as one of the outstanding books written by a Texas
author, 1969.
Publications: Contributed 366 folktales to journals and anthologies. Author of numerous bks., including Negrito,
A Volume of Negro Dialect Poems, 1933; Negro Folktales from Texas, 1942; Dog Ghosts and Other Texas
Negro Folktales, 1958; The Folklore of the North Carolina Negro, 1965; American Negro Folklore, 1968.
Mailing Address: 2824 Laurel Lane, Commerce, Tex. 75428.

BRISBANE, ROBERT HUGHES, Educator
Born: Jacksonville, Fla., Mar. 21, 1913.
Education: B.S., St. John's Univ., 1939; Ph.D., Harvard Univ.,
    1949.
Family: m. Kathryn; d. Phillipa.
Professional Experience: Prof. political science, 1948, chmn.,
    dept. of political science, Morehouse Coll., 1965-; edito-
    rial staff, Encyclopedia Britannica; Fulbright Senior
    Lectr., Aug. 1958, June 1959; Gov. and Pub. Adminstrn.,
    Patna Univ., Patna, Bihar, India.
Memberships: Including Alpha Phi Alpha; AAUP; Am. Political
    Science Assn.; exec. council, ASNLH; Organization of
    Am. Historians; Southern Political Science Assn.
Awards: Merritt Travel Grant, Morehouse Coll., 1955; Non-
    Western Studies Grant to Africa, 1963.
Publications: Contributed articles to journals and books.
    Author, The Black Vanguard, Origins of the Negro Social
    Revolution, 1970; Black Activism in the United States
    (in process).
Mailing Address: 823 Magna Carta Dr., Atlanta, Ga. 30318.

BROOKES, STELLA BREWER, Folklorist, Author
Born: Dallas, Tex.
Education: B.A., Wiley Coll.; M.A., Univ. of Mich., 1930;
    Ph.D., Cornell Univ., 1946.
Family: m. E. Luther Brookes.
Professional Experience: Prof. English, Clark Coll., Atlanta,
    Ga., 1924-; prof. English, Atlanta Univ. (summers); prof.
    English, Alabama State Tchrs. Coll. (summers); lectr.,
    including Spelman Coll., Fisk Univ., Miles Coll., Morris
    Brown Coll., Alabama State Tchrs. Coll.; served as
    Regional Advisory Editor, CLA Journal.
Memberships: Pi Lambda Theta; Phi Delta Gamma; chmn.,
    women's division, NAACP; YWCA; AAUP; CLA; Am.
    Assoc. of African Culture; Internat. Mark Twain
    Soc.
Publications: Contributed numerous articles and book reviews
    to journals and newspapers; Joel Chandler Harris sketch,
    Encyclopedia Britannica, 1957; introduction to Schoken
    Bks'., Uncle Remus Stories. Author, Joel Chandler Har-
    ris: Folklorist, 1950.
Mailing Address: 1120 Chicon St., Austin, Tex. 78702.

BROOKS, CHARLOTTE K., Educational director
Born: Washington, D.C.
Education: A.B., Howard Univ.; M.A., New York Univ., 1951.
Family: m. Walter H.; s. Joseph.

Professional Experience: Tchr. pub. schs., Washington, D.C.;
exchange tchr., England, 1960-61; asst. dir., English
dept., pub. schs., Washington, D.C.; supr. dir., pub. schs.,
Washington, D.C.; cons., Office of Ed.
Memberships: NCTE; Internat. Reading Assn.
Awards: Meyer Travel Award; Fulbright Exchange Grant; Wini-
fred Cullis Lectr. Fellowship.
Publications: Contributed to professional journals. Author, The
Outnumbered, 1969; Search for America, 1969.
Mailing Address: 472 M St., S.W., Washington, D.C. 20011.

BROOKS, GWENDOLYN, Author
Born: Topeka, Kans., June 7, 1917.
Education: Wilson Junior College, 1936; L.H.D. (hon.), Colum-
bia Coll., Chicago, 1964.
Family: m. Henry L. Blakey; children, Henry, Nora.
Professional Experience: Instr. poetry, Columbia Coll., Chi-
cago; instr. poetry, Northeastern Ill. State Coll., Chicago;
reviewer, Chicago Sun Times.
Memberships: Society of Midland Authors.
Awards: Guggenheim Fellowships, 1946, 1947; four Poetry
Workshop awards, Midwestern Writers Conf.; Pulitzer
Prize for Annie Allen, 1950; Woman of the Year, Made-
moiselle, 1947; Poet Laureate of Illinois, 1968-.
Publications: Contributed to journals and periodicals. Author,
A Street in Bronzeville, 1945; Annie Allen, 1949; Maud
Martha, 1953; Bronzeville Boys and Girls, 1956; The
Bean Eaters, 1960; Selected Poems, 1963; Portion of
That Field: The Centennial of the Burial of Lincoln
(with others) 1967; In the Mecca, 1968; Riot, 1971; editor,
Jump Bad: A New Chicago Anthology, 1971.
Mailing Address: 7428 South Evans, Chicago, Ill. 60619.

BROWN, CECIL
Publications: Life and Loves of Mister Jiveass Nigger, 1969.

BROWN, CLAUDE
Publications: Manchild in the Promised Land, 1965.

BROWN, H. RAP
Publications: Die Nigger Die, 1970.

BROWN, PATRICIA L.
Publications: Editor, To Gwen With Love: A Tribute to Gwendolyn Brooks (with others) 1971.

BROWN, STERLING, Author, Educator
Born: Washington, D.C., May 1, 1901.
Education: A.B., Williams Coll., 1925; A.M., Harvard Univ.,
1930.
Family: m. Daisy Turnbull.
Professional Experience: Tchr., Virginia Seminary Coll.,
Lincoln Univ., Mo.; Fisk Univ.; prof. English, Howard
Univ.; vis. prof., New York Univ., New Sch., Sarah
Lawrence Coll., Vassar Coll.; literary editor, Opportu-
nity magazine; editor, Negro Affairs, Federal Writer's
Project.
Memberships: Phi Beta Kappa.
Awards: Guggenheim Fellowship, creative writing.
Publications: Contributed numerous articles to journals.
Author, Southern Road, 1932; Negro Poetry and Drama,
1937; The Negro in American Fiction, 1937; editor (with
others), The Negro Caravan, 1941, 1969.
Mailing Address: Howard University, Washington, D.C. 20001.

BROWN, VIRGINIA SUGGS, Educational director
Born: St. Louis, Mo., July 14, 1924.
Education: B.A., Stowe Teachers Coll., 1947; M.A., Washing-
ton Univ., 1952.
Family: m. Charles F.
Professional Experience: Elementary sch. tchr., kindergarten
and primary grades, pub. schs., St. Louis, 1948-56; tchr.
in charge of Banneker Reading Clinic, pub. schs., St.
Louis; supr. of elementary ed., pub. schs., St. Louis,
1960-65; in-service tchr. of remedial reading techniques,
Harris Tchrs. Coll., St. Louis, 1961-64; staff mem.,
Summer Study Skills Program for rural high sch. stu-
dents, Knoxville Coll., 1963-64; television tchr. of read-
ing for adults, St. Louis, summers 1963-67; dir., Head
Start, Human Development Corp., Office of Economic
Opportunity, St. Louis, 1965-66; cons. in Reading Inst.,
Coll. of the Virgin Is., St. Thomas, 1967, St. Croix, 1968;
dir., Early Childhood Ed., Webster Division, McGraw-
Hill Book Co., 1966-.
Memberships: Nat. Assn. for the Ed. of Young Children; Assn.
for Childhood Ed.; Internat. Reading Assn.
Awards: NCJW, Hannah G. Solomon Award for outstanding ser-
vice to young children, St. Louis, 1966.
Publications: Contributed to professional journals. Senior
author, Skyline Series books: Hidden Lookout, 1965;
Watch Out for C, 1965; Who Cares, 1965; Out Jumped
Abraham, 1967; Teaching Art in the Elementary School,
K-6 Grade (in process).
Mailing Address: 4106-A San Francisco Ave., St. Louis, Mo.
63115.

BRYANT, L. A., Author
Born: Bridgeport, Ind., Oct. 4, 1927.
Family: m. Ella M.
Professional Experience: Mail carrier, U.S. Post Office,
    Chicago; printer; served in U.S. Navy.
Publications: Resurrection, 1959; Restoration of Judah, 1961;
    Black and White Nations, 1966; Know Thyself, 1967.
Mailing Address: 4340 South Cottage Grove, Chicago, Ill.
    60653.

BULLINS, ED, Playwright
Born: Philadelphia, Pa., 1935.
Professional Experience: Formerly playwright-in-residence,
    now assoc. dir, The New Lafayette Theatre, N.Y.C.; co-
    founder and dir., Community Experimental Theater,
    Black Arts/West, San Francisco, Calif.; produced three
    one-act plays, The Electronic Nigger, Clara's Old Man,
    and Son, Come Home (American Place Theater), 1968;
    In New England Winter (N.Y.C.), 1968; edited black
    theater issue, The Drama Review, summer 1968; editor,
    Black Theater magazine; filmmaker with LeRoi Jones.
Memberships: Black Arts School.
Awards: Vernon Rice Award, 1968; Rockefeller Foundation
    grant; American Place Theater grant.
Publications: Contributed essays, short stories and poetry
    to magazines. Author, Five Plays, 1969; comp., New
    Plays from the Black Theater, 1969; Black Quartet
    (with others), 1970; Duplex: A Black Love Fable in Four
    Movements (Phil W. Petrie, ed.), 1971; Hungered One:
    Early Writings, 1971; Four Dynamite Plays, 1972; The
    Theme Is Blackness: The Corner and Other Plays, 1973.
Mailing Address: The New Lafayette Theatre, 137 St. and
    Seventh Ave., New York, N.Y. 10030.

BULLOCK, HENRY ALLEN, Educator
Born: Tarboro, N.C., 1906.
Education: B.A., Virginia Union, 1928; M.A., Univ. of Michigan,
    1929; Ph.D., ibid., 1942.
Family: m. Merle Anderson; children, Henry Allen, Jr., Merle
    Louise, Radney Anderson.
Professional Experience: Prof. social sciences, North Caro-
    lina A & T Coll., 1929-30; prof. sociology, Prairie View
    A & M Coll., 1930-49; prof. sociology, Dillard Univ.,
    1949-50; prof. sociology, Tex. Southern Univ.; prof. his-
    tory and sociology, Univ. of Tex., 1969-.
Memberships: Houston Community Council; Am. Sociol. Assn.;
    Am. Marketing Assn.; Tex. Assn. of College Teachers;
    Internat. Soc. of Criminology; Alpha Kappa Delta.

Awards: Earhart Foundation Fellow, Univ. of Mich.; General
    Ed. Fellow; Piper Teaching Foundation Award; winner
    of Bancroft Prize.
Publications: Contributed to journals. Author, Pathways to the
    Houston Negro Market, 1957; The School in the Social
    Order: A Sociological Introduction to Educational Under-
    standing (with Francesco Cordasco and Maurie Hillson),
    1970.
Mailing Address: Garrison Hall 101, The University of Texas,
    Austin, Tex. 78712.

BURROUGHS, MARGARET T. G., Educator
Born: St. Rose, La., Nov. 1, 1917.
Education: Elementary Ed. Certificate, Chicago Teachers Coll.,
    1937; B.A.E., Art Institute of Chicago; M.A.E., ibid.
Family: m. Charles Gordon; children, Gayle Gosa Toller,
    Paul.
Professional Experience: Tchr., pub. schs., Chicago, 1944-68;
    humanities prof., Kennedy King Coll., Art Institute of
    Chicago and Elmhurst Colls., 1968-70.
Memberships: Nat. Conf. of Artists (founder), 1959; Phi Delta
    Kappa.
Awards: Nat. Endowment for Humanities Fellow, 1968; Am.
    Forum for African Study Fellow, 1968.
Publications: Contributed to journals. Author, What Shall I
    Tell My Children Who Are Black, 1969; Whip Me Whop
    Me Pudding, 1968; Did You Feed My Cow? 1968; Jasper
    the Drummin' Boy, 1970.
Mailing Address: 3806 South Michigan Ave., Chicago, Ill.
    60653.

BUTCHER, MARGARET JUST, Educator
Born: Washington, D. C., Apr. 28, 1913.
Education: Ph.D., Boston Univ., 1947.
Family: d. Sheryl Everett.
Professional Experience: Tchr., Va. Union Univ., 1935-36;
    prof. English, Howard Univ., Washington, D.C.; Ful-
    bright prof., France, 1953-56; lectr., Am. Univ.; dir.,
    English Lang. program, U.S.I.S, Casablanca, Mo-
    rocco.
Memberships: D.C. Bd. of Ed., 1953-56; AAUP; AAUW.
Publications: The Negro in American Culture, 1956.
Mailing Address: 1601 18 St., N.W., Washington, D.C. 20009.

BUTCHER, PHILLIP, Educator
Born: Washington, D.C., Sept. 28, 1918.
Education: A.B., Howard Univ., 1942; M.A., ibid., 1947; Ph.D.,
    Columbia Univ., 1956.

Family: m.; children, 2.
Professional Experience: Literary editor, Opportunity:
    Journal of Negro Life, 1947-48; instr. English, Morgan
    State Coll., 1947-49; asst. prof. English, Morgan State
    Coll., 1949-56; assoc. prof. English, Morgan State
    Coll., 1956-59; vis. prof., South Carolina State Coll.,
    summer 1958; prof. English, Morgan State Coll., 1959-;
    dean, Grad. Sch., Morgan State Coll., 1972-; assoc. edi-
    tor, College Language Association Journal.
Memberships: Am. Studies Assn.; CLA; MLA; Soc. for the
    Study of Southern Literature; NCTE.
Awards: General Ed. Bd. Fellowship (extended), 1948-49; John
    Hay Whitney Opportunity Fellowship (extended), 1951-52;
    CLA Creative Scholarship Award, 1964; several Morgan
    State Coll. Faculty Com. research grants; Am. Philo-
    sophical Soc. research grant, 1968-69.
Publications: Contributed numerous articles to journals.
    Author, George W. Cable: The Northampton Years, 1959;
    George W. Cable, 1962; A William Stanley Brathwaite
    Reader, 1972.
Mailing Address: Morgan State College, Baltimore, Md. 21239.

CAIN, GEORGE
Publications: Blueschild Baby, 1971.

CANNON, C. E.
Publications: St. Nigger, 1972.

CARRINGTON, HAROLD
Publications: Drive Suite, 1970.

CARSON, LULAR L., Executive secretary
Born: Blackstone, Va., April 15, 1921.
Education: New York Univ., 1954-55; Univ. of Southern Calif.,
    1957-58; Pasadena City Coll., 1962; Harvard Univ., 1963-
    64; Certificate, Newspaper Inst. of Am., 1968-69.
Family: s. Ronald Darnell.
Professional Experience: Lib. clerk, RCA, Burlington, Mass.,
    1963-65; steno clerk, JPL Space Laboratory, Pasadena,
    Calif.; exec. sec., Philco-Ford, M.I.T.; Lincoln Labora-
    tory, Lexington, Mass., 1966-.
Memberships: Newspaper Inst. of Am.; The Greater Boston
    Quill Club.
Publications: Contributed articles, short stories, plays to
    journals. Author, The Priceless Gift (in press).
Mailing Address: 75 Brookside Ave., Newtonville, Mass. 02160.

CARTER, MARY KENNEDY, Educational coordinator
Born: Franklin, Ohio, Jan. 13, 1934.
Education: B.S., Ohio State Univ., 1956; M.A., Columbia Univ.,
    1964; London Univ., 1964; Makerere Univ., Kampala,
    Uganda, 1965.
Family: m. Donald Wesley.
Professional Experience: Elementary tchr., pub. schs., Cleve-
    land, 1956-60; demonstration tchr., pub. schs., San Diego,
    Ohio, 1961-63; tutor, supr., Uganda Ministry of Ed.,
    Columbia Univ., 1964-66; instr., research asst., Teachers
    Coll., Columbia Univ., 1966-67; project editor, writer,
    McGraw-Hill Publishers, New York; dist. coordinator,
    tchr. black studies, Roosevelt Sch. Dist., Roosevelt,
    N.Y., 1968-.
Memberships: Pi Lambda Theta; Alpha Kappa Alpha.
Awards: Afro-Anglo-Am. Fellowship, 1963.
Publications: Okelo and Akelo, 1967; Count on Me, 1970; On
    To Freedom, 1970.
Mailing Address: 21917 143 Ave., Laurelton, N.Y. 11413.

CARTER, WILMOTH A., Educator
Born: Reidsville, N.C.
Education: B.A., Shaw Univ., 1937; M.A., Atlanta Univ., 1942;
    Ph.D., Univ. of Chicago, 1959.
Professional Experience: Tchr., Rosenwald Training Sch.,
    Fairmont, N.C., 1938-41; instr., Municipal Coll.,
    Louisville, Ky., Jan.-June, 1943; instr., Southern Univ.,
    Baton Rouge, La., 1944-47; assoc. prof. sociology, Shaw
    Univ., Raleigh, N.C., 1950-57; leader, Institutional Ser-
    vice Unit, Am. Friends Service Com., Pa. Training Sch.,
    Morganza, Pa., summer 1955; prof. sociology, Shaw
    Univ., 1959-63; chmn., Dept. of Sociology, SUNO, New
    Orleans, La., 1963-64; research assoc., race relations,
    Univ. of Mich. and Tuskegee Inst., 1964-66; prof. so-
    ciology and dir., Division of Social Science, Shaw Univ.,
    1966-69; Distinguished Prof. of Urban Science, Shaw
    Univ., 1969-.
Memberships: Am. Sociol. Assn.; Southern Sociol. Soc.; AAUP;
    AAUW; Nat. Council of Women Voters League.
Awards: Alpha Omicron Honor Soc., Shaw Univ.; Alpha Kappa
    Delta Sociol. Honor Soc.; Rosenwald Fellowship, 1947-48;
    Danforth Foundation Fellowship, 1957-59.
Publications: Contributed to journals. Author, The Urban
    Negro in the South, 1961; The New Negro of the South,
    1967.
Mailing Address: Shaw University, The Division of Social
    Sciences, Raleigh, N.C. 27602.

CHALK, OCANIA
Publications: The Black Professional Athlete in Major American Sports: A Study in Courage and Perseverance (in press).

CHANDLER, SUE PINKSTON, Librarian
Born: Nashville, Tenn.
Education: B.A., Xavier Univ., 1949-53; M.A.L.S., George Peabody Coll., 1959-60.
Family: m. Samuel Jones; s. Samuel Keith.
Professional Experience: Lib. asst., 1955-59; asst. cataloger, 1960-61; acting ref. libn., Jan.-June 1961; periodicals libn., 1961-68; ref. libn., 1968-70; asst. libn. for Special Collections, Fisk Univ., 1970-.
Memberships: TLA; Parish Council; Legion of Mary.
Publications: Editor, Living Black American Authors: A Biographical Directory (with Ann Allen Shockley), 1973.
Mailing Address: Special Collections, Fisk University Library, Nashville, Tenn. 37203.

CHERRY, GWENDOLYN
Publications: Portraits in Color: The Lives of Colorful Negro Women (with Ruby Thomas & Pauline Willis), 1962.

CHILDRESS, ALICE, Author, Actress, Director
Born: Charleston, S.C., 1920.
Family: m. Nathan Woodard; d. Jean Lee.
Professional Experience: Actress; dir., the American Negro Theatre, Harlem, N.Y.C., 12 years; Harvard appointment, Radcliffe Institute, 1966-68; play, Wedding Band, produced by Univ. of Mich., 1966.
Awards: OBIE for play, Trouble in Mind, 1956.
Publications: Plays, Florence; Gold Through the Trees; Trouble in Mind; book, Like One of the Family: Conversations from a Domestic's Life, 1956; editor, Black Scenes, 1971.
Mailing Address: 800 Riverside Dr., New York, N.Y. 10032.

CHISHOLM, SHIRLEY ANITA ST. HILL, Congresswoman
Born: Brooklyn, N.Y., Nov. 30, 1924.
Education: B.A., Brooklyn Coll.; M.A., Columbia Univ.
Family: m. Conrad Q.
Professional Experience: Dir., Friends Day Nursery, N.Y.C.; dir., Hamilton-Madison Child Care Center, N.Y.C., 1953-59; ed. cons., Day Care Division, Bureau of Child Welfare, N.Y.S., 1959-64; assemblywoman, N.Y.S., 1964-

68; congresswoman (first black woman elected to Congress) representing the 13th Dist. N.Y., 91st Congress, 1969-.
Memberships: Nat. Assn. of Coll. Women and Key Women, Inc.; NAACP; League of Women Voters.
Awards: Alumna of the Year, Brooklyn Coll. Alumni Bull., 1957; award for outstanding work in Child Welfare, Women's Council of Brooklyn, 1957; Key Woman of Year Award, 1963; Woman of Achievement Award of Key Women, Inc., 1965; ASNLH, Sojourner Truth Award, 1969; NPA, Russwarm Award, 1969.
Publications: Unbought and Unbossed, 1970.
Mailing Address: 1108 Longworth House Office Bldg., Washington, D.C. 20515.

CHRISTIAN, MARCUS BRUCE, Author
Born: Houma, La., March 8, 1900.
Education: Houma Academy; Fed. Writers Project, Dillard Univ. Unit, 1936 (supr., 1939); Rosenwald Fellow, 1943-44.
Professional Experience: Asst. libn., Dillard Univ., 1944-50; established Bruce Printing and Publishing Co., June 1950; writer-in-residence, instr. of Louisiana Negro History and dir., poetry workshop, Louisiana State Univ., New Orleans, 1969-; poetry editor and special feature writer, Louisiana Weekly, 1932-.
Awards: The Common Peoples Manifesto cited in Arthur Spingarn Crisis list as one of the outstanding books of 1948; Sesquicentennial Commission (Battle of New Orleans) bronze medal.
Publications: Contributed poetry to magazines and journals. Author, From the Deep South, 1937; In Memoriam - Franklin Delano Roosevelt, 1945; The Common Peoples Manifesto of World War II, 1948; High Ground, 1958; Negro Soldiers in the Battle of New Orleans, 1965.
Mailing Address: Box 50094, New Orleans, La. 70150.

CLARK, KENNETH B., Educator, Psychologist
Born: Panama, July 24, 1914.
Education: B.A., Howard Univ., 1935; M.A., ibid., 1936. Ph.D., Columbia Univ., 1940.
Family: m. Dr. Mamie Phipps; children, Mrs. Donald Harris, Hilton Bancroft.
Professional Experience: Resident dir., Northside Center for Child Development, 1946-66; prof. psychology, City Coll. of New York, 1942-.
Memberships: Chmn. bd. and founder, HARYOU, 1962-64; Bd. of Regents, N.Y.; Am. Psychological Assn.; Pres. elect, Kappa Alpha Psi; NAACP.

Awards: Spingarn Medal; various honorary degrees.
Publications: Contributed to journals. Author, Prejudice and
    Your Child, 1955; Dark Ghetto, 1965; A Relevant War
    Against Poverty (with Jeannette Hopkins), 1968.
Mailing Address:MARC,60 East 86 St.,New York,N.Y. 10028.

CLARKE, JOHN HENRIK, Author, Educator
Born: Union Springs, Ala., Jan. 1, 1915.
Education: Washington Irving High Sch., N.Y.C., 1933; L.H.D.
    (hon.) Univ. of Denver, 1969; New York Univ., general
    studies, 1951-53.
Family: m. Eugenia Evans; d. Nzingha.
Professional Experience: Master Sgt., Army Air Force, 1941-
    45; administrv. asst. and lectr., African and Am. Negro
    subjects, New Sch. for Social Research, N.Y.C.; traveling
    and research in Africa, 1958; research dir., first Afri-
    can Heritage Exposition to be held in U.S., New York
    Trade Show Bldg., Aug. 6-15, 1959; assoc. editor,
    Freedomways; co-founder and fiction editor, Harlem
    Quarterly; book review editor, Negro History Bulletin;
    feature writer, Pittsburgh Courier and Ghana Evening
    News; contributor, Présence Africaine; book review
    column, "African World Book Shelf"; coordinator and
    special cons., CBS-TV and Columbia Univ. series,
    "Black Heritage, a History of Afro-Americans"; con-
    ductor, eight weeks tchr. training program, "Colloquium
    on Black History, Dimensions of the Black Experience,"
    Columbia Univ., summer 1969; lectr., Urban Leadership
    Training Program, New York Univ.; lectr. African his-
    tory, New Sch. for Social Research, N.Y.C.; adjunct prof.,
    Dept. of Black and Puerto Rican Studies, Hunter Coll.,
    N.Y.C., 1969-; vis. prof. and cons., curricula develop-
    ment, African Research Center, Cornell Univ., 1969-.
Memberships: Harlem Writers' Guild (founding mem.); Black
    Academy of Arts and Letters (founding mem.); African
    Studies Assn.; pres., African Heritage Studies Assn.; In-
    ternat. Soc. of African Culture.
Publications: Contributed numerous articles to books, journals
    and newspapers. Author of numerous books, including The
    Lives of Great African Chiefs, 1958; Rebellion in Rhyme,
    1948; edited works, American Negro Short Stories, 1966;
    Malcolm X, the Man and His Times, 1969; Tales from
    Harlem, 1970.
Mailing Address: 223 West 137 St., New York, N.Y. 10030.

CLEAGE, ALBERT B., JR., Clergyman
Born: Indianapolis, Ind., June 13, 1911.
Education: A.B., Wayne State Univ., 1937; B.D., Oberlin Sch.
    of Theology; Univ. of Southern Calif.; Wayne State Univ.
    Grad. Sch.

Family: m. Doris Graham; children, Kristin, Pearl.
Professional Experience: Social case worker, Dept. of Public
    Welfare, Detroit, Mich., 1931-38; minister, Chandler
    Memorial Church, Lexington, Ky., 1942-43; selected by
    War Service Com., Presbyterian Church, to co-pastor
    Fellowship Church of All Peoples, San Francisco, Calif.,
    1943-44; St. John's Congregational Church, Springfield,
    Mass., 1946-51; St. Mark's Community Church, Detroit,
    Mich., 1951-52; Shrine of the Black Madonna, Detroit,
    Mich., 1952-; co-chairman, Operation Connection to Aid
    Urban Blacks, 1968.
Memberships: Including Round Table Conf. of Christians and
    Jews, Springfield, Mass., 1950-51; NAACP; The Freedom
    Now Political Party, Mich. State Chmn.
Publications: The Black Messiah, 1968; Myths about Malcolm
    X: Two Views (with George Brietman), 1971.
Mailing Address: 2042 Clavert, Detroit, Mich.

CLEAVER, ELDRIDGE, Author, Political activist
Born: Wabbaseka, Ark., 1935.
Education: Junior college; educated in San Quentin, Folsom, and
    Soledad prisons in Calif.
Family: m. Kathleen Neal; s. Antonio Maceo.
Professional Experience: First job as shoe shiner, Phoenix,
    Ariz.; sent to reform school for pushing marijuana, and
    later to Soledad Prison, 1954; released on parole in two
    and a half years; arrested again on charges of assault
    with intent to commit murder, and assault with a deadly
    weapon; sentenced to fourteen years in Folsom Prison;
    paroled, December 1966; senior editor, Ramparts;
    arrested as parole violator, April 1968, for gun battle
    with Oakland Police; freed two months later; ruling over-
    turned by appellate court; left the country for Cuba and
    Africa, November 25, 1968; presidential candidate, Peace
    and Freedom Party, 1968; guest lectr., Univ. of Calif.,
    Berkeley, October 1968, and other colleges and universi-
    ties.
Memberships: Black Panther Party, Minister of Information,
    1967; ex-Black Muslim.
Publications: Eldridge Cleaver, 1967; Soul On Ice, 1968; Post-
    Prison Writing and Speeches, 1969; War Within: Violence
    or Nonviolence in the Black Revolution (with others), 1971.

CLEMONS, LULAMAE, Administrator, health education
Born: Widemer, Ark., Dec. 27, 1917.
Education: Kansas City Gen. Hosp., Diploma, Nursing, 1939-
    42; A.A., Pueblo Jr Coll., 1937-39; B.S., Lincoln Univ.,
    Mo., 1943-45; M.A., Columbia Univ., 1950-51; Ed.D.,
    Univ. of Southern Calif., 1962-64.

Family: s. Frank.
Professional Experience: Dir., health services, Lincoln Univ.,
    Mo., 1945-47; sch. nurse, Dept. of Health, N.Y.C., 1953-
    54; N.Y. Assn. for the Blind, N.Y.C., 1953-56; dir.,
    Health Ed. and Services, Office of Riverside County Supt.
    of Schs., 1956-.
Memberships: NAACP; NEA; Calif. Tchrs. Assn.; AAUW;
    Alpha Kappa Alpha; Soc. of Delta Upsilon; ASHA Fellow.
Awards: Alpha Kappa Alpha Outstanding Woman of the Year;
    Outstanding Headstart Program; NAACP Service Award.
Publications: Contributed to journals. Author, The American
    Negro (American All Series), 1965.
Mailing Address: 5837 Walter St., Riverside, Calif. 92504.

CLEVELAND, E. E.
Publications: Ask the Prophets, 1970; Free at Last, 1970;
    Sparks from the Anvil, 1971.

CLIFT, VIRGIL A., Educator
Born: Princeton, Ind., May 1, 1912.
Education: B.A., Indiana Univ., 1934; M.A., Indiana State Univ.,
    1939; Ph.D., Ohio State Univ., 1944.
Professional Experience: Prof. ed. and head, Dept. of Ed.,
    A & T Coll., Greensboro, N.C., 1939-48; prof. ed. and
    head, Dept of Ed., Morgan State Coll., 1948-63; Ful-
    bright lectr. and tchr. ed., Pakistan, 1954-55; ed. advisor,
    Kingdom of Libya, North Africa, 1956-58; vis. asst. prof.,
    Coll. of Ed., Ohio State Univ., summer 1946; vis. prof.,
    Coll. of Ed., Univ. of Illinois, summer 1962; prof. ed.,
    New York Univ., 1963-; senior editor, Sixteenth Year-
    book, John Dewey Soc., entitled Negro Education in
    America; chmn. com., Selection and Screening Com.,
    Internat. Exchange of persons.
Memberships: Many professional organizations in ed.; Sch.
    Bd., Westbury, N.Y., 1964-66; Phi Delta Kappa; Kappa
    Delta Pi.
Awards: Including General Ed. Bd. Fellowship, 1942-44; Ful-
    bright grant, lectr., Pakistan.
Publications: Numerous professional articles; A Study of
    Library Services for the Disadvantaged in Buffalo,
    Rochester and Syracuse, 1969.
Mailing Address: 3 Washington Square Village, 11-S, New
    York, N.Y. 10012.

COBB, CHARLIE
Publications: Everywhere is Yours, 1971.

COBBS, PRICE M.
Publications: Black Rage (with William H. Grier), 1968; The
    Jesus Bag (with William H. Grier), 1971.

COLEMAN, MERTON H.
Born: Boone, Iowa, Feb. 2, 1889.
Education: Summer High Sch., St. Louis, Mo.
Professional Experience: Coal Miner, 1907-10; laborer, 1912-
    16; Private 1st Class, U.S. Army Expeditionary Forces,
    1918-19.
Memberships: 803rd Pioneer Infantry.
Awards: Meuse-Argonne Offensive.
Publications: That Godless Woman, 1969.
Mailing Address: 17391 Roselawn, Detroit, Mich. 48221.

COLLIER, EUGENIA, Educator
Born: Baltimore, Md., April 6, 1928.
Education: B.A., Howard Univ., 1948; M.A., Columbia Univ.,
    1950; Univ. of Maryland, 1960-65.
Family: m. Charles S.; children, Robert Nelson, Philip
    Gilles.
Professional Experience: Asst. mgr. of Clean Block Cam-
    paign, Afro-American Newspapers, summers 1943-
    49; caseworker, Dept. of Pub. Welfare, Baltimore, Md.,
    and Crownsville State Hosp., Crownsville, Md., 1950-55;
    assoc. prof. English, Morgan State Coll., 1955-66; prof.
    English, Community Coll. of Baltimore, 1966-.
Memberships: CLA.
Awards: Gwendolyn Brooks Award, short story "Marigolds."
Publications: Impressions in Asphalt: Images of Urban
    America (with Ruthe T. Sheffey), 1969; A Bridge to Say-
    ing It Well (with others), 1970; editor, Afro-American
    Writing: An Anthology of Prose and Poetry (with
    Richard A. Long), 1972.
Mailing Address: 2608 Chelsea Terrace, Baltimore, Md.
    21216.

COLTER, CYRUS, Commerce commissioner
Born: Noblesville, Ind., Jan. 8, 1910.
Education: Youngstown (Ohio) Univ.; Ohio State Univ.; LL.B.,
    Chicago-Kent Coll. of Law, 1940.
Family: m. Imogene.
Professional Experience: YMCA, Youngstown, Ohio, 1932-34;
    Chicago YMCA, 1934-40; deputy collector of internal
    revenue, 1940-42; captain, U.S. Army, 1942-46; attorney,
    Chicago, 1946-; asst. commr., Ill. Commerce Commis-
    sion, 1950; commr, ibid., 1951-; chmn., Ill. Emergency
    Transport Board.

Memberships: Including Adminstrv. Conf. of the U.S.; Commn.
on Railroads of the Nat. Assn. of Regulatory Utility
Commrs.; Kappa Alpha Psi; NAACP; Chicago Urban
League; vice-chmn., Citizens Com., Chicago Pub. Lib.;
Chicago Bar Assn.; Cliff Dwellers Club; bd. of trustees,
Chicago Symphony Orchestra; Commercial Club.
Awards: $1,000 fiction prize, Univ. of Iowa, for short story,
"The Beach Umbrella."
Publications: Contributed short stories to periodicals.
Author, The Beach Umbrella, 1970; The River of Eros,
1972; The Hippodrome, 1973.
Mailing Address: 601 East 32 St., Apt. PH-2, Chicago, Ill.
60616.

CONE, JAMES H., Educator, Theologian
Born: Fordyce, Ark., Aug. 5, 1938.
Education: B.A., Philander Smith Coll., 1958; B.D., Garrett
Theological Seminary, 1961; M.A., Northwestern Univ.,
1963; Ph.D., Northwestern Univ., 1965.
Family: m. Rose Hampton; children, Michael Lawrence,
Charles Pierson.
Professional Experience: Asst. prof. religion and philosophy,
Philander Smith Coll., 1964-66; asst. prof. religion,
Adrian Coll., 1966-69; vis. prof. Afro-American history,
Univ. of the Pacific, summer 1969; assoc. prof. theology,
Union Theological Seminary, 1969-; vis. assoc. prof. re-
ligion, Barnard Coll., 1969-; lectr. including The Shrine
of the Black Madonna, Detroit, Mich.; Riverside Church
and The Church of the Master, N.Y.C.
Memberships: Bd. of Dir. and Theological Com., Nat. Com. of
Black Churchmen; Black Methodists for Church Renewal;
Alpha Kappa Mu Honor Soc.; Am. Academy of Religion;
Congress of African Peoples; Rockefeller Doctoral Fel-
lowships in Religion.
Publications: Contributed articles to journals, magazines, and
anthologies. Author, Black Theology and Black Power,
1969; A Black Theology of Liberation, 1970; The Spiritu-
als and the Blues, 1972.
Mailing Address: Union Theological Seminary, 3041 Broadway,
New York, N.Y. 10027.

CONLEY, EVERETT NATHANIEL, Author
Born: Albion, N.J., Sept. 21, 1949.
Education: Camden City High Sch.
Professional Experience: Lance corporal, U.S. Marine Corps,
1967-69.
Publications: A Slice of Black Living, 1970.
Mailing Address: 1489 South 10 St., Camden, N.J. 08104.

COOK, MERCER, Educator
Born: Washington, D.C., Mar. 30, 1903.
Education: A.B., Amherst Coll., 1925; LL.D., ibid., 1965;
    tchrs. diploma, Univ. of Paris (France), 1926; M.A.,
    Brown Univ., 1931; Ph.D., ibid, 1936; LL.D., ibid., 1970.
Family: m. Vashti Smith; children, Mercer, Jacques.
Professional Experience: Asst. prof. romance languages,
    1927-36; prof., Howard Univ., 1945-60; prof. French,
    Atlanta Univ., 1936-43; prof. English, Univ. of Haiti,
    1943-45; foreign rep., Am. Soc. African Culture, 1958-60;
    U.S. Ambassador to Niger, 1961-64, to Senegal and Gam-
    bia, 1964-66; prof., head, dept. Romance Languages,
    Howard Univ., 1970.
Memberships: ASNLH; NAACP; Am. Assn. Tchrs. French;
    ASCAP.
Awards: Decorations, Haitian govt.(1945), Niger Govt.(1964),
    Senegal (1966); Palmer Académiques (France).
Publications: Contributed numerous articles to journals and
    books. Author, Le Noir, 1934; Portraits Americains,
    1938; Five French Negro Authors, 1943. Editor, Haitian
    American Anthology, 1944; Education in Haiti, 1948;
    editor, Introduction to Haiti, 1951; Militant Black Writer
    in Africa and United States (with Stephen E. Henderson),
    1969.
Mailing Address: 4811 Blagden Ave., N.W., Washington, D.C.
    20001.

COOMBS, ORDE
Publications: Editor, We Speak as Liberators: Young Black
    Poets, An Anthology, 1970; editor, What We Must See:
    Young Black Storyteller, An Anthology, 1971; Do You
    See My Love for You Growing? 1972; Eastern Religions
    in the Electric Age (with John H. Garabedian).

COOPER, CLARENCE
Publications: The Scene, 1960; The Dark Messenger, 1962;
    Black: Two Short Novels, 1963.

CORNISH, SAMUEL JAMES, Teacher
Born: Baltimore, Md., Dec. 22, 1938.
Education: Northwestern Univ.
Family: m. Jean Faxon.
Professional Experience: Writing specialist, Enoch Pratt
    Free Library, 1965-66; bookseller, 1966-67; ed. cons.,
    C.A.R.E.L., Washington, D.C., 1967-68; writing special-
    ist, Enoch Pratt Free Library, 1968-69; editor, history,
    Association Press; tchr., Highland Park Free Sch., 1969-.

Publications: Poetry contributed to journals and anthologies.
Author, Angles, 1967; Winters, 1968; Your Hand in Mind,
1970; Generations, 1971; editor (with W. Lucian), Chicory:
Young Voices from the Black Ghetto, 1969.
Mailing Address: 395 Broadway, Cambridge, Mass. 02138.

CORTEZ, JAYNE, Poet
Born: Arizona, May 10, 1937.
Family: s. Denardo Coleman.
Professional Experience: Lectr., including Valley State Coll.,
Queens Coll., Wesleyan Coll., Univ. of Ibadan, Soul
television show, Rehabilitation Center.
Publications: Contributed to anthologies and magazines.
Author, Pisstained Stairs and the Monkey Man's Wares,
1969; Festivals and Funerals, 1971.
Mailing Address: Box 249, Village Station, New York, N.Y.
10014.

COUCH, WILLIAM, JR.
Publications: New Black Playwrights, 1968.

CROMWELL, OTELIA
Publications: Editor, Readings from Negro Authors, for
Schools and Colleges (with Lorenzo Dow Turner & Eva
B. Dykes), 1931; Thomas Heywood: A Study in the Eliza-
bethan Drama of Everyday Life, 1969; Lucretia Mott,
1971.

CROUCH, STANLEY
Publications: Ain't No Ambulances for No Nigguhs Tonight
(with Julius Lester), 1972.

CRUSE, HAROLD W., Author, Educator
Born: Petersburg, Va.
Education: Public schs., Petersburg and N.Y.; Brooklyn Film
Institute.
Professional Experience: U.S. Army, World War II, 1941-45;
free-lance writer, 1940-; organizational and activist
political work, black community, N.Y.C., 1946-67; tchr.
black hist., community free schs.; editor, television
film industry; assisted LeRoi Jones in establishing Jones'
Black Arts Theatre and Sch., 1965-66; film and drama
critic, N.Y. Labor Press; vis. prof. hist., Afro-American
studies, and interim dir., Center for Afro-American and
African studies, Univ of Mich., Ann Arbor, Mich., 1968-;
lectr., including Univ. of London, Univ. of Wales, Univ.
of Sussex, Princeton, Harvard, Yale, Fisk Univ.

Memberships: Phi Kappa Phi.
Publications: Contributed to newspapers, journals and magazines. Author, The Crisis of the Negro Intellectual, 1967; Rebellion or Revolution, 1968.
Mailing Address: 1904 Anderson, Ann Arbor, Mich. 48104.

CUMBO, KATTIE, Teacher
Born: Nov. 3, 1938
Education: A.A., Long Island Univ., 1955-58; B.A., ibid., 1967-70; Afro-Caribbean Certificate, Univ. of West Indies, 1969-70.
Family: Children, Michele Elizabeth, Patricia Denise, Lisarenee Susanne.
Professional Experience: Children's cons., Dept. of Social Services, N.Y.C., 1968-69; asst. to pub. relations dir., Brooklyn Coll. of Pharmacy, 1969; pub. relations cons., Dixwell Community House, summer 1969; typing tchr. (part-time), Brooklyn YMCA, 1968-69; office manager (part-time), Long Island Univ. student newspaper, 1969-70; camp coordinator, Brooklyn YMCA, 1970; instr., Bd. of Ed., N.Y.C., 1970-.
Memberships: Theta Sigma Phi; Harlem Writers' Guild.
Awards: Service Award, Long Island Univ., 1970.
Publications: Contributed to magazines and journals. Poetry in anthologies: Nine Black Poets, 1968; Galaxy of Black Writings, 1970.
Mailing Address: 122 Ashland Pl., Brooklyn, N.Y. 11201.

DANNER, MARGARET (Essie), Poet
Born: Chicago, Ill., Jan. 12, 1915.
Education: YMCA Coll., Chicago, Ill.; Roosevelt Univ., Chicago, Ill.
Family: 1st m. Cordell Strickland; 2nd m. Otto Cunningham; d. Naomi (Ms. Sterling Montrose Washington).
Professional Experience: Editorial asst., Poetry magazine, Chicago, Ill., 1951-55; asst. editor, 1956-57; poet-in-residence, 1961-62; Baha'i teaching com., touring poet, 1964-66; poet-in-residence, Virginia Union Univ., Richmond, 1968-69.
Memberships: Pres., Writer's Inc., Nologonya African Cultural Organization.
Awards: John Hay Whitney fellow, Senegal, Paris, 1966; Poetry Workshop, Midwestern Writer's Conf., 1945; Women's auxiliary, Afro-American Interest grant, 1950; African Studies Assn., 1950; Harriet Tubman, 1965; Am. Soc. of African Culture, 1960; African Studies Assn., 1961; Poets in Concert, 1968.

Publications: Contributed to magazines. Author, Impressions of African Art, 1961; To Flower: Poems, 1963; Poem Counterpoem (with Dudley Randall), 1966, 1969; Iron Lace, 1968; editor, Brass Horses, 1968; Regroup, 1969.
Mailing Address: 626 East 102 Pl., Chicago, Ill. 60628.

DARBEN, ALTHEA GIBSON, Sports consultant
Born: Silver, S.C., Aug. 25, 1927.
Education: B.S., Florida A & M Coll., 1949-53.
Family: m. William A.
Professional Experience: Community relation rep., Ward Baking Co., N.Y.C., 1959-64; special sports cons., Essex County Parks Commission, Newark, N.J., 1970-.
Memberships: NAACP; Alpha Kappa Alpha.
Awards: Woman Athlete of the Year, 1957 and 1958; tennis championship.
Publications: I Always Wanted to be Somebody, 1958.
Mailing Address: 275 Prospect St., East Orange, N.J. 07017.

DARITY, WILLIAM A., JR., Student
Born: Norfolk, Va., April 19, 1953.
Education: Amherst Regional High Sch.; Brown Univ.
Memberships: Student Council; pres., Western Mass. Assn. of Student Councils; Debating Club; Nat. Honor Soc.
Awards: Harvard Book Award; Mass. State Debating Champion, 1969; Nat. Merit Letter of Commendation.
Publications: The Shades of Time, 1969.
Mailing Address: 105 Heatherstone Rd., Amherst, Mass. 01002.

DAVIS, ALLISON, Anthropologist, Psychologist
Born: Washington, D.C., Oct. 10, 1902.
Education: A.B., Williams Coll., 1920-24; M.A., Howard Univ., 1925; Ph.D., Univ. of Chicago, 1942.
Family: m. Lois L.; children, Albion S., Gordon J.
Professional Experience: John Dewey Distinguished Service Prof. of Ed., Univ. of Chicago (mem. of faculty since 1939); vis. prof. sociology, Columbia Univ., Univ. of Mich.; vis. prof. psychology, Univ. of Calif., Berkeley; George A. Miller Distinguished Service Prof., Univ. of Ill., 1965; served on Conf. to Insure Civil Rights, 1965, and on the White House Task Force on the Gifted, 1968; vice chmn., adv. com. on Counselling, Assessment and Selection of the Manpower Adminstrn., U.S. Dept. of Labor, 1970; lectr., Alexander Inglis Memorial, Howard Univ.; Billings Lectr., Smith Coll.; Horace Mann Lectr., Univ. of Pittsburgh; DuPont Lectr., Univ. of Del.
Awards: Fellow, Am. Academy of Arts and Sciences (first elected from the field of education); fellow, Center for Advanced Study in the Behavioral Sciences.

Publications: Contributed numerous articles to professional
  journals. Author, Children of Bondage (with John Dol-
  lard), 1940; Deep South: A Social Anthropological Study
  of Caste and Class (with Burleigh B. Gardner and Mary
  R. Gardner), 1941; Father of the Man (with Robert J.
  Havighurst), 1947; Social-Class Influences upon Learn-
  ing, 1948; Intelligence and Cultural Differences (with
  Kenneth Eells, R. J. Havighurst and Ralph Tyler), 1951;
  Davis-Eells Test of General Intelligence (with Kenneth
  Eells), 1953; Psychology of the Child in the Middle
  Class, 1960; Relationships Between Achievement in High
  School, College and Occupation: A Follow-up Study,
  1963.
Mailing Address: University of Chicago, Graduate School of
  Education, 5835 Kimbark Ave., Chicago, Ill. 60637.

DAVIS, ARTHUR P., Educator
Born: Hampton, Va., Nov. 21, 1904.
Education: A.B., Columbia Coll., 1923-27; M.A., Columbia
  Univ., 1929; Ph.D., ibid., 1942.
Family: m. Clarice Winn; s. Arthur P., Jr.
Professional Experience: Prof. English, North Carolina
  Coll., Durham, 1927-28; prof. English, Va. Union Univ.,
  Richmond, 1929-44; prof. English, grad., Hampton In-
  stitute, summers 1943-49; prof. English, 1944-68; prof.,
  Howard Univ., 1969-; columnist, "With a Grain of Salt,"
  Journal and Guide newspaper, 1933-50; conducted a
  series of 26 radio talks, "Ebony Harvest," WAMU-FM,
  Washington-Baltimore, Oct. 2, 1972 to April 2, 1973.
Memberships: MLA; CLA.
Awards: General Ed. Bd. Fellowships, 1932-33, 1936-37, for
  study in England; Proudfit Fellowship, Columbia Univ.,
  1937; Nat. Hampton Alumni Award, 1947.
Publications: Contributed numerous articles, book reviews
  and short stories to professional journals, magazines
  and anthologies. Author, Isaac Watts: His Life and
  Works, 1943, 1948 (London); editor, The Negro Caravan
  (with Sterling Brown and Ulysses Lee), 1941; editor,
  Cavalcade: Negro American Writers from 1760 to the
  Present (with Saunders Redding), 1971.
Mailing Address: 453 Luray Pl., N.W., Washington, D.C. 20010.

DAVIS, GEORGE
Publications: Coming Home, 1972.

DAVIS, LENWOOD G., Educator
Born: Beaufort, N.C., Feb. 22, 1939.
Education: B.A., North Carolina Central Univ., 1961; M.A.,
  ibid., 1968; Univ. of Ghana, summer 1969; Northwestern
  Univ., summer 1970.

Family: m. Glenda F. Manning; d. Tatia Mia.
Professional Experience: U.S. Army, 1964-66; instr. history,
Livingston Coll., 1968-70; instr. history, Portland State
Univ., 1970-; cons., Black Studies program, N.C.; cons.,
Six Institutions, Consortium for African and Afro-Amer-
ican Studies Curriculum Project.
Memberships: Am. Historical Assn.; Organization of Am.
Historians; The Academy of Political Science; AAUP;
ASNLH.
Publications: I Have a Dream: The Life and Times of Martin
Luther King, Jr., 1969.
Mailing Address: 1825 S.W. Main St., Portland, Ore. 97214.

DAVIS, OSSIE, Actor, Playwright
Born: Cogdell, Ga., Dec. 18, 1917.
Education: Howard Univ., 1935-38.
Family: m. Ruby Ann Wallace (Ruby Dee); children, Nora,
Guy, LaVerne.
Professional Experience: Actor, Rose McClendon Players,
Harlem, 1938; janitor, shipping clerk, stock clerk; surgi-
cal technician, Special Services, U.S. Army, World War
II, 1942-45; acted in such plays as Jeb (1946), The Lead-
ing Lady (1948), The Smile of the World (1949), The
Wisteria Trees (1950), A Raisin in the Sun (1959), Purlie
Victorious (1962); stage manager, The World of Sholem
Aleichem, 1954-55; acted in movies, including No Way
Out (1950), Fourteen Hours (1951), The Joe Louis Story
(1953), The Cardinal (1963), Slaves (1969), Gone Are the
Days (1963); coproducer, Ballad for Binshire, 1963.
Memberships: Actor's Equity Assn.; NAACP; advisory bd.,
CORE.
Publications: Play, Purlie Victorious, 1961.
Mailing Address: 44 Cortlandt Ave., New Rochelle, N.Y.
10801.

deCOY, ROBERT H.
Publications: Nigger Bible, 1967; The Big Black Fire,1969;
Cold Black Preach, 1971.

DELANY, SAMUEL R.
Publications: Captives of the Flame, 1963; The Towers of
Toron, 1964; The Ballad of Beta-2, 1965; City of a
Thousand Suns, 1965; Babel-17, 1966; Empire Star, 1966;
The Einstein Intersection, 1967; Nova, 1968; The Fall of
the Towers, 1972; The Jewels of Aptor, 1972.

DEMBER, JEAN WILKINS, Housewife
Born: Brooklyn, N.Y., Jan. 29, 1930.
Education: Lincoln Sch. for Nurses.

Family: m. Clarence R.; children, Clarence Jr., Judith, Regi-
nia, Lila, Theresa, Zelie, Clemancia.
Professional Experience: Editor, NAACP Bulletin; sec., Bd. of
Amityville Copiague E. Farmingdale Commn. Action, 2
yrs.; housewife-.
Memberships: Diocesan Commn. Interracial Center Affairs;
mem. at large, L.I. Council of Churches Social Minis-
tries; Bd. of Regina Residence, Welfare Com. and Home
for Unwed Mothers; exec. com., NAACP, Central L.I.
Branch; Black Bay Catholics of Am.
Awards: Am. Legion Citation for Meritorious Service, Hunter-
Squire-Jackson Post 1218.
Publications: Poems published in Uptight.
Mailing Address: 5 Jefferson St., Copiague, N.Y. 11726.

DEMBY, WILLIAM, Author
Born: Pittsburgh, Pa., 1922.
Education: West Virginia State Coll.; B.A., Fisk Univ., 1947;
Univ. of Rome.
Professional Experience: Served in World War II, U.S. Army,
North Africa and Italy; writer, Stars and Stripes during
service; jazz musician and screen writer for Roberto
Rossellini in Rome; advertising agent, N.Y., 1963; tchr.,
Staten Island Community Coll., N.Y.
Memberships: Alpha Phi Alpha.
Publications: Beetlecreek, 1950; The Catacombs, 1965.

DEMILLE, DARCY (Mrs. Wilma Jackson), Literary agent,
Author
Born: Chicago, Ill., Dec. 17, 1929.
Education: Wilson Jr. Coll., Chicago; graduate, Walker Coll.
of Cosmetology; Flint Community Jr. Coll.
Professional Experience: Owner-operator, Wilma's Beauty Box,
Flint, Mich.; columnist (social news) Flint Herald, 1956-
58; columnist, features, articles, the Chicago Defender
newspaper, 1959-60; woman's editor, ANP, 1958-60; syndi-
cated theatrical columnist, "Data 'N Chatter, " ANP,
1958-61; NPI, 1961-63; stringer for ANP until July 1964;
columnist, "Guess Who?," Hep magazine, 1964-71;
former exec. editor, the Circle newspaper, Flint Urban
League; conducted research market interviews, Barlow
Surbey Service, Chicago, 1958-60; owner, Medi-Rary
Literary Agency, Flint, Mich.
Awards: Top Magazine Writer, Flint Writer's Club (magazine
category), 1959-70.
Publications: Contributed articles to Tan, Negro Digest, Ebony,
Sepia and Hep.
Mailing Address: 2018 Whittlesey St., Flint, Mich, 48503.

DENT, TOM
Publications: Free Southern Theater (with Richard Schechner),
1969.

DODSON, OWEN VINCENT, Educator, Dramatist, Author
Born: Brooklyn, N.Y., Nov, 28, 1914.
Education: B.A., Bates Coll., 1932-36; M.F.A., Yale Univ.,
1936-39; D.Litt. (hon.), Bates Coll., 1967.
Professional Experience:Instr.,Atlanta Univ.,summers 1938-
39,full-time,1939-42; instr., Hampton Inst., 1942-43;
dir. drama, Atlanta Univ., Hampton Inst., and Spelman
Coll.; lectr. including Iowa Univ., Vassar, Kenyon, Cor-
nell; conductor of seminars in theatre and playwriting;
dir.,summer theater,The Theater Lobby, Washington,
D.C., Lincoln Univ. (Mo.), Howard Univ.; prof. drama,
Howard University 1936-69; poet-in-residence, Ruth
Stephan Poetry Center, Univ. of Arizona, spring 1969.
Memberships: Exec. sec., the Com. for Mass Ed. in Race
Relations of the American Film Center, N.Y.C.
Awards: Rosenwald Fellowship; General Ed. Bd. Fellowship;
Guggenheim Fellowship, 1953; Paris Review prize for
short story "The Summer Fire"; named Poet Laureate
by Her Majesty the Queen of England, 1968.
Publications:Numerous poems, plays, fiction, represented
in over thirty anthologies. Most recent publications,
Boy at the Window, 1951; Powerful Long Ladder, 1970;
The Morning Duke Ellington Praised the Lord and Seven
Little Davids Tap Danced Unto (in process).
Mailing Address: 600 West End Ave., Apt. 2D, New York, N.Y.
10024.

DRAKE, ST. CLAIR, Educator
Born: Suffolk, Va., Jan. 2, 1911.
Education: B.Sc., Hampton Inst., 1931; Ph.D., Univ. of Chicago, 1937-48.
Family: m. Elizabeth; children, Sandra, Kail.
Professional Experience: Research assoc., Carnegie-Myrdal
Study of the Negro in America, Sept. 1940-June 1941;
instr., Dillard Univ., Sept. 1935-June 1946; asst. prof.,
ibid., Sept. 1941-June 1942; warrant officer, U.S. Mari-
time Service, Sept. 1943-Dec. 1945; asst. prof., Roose-
velt Univ., Sept. 1946-Jan. 1954; vis. prof., Univ. of Li-
beria,Jan.-June 1954;prof.,Roosevelt Univ.,Sept.1955-
Oct. 1958; head, dept. of sociology, Univ. of Ghana,
West Africa, Oct. 1958-Feb. 1961; prof., Roosevelt
Univ., Feb. 1961-Oct. 1969; prof. sociology and anthropology, Stanford Univ., Oct. 1969-; training staff of Peace
Corps tchrs., Ghana, 1961, 1962, 1964.

Memberships: African Studies Assn.; Am. Anthropological Assn.
Awards: Ford Foundation Fellow for study of mass media in West Africa, 1954-55.
Publications: Contributed numerous articles to journals and books. Author, Churches and Voluntary Associations Among Negroes in Chicago, 1940; Black Metropolis (with Horace Cayton), 1945, revised and enlarged, 1962, 1970; Social Work in West Africa (with Dr. Peter Omari), 1963; Race Relations in a Time of Rapid Social Change, 1966.
Mailing Address: 245 Leland Ave., Palo Alto, Calif.

DUNHAM, KATHERINE, Dancer, Choreographer
Born: Chicago, Ill., 1910.
Education: Univ. of Chicago; Northwestern Univ.
Professional Experience: Formed Negro Sch. of the Dance; first public appearance, Negro Rhapsody, Chicago Beaux Arts Ball, 1931; first major dance performance, Chicago World's Fair, 1934; Chicago Opera Co., 1935-36; supr., City Theater writer's project, cult studies, Chicago, 1939; dance dir., Labor Stage, N.Y.C., 1939-40; movies including Cabin in the Sky, 1940-41; Carnival of Rhythm, 1941; Stormy Weather, 1943; choreographer, Pardon My Sarong, 1942; formed Katherine Dunham Sch. Cultural Arts, Inc., N.Y.C., 1945; producer, dir., Katherine Dunham Dance Co.; starred in own production, Bal Negre, 1946-47, which toured country, Jan.-April 1948; choreographer, Aida, Metropolitan Opera, 1964; state dept. advisor, First World Festival Negro Art, Dakar, 1966; artistic and tech. advisor to the president, Senegal, 1966-67; artist-in-residence, fine arts div., Southern Ill. Univ., 1967; dir., Performing Arts Training Center, Southern Ill. Univ., East St. Louis, Ill.
Memberships: including Lincoln Academy; Am. Guild of Musical Artists; gov. bd., Am. Federation of Radio Artists; Actors' Equity.
Awards: Julius Rosenwald Travel Fellowship to West Indies, 1936-37.
Publications: Contributed articles to periodicals. Author, Katherine Dunham's Journey to Accompong, 1946; Dances of Haiti: An Analysis of Their Form and Function, (not published in U.S.), 1946, 1948; A Touch of Innocence, 1959.
Mailing Address: Performing Arts Training Center, Southern Illinois University, East St. Louis, Ill.

DUSTER, ALFREDA M. BARNETT, Social worker
Born: Chicago, Ill., Sept. 3, 1904.
Education: Ph.B., Univ. of Chicago, 1921-24.

Family: m. Benjamin C. (deceased); children, Charles E.,
Donald L., Alfreda M. Duster Ferrell, Troy S.
Professional Experience: Sociologist I, Ill. Youth Commn.,
1947-65; asst. to dir., Woodlawn Community Ser-
vices Agency, 1965-67; community rep., Catalyst for
Youth, 1967-68; dir., Community Relations Opportunity
Centers, 1968-; dir. girls' activities, Camp Illini,
summers 1950-70.
Memberships: YWCA, Chicago Internat. Program; Wesleyan
Service Guild (now United Methodist Women); former
chmn., Model Area Council of Woodlawn; Alfreda Wells
Duster Civic Club, Chicago, Northern District; Nat.
Assn. of Colored Women.
Awards: Mother of the Year, 1950, 1970; Bootstrap Award,
1970; Rust Coll. Assoc., 1971; Royal Plaza Retirement
Hotel Award for Concern for Senior Citizens.
Publications: Editor, Crusade for Justice: The Autobiography
of Ida B. Wells.
Mailing Address: 6632 South Greenwood Ave., Chicago, Ill.
60637.

DUSTER, TROY, Educator
Born: Chicago, Ill., July 11, 1936.
Education: B.S., Northwestern Univ., 1953-57; M.A., Univ. of
Calif., Los Angeles, 1957-59; Ph.D., Northwestern Univ.,
1959-62.
Family: m. Marie E.
Professional Experience: Research assoc., Nat. Academy of
Sciences, Disaster Research Study, Nat. Research Study,
Washington, D.C., 1961; research fellow, Nat. Inst. of
Mental Health, 1961-62; fellow of Swedish Government,
Sociologiska Institutionen, Uppsala Univ., Uppsala,
Sweden, 1962-63; cons., Pacific State Hosp., Mental Re-
tardation Study Rehabilitation Center, Drug Addiction
Research, Corona, Calif.; assoc. editor, The American
Sociologist, 1968-70; research sociologist, Center for
Research and Development in Higher Ed., Univ. of Calif.,
Berkeley, 1966-.
Memberships: Am. Sociol. Assn.; Am. Federation of Scientists;
Am. Academy of Political and Social Science.
Awards: Haynes Foundation Fellowship, 1965.
Publications: Contributed to journals. Author, The Legislation
of Morality, 1969.
Mailing Address: Dept. of Sociology, University of California,
Berkeley, Calif. 94720.

ECKELS, JON [ASKIA AKHNATON]
Publications: Home is Where the Soul Is, 1969; Our Business
in the Streets, 1971.

EDMONDS, HELEN G., Educator
Born: Lawrenceville, Va., Dec. 3, 1911.
Education: A.B., Morgan State Coll., 1931-33; M.A., Ohio State
Univ., 1936-38; Ph.D., ibid., 1941-46; post-doctoral
study, Univ. of Heidelberg; LL.D. (hon.), Morgan State
Coll., 1958.
Professional Experience: Dean of women, prof. Greek and
Latin, Va. Seminary and Coll., Lynchburg, 1934-35;
instr. history, Saint Paul's Coll., Lawrenceville, Va.,
1935-40; cons., social science, Va. State Dept. of Ed.,
summer 1940; prof. history, North Carolina Central
Univ., 1941-48; grad. prof. history, ibid, 1948-64; chmn.,
dept. of history and social science, ibid., 1963-64; dean,
grad. sch. of arts and sciences, ibid., 1964-71; distin-
guished prof. history, ibid., 1971-; leader specialist,
U.S. State Dept., Internat. Ed. Exchange Program,
Austria, Denmark, France, Germany, and Sweden; U.S.
Alternate Delegate, General Assembly, U.N., Sept. 13-
Dec. 18, 1970.
Memberships: Including Am. Historical Assn.; ASNLH, exec.
council; Assn. of Social Science Tchrs.; Nat. Assn. Coll.
Deans and Registrars; NEA; N.C. Assn. of Academic
Deans; Organization of Am. Historians; Southern His-
torical Assn.; Peace Corps, Nat. Adv. Com., now
ACTION; Delta Sigma Theta; Nat. Council of Negro
Women; nat. pres., the Links, Inc., July 1, 1970; Nat.
Council of Women of U.S.A.
Awards: Including General Ed. Bd., Rockefeller Foundation,
1943-45; Southern Fellowships Fund, Inc., research
grant, 1948; Fund for the Advancement of Ed., 1954-55;
Southern Fellowships Fund, Inc., research grant, 1969-
70; Nat. Foundation for the Humanities, senior fellow,
1970-71.
Publications: Contributed articles to professional journals.
Author, The Negro and Fusion Politics in North Caro-
lina, 1951; Black Faces in High Places, 1971.
Mailing Address: North Carolina Central University, Durham,
N.C. 27707.

EDWARDS, CHARLESZIME SPEARS, Nutritionist
Born: Indianapolis, Ind., April 17, 1907.
Education: B.S., Bradley Univ., 1928.
Family: m. Rutherford B.; children, Mach C., John W.,
Charles A., Arthur K.
Professional Experience: Tchr. home economics, Livingstone
Coll., 1928-29; Head Start, nutrition, OEO, Bd. of Ed.,
Kansas City, Kan., 1967-70.
Memberships: YWCA; NAACP; Alpha Kappa Alpha.
Publications: How to Wear Colors with Emphasis on Dark
Skin, 1965.
Mailing Address: 1514 North 7 St., Kansas City, Kan. 66101.

EDWARDS, HARRY
Publications: Black Students, 1970; Revolt of the Black Athlete,
1970; Healing Intelligence, 1971.

EGYPT, OPHELIA SETTLE, Social worker, Consultant
Born: Clarksville, Texas, Feb. 20, 1903.
Education: B.A., Howard Univ., 1921-25; M.A., Univ. of Pa.,
1926; N.Y. Sch. of Social Work, 1938-44; Sch. of Social
Work, Univ. of Pa., 1949-50.
Family: m. Ivory Lester; s. Ivory, Jr., stepson, Thurman Lee
Egypt.
Professional Experience: Tchr., Orange County Training Sch.,
Chapel Hill, N.C., 1925-26; instr. and researcher, Fisk
Univ. Social Science Dept., 1928-33; asst. cons., St.
Louis Provident, St. Louis, Mo., 1933-35; dir., Social
Service Dept., Flint Goodridge Hospital, New Orleans,
La.; asst. prof. and field work supr., medical social
curriculum, Howard Univ., 1939-51; probation officer,
Juvenile Court, Washington, D.C., 1950-52; exec. dir.,
Iona R. Whipper Home, 1952-54; case worker, special
project, unmarried mothers, Washington, D.C., 1954-56;
community ed., founder and dir., Parklands Neighbor-
hood Clinic, Planned Parenthood of Metropolitan Wash-
ington, D.C. (ret.), 1956-68; cons., Civil Service Com.,
summer 1940; family planning, OEO, HEW, and planned
parenthood, 1968-70.
Memberships: Nat. Assn. of Social Workers; Academy of
Certified Social Workers; Black Writer's Workshop;
ASNLH; NAACP; Planned Parenthood of Metropolitan
Washington, D.C.; Garfield-Douglass Civic Assn.;
Washington Performing Arts Soc.
Publications: Contributed articles to journals. Author, James
Weldon Johnson, 1973.
Mailing Address: 1933 Alabama Ave., S.E., Washington, D.C.

ELAM, DOROTHY ALLEN CONLEY, Teacher
Born: Philadelphia, Pa., July 23, 1904.
Education: B.S., Glassboro State Coll., 1956.
Family: m. Rev. A.W. Elam; children, Dr. Harold W. Conley,
Nathaniel Conley.
Professional Experience: Tchr., Bd. of Ed., Maryland, 1924-
25; tchr., Bd. of Ed., New Jersey, 1927-64; tchr.,
Camden City, Bd. of Ed., 1968-69.
Memberships: chmn., Negro History, Phi Delta Kappa, Eta
Chapter; organizer, pres., Camden Co. Intercultural
Council.
Awards: New Jersey Organization of Tchrs. Distinguished
Alumni Award, Glassboro State Coll.; New Jersey State
Fed. of Women's Club, 1967; Distinguished Citizen
Award, Tenth St. Baptist Church, Camden, N.J.

Publications: Articles included in Negro History Bulletin, record and filmstrip Historical Interpretation of Negro Spirituals.
Mailing Address: R. 2, Box 371C, Berlin, N.J. 08009.

ELDER, LONNE, III, Author
Born: Americus, Ga.
Education: Yale Univ. Sch. of Drama.
Family: m. Judith Ann; s. David DuBois.
Professional Experience: Television writer for N.Y.P.D. series, ABC Network.
Memberships: Harlem Writers' Guild—New Dramatists Com.; Black Academy of Arts and Letters.
Awards: John Hay Whitney Fellowship in Creative Writing; Stanley Drama Award, Wagner Coll.; Am. Nat. Theatre Academy Hamilton K. Bishop Award in playwriting; Joseph E. Levine Fellowship in film writing, Yale Univ.; John Golden Fellowship in playwriting, Yale Univ.; the Outer Critics Circle Award, Drama Desk Vernon Rice Award, Stella Holt Memorial Award (all for Ceremonies in Dark Old Men which was second in the voting for the 1969 Pulitzer Prize).
Publications: Contributed articles to the New York Times. Author, play, Ceremonies in Dark Old Men; Deadly Circle of Violence, television play.
Mailing Address: 55 West 14 St., New York, N.Y. 10011.

ELLISON, RALPH WALDO, Author
Born: Oklahoma City, Okla., March 1, 1914.
Education: Tuskegee Institute, 1933-36; Ph.D. in Humane Letters (hon.), Tuskegee Institute, 1963; D.Litt. (hon.), Rutgers Univ., 1966; D.Litt. (hon.), Univ. of Mich., 1967; L.H.D. (hon.), Grinnell Coll., 1967.
Family: m. Fanny McConnell.
Professional Experience: Lectr., Salzburg Seminar in Am. Studies, Austria, 1954; USIA Dept. of State, tour of Italian Cities, 1956; Alexander White Professor, Univ. of Chicago, winter 1961; lectr., Bard Coll., 1958-61; lectr., Rutgers Univ., 1962-64; hon. cons. in Am. Letters, Lib. of Congress, 1966.
Memberships: Charter mem., Nat. Council on the Arts; charter mem., Carnegie Commn. on Ed. TV; Nat. Advisory Council, Hampshire Coll.; bd. mem., Am. P.E.N.; bd. mem., WNDT, Channel 13; bd. mem., Associated Council of the Arts; trustee, John F. Kennedy Center for Performing Arts; trustee, Bennington Coll.
Awards: Fellow, Nat. Inst. of Arts and Letters; Am. Academy of Arts and Sciences; Stillman Coll.; Yale Univ.; Rosenwald Fellowship, 1945-47; Am. Academy in Rome, 1955-

57; Rockefeller Foundation, 1964; awards for Invisible
Man, Nat. Book Award, 1953, Russwurm Award, 1953,
NNPA Award, 1954, N.Y. Herald Tribune Book Week
Consensus of Authors and Critics Poll, "Book Most
Cited in 1965"; Medal of Freedom, Civilian Award from
Pres. Lyndon B. Johnson, 1969; Chevalier de l'Ordre
Arts et Lettres from the Minister of Cultural Affairs,
France, 1969.
Publications: Contributed to journals. Author, Invisible Man,
1952; Shadow and Act, 1964.
Mailing Address: 730 Riverside Dr., New York, N.Y. 10031.

EMANUEL, JAMES A., Educator
Born: Alliance, Neb., June 14, 1921.
Education: B.A., Howard Univ., 1946-50; M.A., Northwestern
Univ., 1950-53; Ph. D., Columbia Univ., 1953-62.
Family: m. Mattie Etha; s. James A., Jr.
Professional Experience: Weighmaster, Bradley Iron and
Metal Co., Rock Is., Ill., 1940-42; confidential sec.,
Gen. Benjamin O. Davis, Sr., Office of the Inspector
General, Washington, D.C., 1942-44; staff sgt., 93rd
Infantry Division, 1944-46; supr., Main Army and Air
Force Induction, 1951-53; instr., YWCA Secretarial Sch.,
N.Y.C., 1955-56; assoc. prof., City Coll. of N.Y., 1957-.
Memberships: AAUP; NAACP.
Awards: John Hay Whitney Foundation Opportunity Fellow,
1952-54; Eugene F. Saxton Memorial Trust Fellowship,
1965; Fulbright Prof. of Am. Lit., upon invitation,
Univ. of Grenoble, France, 1968-69.
Publications: Contributed to journals. Author, Langston
Hughes (Twayne's U.S. Authors Series, Vol. 123),
1967; Dark Symphony: Negro Literature in America
(edited with Theodore L. Gross), 1968; The Treehouse
and Other Poems, 1968.
Mailing Address: 405 Nuber Ave., Mt. Vernon, N.Y. 10553.

EVANS, MARI, Author
Born: Toledo, Ohio.
Education: Univ. of Toledo.
Professional Experience: Cons., Discovery Grant Program,
Nat. Endowment of the Arts; lectr., producer, dir.,
writer-in-residence, instr. black literature, Indiana
and Purdue Universities.
Awards: John Hay Whitney Fellow, 1965-66; Woodrow Wilson
Foundation Grant, 1968.
Publications: I Am a Black Woman, 1970.
Mailing Address: 750 West Tenth St., B-1, Indianapolis, Ind.
46202.

FABIO, SARAH WEBSTER, Educator
Born: Nashville, Tenn., Jan. 20, 1928.
Education: B.A., Fisk Univ., 1946; M.A., San Francisco State
    Coll.
Family: Children, Cheryl, Ronnie, Renee Angela, Leslie,
    Thomas.
Professional Experience: Tchr. Afro-American lit., Merritt
    Junior Coll., Oakland, Calif.; tchr. Afro-American
    studies, Univ. of Calif., Berkeley; participated in First
    World Festival of Negro Art, Dakar, Senegal, 1966;
    Third Annual Writers' Conf., Fisk Univ., 1968; editor,
    Phase II, Journal of Black Arts Renaissance.
Publications: Contributed to magazines and journals. Author,
    A Mirror a Soul; Black Is a Panther Caged; Race Results,
    U.S.A., 1966.
Mailing Address: 2536 Baylor East, Palo Alto, Calif.

FAIR, RONALD, Author
Born: Chicago, Ill., Oct. 27, 1932.
Education: Chicago Pub. Schs.; business sch.
Professional Experience: Hospital corpsman, U.S. Navy;
    court reporter.
Awards: Arts and Letters, 1970, for World of Nothing.
Publications: Contributed to journals and magazines. Author,
    Many Thousand Gone, 1965; Hog Butcher, 1966; World
    of Nothing, 1970; We Can't Breathe, 1972.
Mailing Address: Ca Rica, 6951 Lopagno, Ticino, Switzerland.

FAUSET, ARTHUR HUFF, Author, Anthropologist
Born: Flemington, N.J., Jan. 20, 1899.
Education: A.B., M.A., Ph.D., Univ. of Pa.
Professional Experience: Tchr., principal, Philadelphia Pub.
    Schs., 1918-46; volunteer, AUS, World War II (promotion
    to 2nd lt. denied because of previous activity in Civil
    Liberties field in Philadelphia, Pa.).
Memberships: Alpha Phi Alpha.
Awards: Fellow, Am. Anthropological Assn.; Am. Folklore
    Soc., studied folklore extant among blacks in Philadel-
    phia, British West Indies, Nova Scotia and in the south,
    1931; prize short story "Symphonesque" reprinted in
    various publications, including O'Brien Best Short
    Stories and O. Henry Best Short Stories.
Publications: Contributed numerous short stories, essays,
    articles and reviews to Opportunity and Crisis maga-
    zines. Author, Sojourner Truth: God's Faithful Pilgrim,
    1938; For Freedom: A Biographical Story of the Ameri-
    can Negro, 1927; Folklore of Nova Scotia, 1931; Black
    Gods of the Metropolis: Negro Religious Cults of the

Urban North, 1944, 1970; America, Red, White, Black
and Yellow (with Nella B. Bright).
Mailing Address: 333 East 30 St., Apt. 8-K, New York, N.Y.
10016.

FAX, ELTON CLAY, Illustrator, Author
Born: Baltimore, Md., Oct. 9, 1909.
Education: B.F.A., Syracuse Univ., 1931.
Family: d. Betty Louise.
Professional Experience: Book illustrator; "Chalk Talks"
lectr., high schs., Sch. Assembly Service of Chicago, Ill.,
and Rochester, N.Y.; New York Times children's book
programs; U.S. Dept. of State specialist, South America
and Caribbean 1955, East Africa 1964; rep. of Am.
Soc. of African Culture on tour of Nigeria, 1963; par-
ticipates in international educational exchange.
Memberships: Am. Soc. of African Culture; International
Platform Assn.
Awards: Coretta Scott King award for Seventeen Black Artists.
Publications: Contributed numerous writings and illustrations
to books. Author, West Africa Vignettes, 1963; Contemporary Black Leaders, 1970; Seventeen Black Ar-
tists, 1971; Garvey: Story of a Pioneer Black National-
ist, 1972.
Mailing Address: c/o Dodd Mead, 79 Madison Ave., New
York, N.Y. 10016.

FEELINGS, MURIEL, Teacher
Born: Philadelphia, Pa., July 31, 1938.
Education: Philadelphia Museum Sch. of Art, 1957-59; B.A.,
Los Angeles State Coll., 1963.
Family: m. Thomas; s. Zamani.
Professional Experience: Tchr., Bd. of Ed., N.Y., 1964-65;
tchr., Uganda, E. Africa, 1965-67; tchr. Spanish, Ocean-
Hill Brownsville Experimental Sch. District, N.Y., 1968-
70.
Memberships: Columbian Design Soc., N.Y.
Publications: Zamani Goes to Market, 1970; Moja Means One:
The Swahili Counting Book, 1971.
Mailing Address: 320 Eastern Parkway, Brooklyn, N.Y. 11225.

FEELINGS, TOM, Free-lance illustrator
Born: Brooklyn, N.Y., May 19, 1933.
Education: George Washington Vocational High Sch., 1947-51;
Cartoonist Illustrators Sch., 1951-53; Sch. of Visual
Arts, 1958-60.
Family: m. Muriel; children, Zamani, Kamali.

Professional Experience: U.S. Air Force, A/1c, 1953-57;
   free-lance comic strip, "Tommy Traveler in the World
   of Negro History, " New York Age, 1958-59; illustrator,
   African Review, gov. magazine, Ghana, West Africa,
   1964-66; free-lance magazine illustrator, 1959-70; art
   dir., children's textbooks, 1971-; illustrator, gov. of
   Guyana, South America.
Awards: ALA Caldecott candidate for best illustrated chil-
   dren's book, Moja Means One, 1972; candidate for
   fourth Coretta Scott King Award for book, Black Pil-
   grimage; ALA Notable Children's Books, 1972, Black
   Pilgrimage.
Publications: Contributed to periodicals; illustrated "The
   Negro in America," Look magazine, 1962; illustrated
   over ten books, including To Be a Slave, 1968; Black
   Folktales, 1969; Zamani Goes to Market, 1970; Moja
   Means One, 1972; We Are One, 1972. Author, Black
   Pilgrimage, 1972.
Mailing Address: c/o Anna Morris, 21 St. James Place,
   Brooklyn, N.Y. 11225.

FELTON, B.
Publications: Ghetto Waif.

FERGUSON, BLANCHE E., Educator
Born: New York, N.Y., July 7, 1906.
Education: A.B., Syracuse Univ., 1922-26; M.A., Butler Univ.,
   1944.
Family: m. Jacque Ferguson.
Professional Experience: Instr. English, Wiley Coll., Mar-
   shall, Tex., 1926-28; tchr., Indianapolis Publ. Schs.,
   1928-71; dir. publications, radio coordinator, Attucks
   High Sch., Indianapolis, Ind.; radio columnist, the
   Indiana Teacher.
Memberships: AAUW; Phi Kappa Phi.
Awards: Indiana Univ. Writer's Conf., 1963.
Publications: Countee Cullen and the Negro Renaissance,
   1966.
Mailing Address: 5672 N. Illinois St., Indianapolis, Ind.
   46208.

FIELDS, JULIA, Author, Poet.
Born: Bessemer, Ala.; Jan. 18, 1938.
Education: B.S., Knoxville Coll., 1961; M.A., Bread Loaf Sch.
   of English, 1972; Univ. of Edinburgh, Scotland.
Professional Experience: Bread Loaf Writer's Conf.; tchr.,
   Westfield High Sch., Birmingham, Ala.; poet-in-
   residence, Miles Coll., Hampton Institute, St. Augustine

Coll., and East Carolina Univ.; play produced, All Day
Tomorrow, Knoxville Coll., 1966.
Awards: $1,500 grant, Nat. Endowment for the Arts, 1968;
Seventh Conrad Kent Rivers Memorial Fund Award,
1972.
Publications: Contributed poetry to magazines and anthologies.
Author, Poems, 1968; I Heard a Young Man Saying.
Mailing Address: Box 209, Scotland Neck, N.C.

FLEMING, GEORGE JAMES, Educator
Born: Virgin Is., U.S.A., Feb. 15, 1904.
Education: B.A., Univ. of Wisconsin, 1931; A.M., Univ. of
Pa., 1944; Ph.D., ibid., 1948.
Professional Experience: Editorial staff, newspapers
(Journal and Guide, Norfolk, Va., Amsterdam News,
N.Y.C., Philadelphia Tribune, 1931-41); editor, Kappa
Alpha Psi Journal, 1938-50; head, press relations for
Mayor's Com. on Conditions in Harlem, 1935; staff,
The Negro in America, research project sponsored by
the Carnegie Corp. of N.Y., 1939; field examiner,
FEPC, 1941-43, regional dir., 1943-45; sec. of Race
Relations Com. of Am. Friends Service Com., 1945-50;
editor, Who's Who in Colored America, 1950; supr.
editor, Who's Who in the United Nations; vis. lectr.,
West and East Africa and Israel, 1965-66; founder-dir.,
Inst. for Political Education, 1959-66; vis. prof., Univ.
of Pa., 1966-68, Lincoln Univ., Pa., 1968-70; prof.
political science, Morgan State Coll., Baltimore, Md.
Memberships: Including bd. of trustees, Coll. of the Virgin
Is., 1969; Am. Academy of Political and Social Science;
Southern Political Science Assn.; Am. Soc. for Pub. Ad-
minstrn.; Am. Assn. for Public Opinion Research; Kappa
Alpha Psi.
Awards: Public Service, Wisconsin Alumnus, 1949; Hampton
Inst. Distinguished Service Award, 1948.
Publications: Contributed numerous articles to journals,
newspapers, and periodicals. Author, An All-Negro
Ticket in Baltimore, 1960; Why Baltimore Failed to
Elect a Black Mayor in 1971, 1972.
Mailing Address: Dept. of Political Science, Morgan State
College, Baltimore, Md. 21239.

FOSTER, CRAIG CURTIS, Student
Born: New York City, July 14, 1947.
Education: B.A., Yale Univ., 1965-69.
Professional Experience: Univ. financing; researched and
created Yale's Afro-American major studies program.
Memberships: Black Student Alliance, Yale Univ.

Publications: Contributed to Yale Alumni magazine. Author,
Black Studies in the University, 1969.
Mailing Address: Apt. 588, 2333 Fifth Ave., New York, N.Y.
10037.

FRANKLIN, JOHN HOPE, Author, Educator
Born: Rentiesville, Okla., Jan. 2, 1915.
Education: B.A., Fisk Univ., 1935; M.A., Harvard Univ., 1936;
Ph.D., ibid., 1941; LL.D. (hon.), Morgan State Coll.,
1960; LL.D. (hon.), Virginia State Coll., 1961; LL.D.
(hon.), Lincoln Univ., 1961; LL.D. (hon.), Tuskegee
Inst., 1964; LL.D. (hon.), Lincoln Coll., 1965; LL.D.
(hon.), Hamline Univ., 1965; LL.D. (hon.), Fisk Univ.,
1966; LL.D. (hon.), Rhode Island Coll., 1967; LL.D.
(hon.), Dickinson Coll., 1968; LL.D. (hon.), Howard
Univ., 1968; LL.D. (hon.), Johnson C. Smith Univ., 1968;
Litt.D. (hon.), Tougaloo Coll., 1967; L.H.D. (hon.),
Univ. of Mass., 1964; L.H.D. (hon.), Long Island Univ.,
1964.
Family: m. Aurelia Whittington; s. John Whittington.
Professional Experience: Instr., Fisk Univ., 1936-37; prof.
history, St. Augustine's Coll., 1939-43; prof. history,
North Carolina Coll., 1943-47; prof. history, Howard
Univ., 1947-56; prof. and chmn., Dept. of History, Brook-
lyn Coll., 1956-64; prof. American history and chmn.,
Dept. History, Univ. of Chicago, 1967-.
Memberships: Chmn., Bd. of Trustees, Fisk Univ.; Nat. Ed.
Television Bd.; Am. Historical Assn.; Southern His-
torical Assoc.; AAUP; ASNLH; ACLS; Am. Studies Assn.
Awards: Edward Austin Fellow, 1937-38; Rosenwald Fellow,
1937-39; Guggenheim Fellow, 1950-51; President's
Fellow, Brown Univ., 1952-53; Fulbright Prof., Austra-
lia, 1960.
Publications: Contributed numerous articles to books and
journals. Most recent publications, Reconstruction After
the Civil War, 1961; The Emancipation Proclamation,
1963; Land of the Free, 1966; From Slavery to Freedom:
A History of American Negroes, 1967; Illustrated History
of Black Americans, 1970.
Mailing Address: 5805 Blackstone Ave., Chicago, Ill. 60637.

FULLER, HOYT (William), Editor, Author
Born: Atlanta, Ga., Sept. 10, 1928.
Education: B.A., Wayne State Univ., 1946-50.
Professional Experience: Reporter, feature editor, Detroit
Tribune, 1949-51; feature editor, Michigan Chronicle,
1951-54; assoc. editor, Ebony magazine, 1954-57; resi-
dent of Spain, corr., Haagse Post, Dutch newspaper in
West Africa, 1957-60; asst. ed., Collier's Encyclopedia;

exec. editor, Black World (formerly Negro Digest), 1961-; tchr., fiction writing seminar, Columbia Coll., Chicago; tchr., Afro-American Lit., Northwestern Univ. and Indiana Univ.
Memberships: Founder of the Organization of Black Am. Culture.
Awards: John Hay Whitney Opportunity Fellowship, travel in West Africa, 1965-66.
Publications: Contributed articles and stories to journals, periodicals, newspapers and anthologies. Author, Journey to Africa, 1971.
Mailing Address: 3001 South Martin Luther King Drive, Apt. 1902, Chicago, Ill. 60616.

GAINES, ERNEST J., Author
Born: Oscar, La., Jan. 15, 1933.
Education: B.A., San Francisco State College, 1957; Stanford Univ., 1958-59.
Professional Experience: Writing, odd jobs; military service, U.S. Army, 1953-55.
Awards: Wallace Stegner Creative Writing.
Publications: Contributed short stories and novellas to magazines. Author, Catherine Carmier, 1964; Of Love and Dust, 1967; Bloodline, 1968; Long Day in November, 1971; Autobiography of Miss Jane Pittman, 1971.
Mailing Address: 998 Divisadero St., San Francisco, Calif. 94115.

GAMBLE, QUO VADIS GEX, Radio news director
Born: New Orleans, La., Oct. 27, 1950.
Education: Boston Univ., 1969-70; Radio Engineering Inst., 1st phone license.
Family: m. Otis James.
Professional Experience: Tchr. asst., Boston Univ., June - September 1970; chief instr., WBUR, Boston Univ. radio station, Nov. 1970 - Aug. 1971; news dir., WYLD radio station, New Orleans, La., June 1972-.
Memberships: Media Women; AFTRA.
Awards: Merit Award, Housing Authority, New Orleans.
Publications: Contributed to Nkombo publications and New Orleans States Item newspaper. Author, Dark Waters, 1969.
Mailing Address: 3000 Lowerline St., New Orleans, La. 70118.

GANT, LISBETH, Author
Born: Chicago, Ill., Apr. 16, 1948.
Education: B.A.,Kalamazoo Coll., 1964-68; M.A., Columbia Univ., 1969-70.

Professional Experience: Reporter, Nat. Black Network;
  writer, Afro World Associates (U.N.); free-lance writer;
  book and play reviewer.
Awards: Coretta Scott King Award, AAUW, 1969; nomination,
  Outstanding Young Women of America, 1969; Richard
  Wright-Amiri Baraka Award for Literary Criticism,
  Black World, 1972.
Publications: Contributed articles to periodicals and journals.
  Author, A Bibliography of Black American Literature,
  1746-1971 (in press); Fight on Resistance to the African
  Slave Trade (in press).
Mailing Address: 15 West 72 St. #4L, New York, N.Y. 10023.

GARLAND, PHYL (Phyllis T.), Editor
Born: McKeesport, Pa., Oct. 27, 1935.
Education: B.S.J., Northwestern Univ.
Professional Experience: Jr. editor, Pittsburgh Courier,
  1955-57; feature editor, columnist, reporter, feature
  writer, Pittsburgh Courier, 1958-65; lectr. Theta Sigma
  Phi Nat. Writers' Conf., 1970; lectr., Music Educators'
  Nat. Conf., 1970; lectr., Univ. of Indiana Com. on Black
  Music, 1970; asst. editor, Ebony magazine, 1965-67;
  assoc. editor, Ebony magazine, 1967-69; New York
  editor, Ebony magazine, 1969-.
Memberships: Theta Sigma Phi (journalist organization for
  women); Delta Sigma Theta; Media Women.
Awards: Golden Quill for outstanding feature writer on
  Western Pennsylvania, 1962.
Publications: The Sound of Soul, 1969.
Mailing Address: 433 West 24 St., New York, N.Y. 10011.

GARY, MADELEINE SOPHIE, Author
Born: Chicago, Ill.
Publications: Vignettes: Of the Beam in a Niggers' Eye,
  1970.
Mailing Address: Box 78261, Los Angeles, Calif. 90016.

GAYLE, ADDISON, JR., Educator
Born: Newport News, Va., June 2, 1932.
Education: B.A., City Coll. of N.Y.; M.A., Univ. of Calif., 1966.
Family: m. Rosalie.
Professional Experience: Porter, Brooklyn Army Base, 1959-
  60; admin. asst., CCNY program to enable young people
  from culturally different areas to attend coll., June
  1965 - Aug. 1965; reader, dept. of English, Univ. of
  Calif., Los Angeles, Sept. 1965 - Jan. 1966; research
  asst., training laboratory animals, ibid., Sept. 1965 -
  June 1966; lectr., dept. of English, CCNY, Sept. 1966 -

June 1969; lectr., "Age of Richard Wright, " dept. of
English, Univ. Coll., Bronx, N.Y., Feb. - June 1969; vis.
prof. American and Afro-American Literature, dept.
of English, Univ. of Washington, June - Aug. 1971; asst.
prof. creative writing, dept. of English, Livingston Coll.,
Rutgers Univ., Sept. 1971 - June 1972; assoc. prof.
composition and literature courses, dept. of English,
Baruch Coll., N.Y.C., 1969-; lectr., including "Black
Heritage," Channel 2 TV, Oberlin Coll., Univ. of Va.,
Yale Univ., Dunbar Centenary, Univ. of Calif., Irvine;
cons., Minority Writers, Doubleday and Random House;
editorial staffs, Amistad magazine, Third World Press,
Black Lines magazine; annual donor of Richard Wright-
Amiri Baraka Award, for best critical essay published
in Black World magazine; sponsor of the Richard Wright
Award for SEEK student with highest average each
semester.
Memberships: Including Presidential Com. on Student Unrest,
Spring 1970; Baruch Coll. Affirmative Action Com.;
P & B Com., dept. of Compensatory Ed.
Publications: Contributed numerous articles and reviews to an-
thologies, journals and magazines. Author, Black Ex-
pression: Essays By and About Black Americans in the
Creative Arts, 1969; The Black Situation, 1970; The
Black Aesthetic, 1971; Bondage, Freedom and Beyond,
1971; Oak and Ivy: A Biography of Paul Laurence Dunbar,
1971; Claude McKay; The Black Poet at War, 1972; A
History of the Black Novel (in process).
Mailing Address: 100 East Hartsdale Ave., Hartsdale, N.Y.
10530.

GIBSON, CHARLINE, Housewife
Born: Omaha, Neb., April 22, 1937.
Education: Omaha Univ.
Family: m. Robert; children, Anita Renee, Annette Suzanne.
Professional Experience: Bureau of Internal Revenue (3 yrs.).
Memberships: Black Women Unlimited; Bd. of Planned Parent-
hood; Omaha Human Relations Bd.; Panel of American
Women; Headstart.
Publications: A Wife's Guide to Baseball, 1970.
Mailing Address: 3624 South 94 St., Omaha, Neb. 68124.

GILLESPIE, MARCIA ANN, Editor
Born: Long Island, N.Y., July 10, 1944.
Education: B.A., Lake Forest Coll., 1966.
Professional Experience: Research reporter, Time Inc.,
Time Life Books, 1966-70; managing editor, 1970-71,
editor-in-chief, Essence, 1971-.

Memberships: Am. Soc. of Magazine Editors; advisory bd.,
    Community News Service, N.Y.C.; bd., Malcolm King
    Coll., N.Y.C.
Publications: Assisted with Illustrated History of Black Ameri-
    cans, 1970.
Mailing Address: 300 East 42 St., New York, N.Y. 10017.

GIOVANNI, NIKKI (Yolande C., Jr.), Author
Born: Knoxville, Tenn., June 7, 1943.
Education: B.A., Fisk Univ., 1967.
Family: s. Thomas Watson.
Professional Experience: Asst. prof., Queens Coll., 1968-69;
    assoc. prof., Rutgers Univ., Livingston Coll., 1969-.
Awards: Nat. Council of the Arts, 1970; Harlem Cultural
    Council, 1969; Amsterdam News, one of ten most ad-
    mired Black Women, 1969.
Publications: Contributed numerous poems and articles to
    magazines and anthologies. Author, Black Feeling Black
    Talk, 1968; Black Judgement, 1969; Re: Creation, 1970;
    Black Feeling Black Talk Black Judgement, 1970; Night
    Comes Softly; Anthology of Black Female Voices, 1970;
    Spin a Soft Black Song: Poems for Children, 1971;
    Gemini, 1972; My House: Poems, 1972.
Mailing Address: 38 West 94 St., New York, N.Y. 10025.

GLOSTER, HUGH MORRIS, College president
Born: Brownsville, Tenn., May 11, 1911.
Education: B.A., Morehouse Coll., 1931; M.A., Atlanta Univ.,
    1933; Ph.D., New York Univ., 1943; doctorate (hon.),
    Univ. of Haiti, 1968.
Family: 2nd m. Beulah Victoria Harold; children, 1st m., Alice
    Louise, Evelyn Elaine; 2nd m., Hugh Morris.
Professional Experience: Instr., assoc. prof. English, LeMoyne
    Coll., 1933-41; prof. English, Morehouse Coll., 1941-43;
    program dir., USO, Ft. Huachuca, Arizona, 1943-44; prof.
    English and chmn., dept. lang. and lit., Hampton Institute,
    1946-67; dean faculty, Hampton Inst. 1963-67; pres.,
    Morehouse Coll., 1967-; guest prof. English, New York
    Univ., summers 1949, 1962; vis. prof. Am. Lit., Univ.
    of Warsaw, 1961-62; contributing editor, Phylon, 1948-
    53; adv. editor, College Language Association journal,
    1957-.
Memberships: Including commn. on coll. adminstrn., Assn.
    Am. Colls.; vice pres., Assn. Prot. Colls. and Univs.
    in Ga.; bd. dirs., Nat. Assn. for Equal Opportunity in
    Higher Ed.; bd. dirs, trustee, United Negro Coll. Fund;
    Coll. Entrance Exam Bd., Educational Testing Service;
    founder and pres., CLA, 1937-38, 1948-50; Alpha Phi
    Alpha; Am. Assn. Higher Ed., exec. com., 1967-69; Am.
    Assoc. Univ. Adminstrs.

Awards: Research grant, Alpha Phi Alpha, summer 1940; research grant, Carnegie Foundation, 1950-51; distinguished contributor's award, CLA, 1958; Centennial medallion, Hampton Inst., 1968; Alumnus of Year award, LeMoyne Coll., 1967.
Publications: Contributed to journals. Author, Negro Voices in American Fiction, 1948; co-editor, The Brown Thrush: An Anthology of Verse by Negro College Students, 1935; My Life, My Country, My World: College Readings for Modern Living, 1952.
Mailing Address: Morehouse College, Atlanta, Ga. 30314.

GODDARD, NETTYE GEORGE, Teacher
Born: Gadsden, Ala., May 22, 1923.
Education: A.B., Talladega Coll., 1942; San Jose State; Univ. of Pacific.
Family: m. George; children, Rosalind Kent, Radcliffe Kirsten.
Professional Experience: Tchr. English, Gadsden, Ala., 1942-43; tchr. English, San Jose Unified Sch. Dist., 1957-69; tchr. Black experience, extension faculty, San Jose State Coll.; tchr. the Black experience and linguistics-transformational grammar; cons., summer faculty, Coll. of Notre Dame, Belmont, Calif.; cons., Black curriculum, San Jose Unified Sch. Dist., 1969-.
Publications: Black Literature (in process).
Mailing Address: 10183 Kenny Lane, San Jose, Calif. 95127.

GOODE, KENNETH, Educational administrator
Born: New Orleans, La., 1932.
Education: B.A., Univ. of Ariz., 1957; LL.B., ibid., 1960; J.D., ibid., 1960; Air Police Security Sch., Tyndall Air Force Base, Tyndall, Fla.
Professional Experience: Management Internship Program, U.S. Atomic Energy Commn.; research attorney, Univ. of Calif., Berkeley, 1960-63; contract adminstr., U.S. Atomic Energy Commn., Berkeley, Calif., 1963-67; instr. political science and Afro-American history, Merritt Coll., Oakland, Calif., 1964-67; instr. political science and Afro-American history, Laney Coll., Oakland, Calif., 1967; instr. Afro-American history, Univ. of Calif., extension division, Berkeley, 1967-68; asst. to the exec. vice chancellor, Univ. of Calif., Berkeley, 1968-69; asst. chancellor, special programs, Univ. of Calif., Berkeley, 1969-.
Memberships: Numerous organizations, including Am. Academy of Social and Political Science; Am. Political Science Assn.; ASNLH; U.N. Assn.; Kappa Alpha Psi.
Publications: From Africa to the United States and Then, 1969.
Mailing Address: University of California, Berkeley, Calif. 94720.

GORDON, EDMUND WYATT, Minister, Psychologist
Born: Goldsboro, N.C., June 13, 1921.
Education: B.S., Howard Univ., 1942; B.D., ibid., 1945; M.A.,
    Am. Univ., 1950; Ed.D., Columbia Tchrs. Coll., 1957.
Family: m. Susan Elizabeth Gitt; children, Edmund T.,
    Christopher W., Jessica G., Johanna S.
Professional Experience: Ordained, Presbyterian Church,
    1945; field missionary, bd. nat. missions, Presby-
    terian Church, 1945-46; asst. dean of men, Howard
    Univ, 1946-50; asst. dir. and counseling psychologist,
    Morningside Community Center and Mental Health
    Service, N.Y.C., 1951-52; part-time clinical asst.,
    psychiatry, senior psychologist and supr., Jewish
    Hosp., Brooklyn, N.Y., 1952-60; co-founder, Harriet
    Tubman Clinic for children, N.Y.C., 1953-59; chmn.,
    dept. of special ed., Yeshiva Univ., 1959-61; research
    asst. prof., Albert Einstein Coll. Medicine, 1963-;
    chmn., dept. guidance and prof. ed., Tchrs. Coll.,
    Columbia Univ., 1968-; cons.
Memberships: Research grants review panel, U.S. Office
    Ed., 1964-; NAACP, pres. Rockland County branch, N.Y.,
    1956-61; N.Y. State Psychol. Assn., pres. of applied so-
    cial div., 1965-66; Am. Orthopsychiat. Assn; Soc. Re-
    search Child Development; A.A.A.S.; Am. Personnel and
    Guidance Assn.
Awards: Fellow research conf., learning and ed. process,
    Stanford, 1964; fellow, Am. Psychol. Assn.
Publications: Contributed numerous articles to journals.
    Author, Compensatory Education for the Disadvantaged:
    Programs and Practices - Preschool Through College
    (with Doxey A. Wilkerson), 1966.
Mailing Address: Columbia University, Teachers College,
    523 West 120 Street, New York, N.Y. 10027.

GORDONE, CHARLES
Publications: No Place to Be Somebody; A Black Comedy in
    Three Acts, 1969.

GRAHAM, LE
Publications: Black Narrator.

GRAHAM, LORENZ, Author
Born: New Orleans, La., Jan. 27, 1902.
Education: Univ. of California, Los Angeles, 1922-24; B.A.,
    Va. Union Univ., 1936; New York Sch. of Social Work,
    1954; New York Univ., 1955-57.
Family: m. Ruth Morris; children, Mrs. Joyce Johnson, Mrs.
    Ruth May, Charles M.

Professional Experience: Tchr., Monrovia Coll., Liberia, 1925-
29; probation officer, Los Angeles County, 1957-66;
social worker, Federation of Churches, N.Y., 1949-56;
real estate business, Long Island, N.Y., 1946-48; camp
ed. adviser, Civilian Conservation Corps, Va., 1934-45.
Memberships: Authors' League of America; P.E.N. Internat.;
Southern Calif. Writers' Guild; Kappa Alpha Psi.
Awards: Thomas Alva Edison Foundation Citation, 1956;
Charles W. Follett Award, 1958; Child Study Assn. of
America Award, 1958; Vassie D. Wright Award, 1967;
Southern Calif. Council of Literature for Children and
Young People Award, 1968; Book World, first prize, 1969.
Publications: Numerous books, latest, Southtown, 1958; I,
Momolu, 1966; North Town, 1965; Whose Town? 1969;
Every Man Heart Lay Down, 1970; John Brown at Harpers
Ferry, 1971.
Mailing Address: 4911 Sixth Ave., Los Angeles, Calif. 90043.

GRAHAM, SHIRLEY LOLA (Mrs. W. E. B. DuBois), Author,
Composer
Born: Indianapolis, Ind., Nov. 11, 1906.
Education: Advanced musical training, Paris, 1926-28; French
Certificate, Sorbonne Univ., 1929; B.A., Oberlin Coll.,
1934; M.A. ibid., 1935; Yale Univ. Drama School, 1938-
40; L.H.D. (hon.), Univ. of Mass., 1973.
Family: 1st m. Shadrach T. McCunts; 2nd m. W. E. B. DuBois;
s., 1st m., David Graham.
Professional Experience: Head, Fine Art Dept., Tenn. State
Coll., 1935-36; dir., Negro unit, Chicago Federal Theater,
1936-38; USO dir.; YWCA dir., 1940-42; field sec.,
NAACP, 1942-44; organizing dir., Ghana Television,
1964-66; founding editor, Freedomways, 1960-63; English editor, Afro-Asian Writers Bureau, Peking, China,
1968.
Memberships: Kappa Delta Pi; Sigma Delta Theta; P.E.N.
Awards: Julius Rosenwald Fellow, Yale Univ. Drama School,
1938-40; Guggenheim Fellow for historical research,
1945-47; Julian Messner award, There Was Once a
Slave, 1950; Anisfield-Wolf Award, Your Most Humble
Servant, 1950.
Publications: Contributed to numerous journals and news-
papers; composer, music drama, Tom Tom, 1932.
Author, Dr. George Washington Carver, Scientist,
1944 (with George Lipscombe); Paul Robeson, Citizen
of the World, 1946; There Was Once a Slave, 1947; The
Story of Phyllis Wheatley, 1949; Your Most Humble
Servant, 1949; Jean Baptiste Point de Sable, Founder of
Chicago, 1953; The Story of Pocahantas, 1954; Booker
T. Washington, Educator, 1955; His Day Is Marching On:
A Memoir of W. E. B. DuBois, 1971; Gamal Abdel
Nasser: Son of the Nile, 1972; The Zulu Heart (in press).
Mailing Address: 76 Nile Street, Apt. 24, Giza, Cairo, Egypt.

GREEN, ROBERT L., Educational director
Born: Detroit, Mich., Nov. 23, 1933.
Education: B.A., San Francisco State Coll., 1958; M.A., ibid.,
    1960; Ph.D., Michigan State Univ., 1963.
Family: m. Lettie; children, Robert, Melvin, Kurt.
Professional Experience: Research asst., Langley Porter
    Research Inst., Univ. of Calif., San Francisco, 1959-60;
    sch. psychology intern, pub. schs., Oakland, Calif., 1959-
    60; group counselor, juvenile court, San Francisco, Calif.,
    June-September 1960; psychologist, Lansing Child Guid-
    ance Clinic, part-time, Lansing, Mich., 1961-62; instr.
    ed. psychology, Mich. State Univ., 1960-62; asst. prof.
    ed., Mich. State Univ., half-time, while serving as prin-
    cipal investigator on research grant for focusing on the
    ed. status of school-deprived Black children, Prince
    Edward County, Va., 1963-65; ed. dir., SCLS, Atlanta,
    Ga., 1965-66; dir., OE Grant, Chicago Adult Ed. Project
    for SCLS, June-October 1967; prof. ed. psychology, asst.
    provost, and dir., Center for Urban Affairs, Mich. State
    Univ., 1968-; served as cons. and on numerous commit-
    tees, such as President's Youth Opportunity Commn.,
    Mich. State Dept. of Ed.
Memberships: Cochairman, Assn. of Black Psychologists; Am.
    Psychological Assn.; Society for the Psychological Study
    of Social Issues; Am. Ed. Research Assn.
Awards: Mich. State Univ. Faculty Award, 1968.
Publications: Contributed to journals. Author, Racial Crisis
    in American Education, 1969; Famous Negro American
    Series, 1970.
Mailing Address: 1170 Bryant Dr., East Lansing, Mich. 48823.

GREENE, LORENZO J., Educator
Born: Ansonia, Conn., Nov. 16, 1899.
Education: A.B., Howard Univ., 1924; M.A., Columbia Univ.,
    1926; Ph.D., ibid., 1942.
Family: m. Thomasina T.; s. Lorenzo Thomas.
Professional Experience: Research Assoc. for Dr. Carter G.
    Woodson, 1928-33; asst. prof. history, Lincoln Univ.,
    Mo., 1933-45; vis. prof. history, summer session,
    Tennessee A & I Coll., 1945; cons., Afro-American his-
    tory, pub. sch. systems of Alton, Ill., Pittsburgh, Pa.,
    Springfield and Columbia, Mo.; cons., Black Frontier
    study, Univ. of Nebraska; cons. to pub. sch. theatrical
    group, Kansas City, Mo., and to various colleges on
    black history; vis. prof. history, Southern Ill. Univ.,
    Edwardsville, 1968; vis. prof. history, Univ. of Kansas,
    spring 1969-.
Memberships: ASNLH; Am. Historical Assn.; Mo. State His-
    torical Assn.; NAACP; Organization of Am. Historians.
Awards: Rosenwald Fund; General Ed. Bd., ASNLH.

Publications: Contributed numerous articles to professional journals. Author, latest publications, The Negro in Colonial New England, 1620-1776, 1942; Desegregation of Schools in Missouri, 1954-1959.
Mailing Address: Lincoln University, Jefferson City, Mo. 65101.

GREENFIELD, ELOISE, Author
Born: Parmele, N.C., May 17, 1929.
Education: Miner Tchrs. Coll., 1946-49.
Family: m. Robert J. Greenfield; children, Steven R., Monica Joyce.
Professional Experience: Clerk-typist, 1949-56; supervisory patent asst., U.S. Patent Office, 1956-60; case control technician, Work and Training Opportunity Center, 1967-68; adminstrv. asst., Dept. of Occupations and Professions, 1968.
Memberships: Co-chmn., D.C. Black Writers' Workshop.
Publications: Contributed to journals. Author, Bubbles, 1972.
Mailing Address: 830 Buchanan St., N.E., Washington, D.C. 20017.

GREENIDGE, EDWIN, Housing administr.
Born: New York, N.Y., April 17, 1929.
Education: B.S., Long Island Univ., 1947-55; Long Island graduate sch., 1958-60.
Family: m. Lillian; s. Cyril George II.
Professional Experience: Staff sgt., U.S. Army Adminstn., 1951-53; district supr., Bd. of Ed., N.Y.C., 1955-68; deputy Commr., N.Y.C., Youth Services Agency, 1968-70; cons., President's Council on Physical Fitness; Roving Leader Institute, Univ. of Illinois; deputy adminstr., N.Y.C. Housing and Development Adminstrn., 1970-.
Memberships: Past pres., Courtsman A.A., Inc.; Bd. of Dirs., Vermont Youth Project, Inc., N.Y.C.; Bd. of Dirs., Manpower and Minority Caucus Chmn.; N.Y. Urban Coalition, Inc., Bd. of Dirs.; Coalition-Jobs.
Awards: Wagner Youth and Adult Center, Testimonial Award, 1963; Certificate of Honor, Operation Better Block, 1969; Courtsman A.A., Community Achievement Award; A.W.V.S. Community Service Award; Morrisania Youth and Community Service Center, Inc., Man of the Year Award, 1969; P. Ballantine and Sons, Service to Youth Award, 1970; Council Against Poverty, Testimonial Award, 1970.
Publications: If Not Now, When? 1969.
Mailing Address: 100 Gold St., Room 9009, New York, N.Y. 10038.

GREENLEE, SAM, Author
Born: Chicago, Ill., July 13, 1930.
Education: B.S., Univ. of Wisconsin, 1952; Univ. of Chicago,
    1954-57; Univ. of Thessaloniki, Greece, 1963-64.
Family: m. Nienke.
Professional Experience: 1st lt., infantry, U.S. Army, 1952-54;
    foreign service officer, U.S. Information Agency, 1957-
    65; deputy dir., LMOC, 1965-69.
Awards: Meritorious Service Award, USIA; Book of the Year,
    British Press, 1969.
Publications: Contributed articles and short stories to maga-
    zines, journals and newspapers. Author, The Spook Who
    Sat By the Door, 1969; Blues for an African Princess,
    1970.
Mailing Address: 6240 South Champlain Ave., Chicago, Ill.,
    60637.

GREGORY, DICK, Comedian, Author
Born: St. Louis, Mo., 1932.
Education: Southern Ill. Univ., 1951-53, 1955-56.
Family: m. Lillian Smith; children, Michele, Lynne, Paula,
    Pamela, Stephanie, Gregory, Miss, Christian, Ayanna,
    Yohance.
Professional Experience: AUS, 1953-55; entertainer; master
    of ceremonies, Roberts Show Club, Chicago, 1959-60;
    Playboy Club, Chicago, 1961; lectr., colleges and uni-
    versities; Peace and Freedom Party candidate, 1968.
Awards: Winner, mile championship, 1951, 52; Outstanding
    Athlete, Southern Ill. Univ., 1953.
Publications: Nigger, 1964; From the Back of the Bus, 1964;
    What's Happening, 1965; The Shadow that Scares Me,
    1971; Write Me In, 1971; No More Lies, 1971; Dick
    Gregory's Political Primer, 1972.
Mailing Address: 1415 East 55 St., Chicago, Ill. 60637.

GRIER, WILLIAM H.
Publications: Black Rage (with Price Cobbs), 1968; The Jesus
    Bag (with Price Cobbs), 1971.

GROSVENOR, KALI
Publications: Poems by Kali, 1970.

GROSVENOR, VERTA MAE, Author
Born: Fairfax, Allendale County, South Carolina, April 4, 1938.
Education: Kensington High Sch., Philadelphia, Pa.

Family: Children, Kali, Chandra.
Professional Experience: Food columnist, Amsterdam News,
    Chicago Courier.
Memberships: PUSH.
Publications: Contributed articles and stories to newspapers,
    magazines and anthologies. Author, Vibration Cooking,
    1970; Thursdays and Every Other Sunday Off, a Domestic
    Rap, 1972.
Mailing Address: 286 East 2 St., New York, N.Y. 10009.

GWAITNEY, JOHN LANGSTON, Educator
Born: Orange, N.J., Sept. 25, 1928.
Education: B.A., Upsala Coll., 1952; M.A., New School for
    Social Research, 1957; Ph.D., Columbia Univ., 1967.
Family: m. Judith; children, Karen, Peter.
Professional Experience: Ethnographic fieldwork among
    Chinantec of Oaxaca, Mex., and Shinnecock and Poospa-
    tuck marginals of Long Island; assoc. prof., State Univ.
    of New York, Cortland, 1967-.
Memberships: Am. Anthropological Soc.; Am. Ethnological
    Soc.; Soc. for Applied Anthropology.
Awards: John Hay Whitney Fellow; Ruth Benedict Memorial
    Award; Nat. Inst. of Health Fellow; N.Y.S. Univ. Council
    Grant; N.Y.S. Ed. Dept. Grant; Columbia Univ. Ansley
    Dissertation Award.
Publications: The Thrice Shy: Cultural Accommodations to
    Blindness and Other Disasters in a Mexican Village,
    1970; Role of Expectation of Blindness in an Oaxaca
    Village, 1970.
Mailing Address: 15 Graham Ave., Cortland, N.Y. 13048.

HAIRSTON, LOYLE, Author
Born: Macon, Miss., July 1, 1926.
Education: Macon High Sch., 1932-43; Robert Louis Stevenson,
    N.Y.C., 1949-51.
Family: m. Yael; children, Mark, Jonathan, Ilana Susie.
Professional Experience: Seaman, U.S. Naval Reserves serving
    in the Pacific theater, Carolines, Marianas, Okinawa in
    black work battalion, logistics, 1944-46.
Memberships: NAACP; CORE; SCLS; Malcolm X's Nationalist
    Forum.
Publications: Contributed to newspapers and journals. Author
    of short stories in Anthology: Harlem, U.S.A. and Ameri-
    can Negro Short Stories, 1966; essay in William Styron's
    Nat Turner: Ten Black Writers Respond, 1968.
Mailing Address: 1414 Brooklyn Ave., Brooklyn, N.Y. 11210.

HALE, FRANK W., JR., College president
Born: Kansas City, Mo., Mar. 24, 1927.
Education: A.B., Univ. of Nebraska, 1950; M.A., ibid., 1951;
    Ph.D., Ohio State Univ., 1955; Univ. of London, summer
    1960.
Family: m. Ruth Colleen; children, Mrs. Ruth Hale Carey,
    Frank W., III, Sherilyn Renene.
Professional Experience: Instr. English and speech, Oakwood
    Coll., Huntsville, Ala., 1951-53; dir., pub. relations,
    Oakwood Coll., 1952-53; asst. instr. speech, Ohio State
    Univ., 1954-55; prof. and head, Dept. of Speech, Oakwood
    Coll., 1955-59; vis. prof. speech, Andrews Univ., Wash-
    ington, D.C., summer 1957; prof. and chmn., Dept. of
    English, Central State Coll., Wilberforce,Ohio, 1959-66;
    pres., Oakwood Coll., 1966-; served as cons., Bd. of Ed.,
    Xenia, Ohio, 1964; book cons., Choice; communications
    cons., Career Development branch, U.S. Air Force,
    Wright-Patterson Air Force Base, Ohio, 1965-66; served
    on numerous boards, including Ala. Center for Higher
    Ed., 1967; Mental Health Assn., 1968-; Riverside Hospi-
    tal, Nashville, Tenn., 1966-.
Memberships: Am. Assn. of Colleges and Universities; ASNLH;
    Am. Assn. of Sch. Administrators; NCTE; MLA; Speech
    Assn. of America; Ohio Speech Assn.; Ohio English
    Assn.
Awards: Assistantship, Ohio State Univ., 1954; British Council
    Award, 1960; Distinguished Alumnus of the Year, Dept
    of Speech, Ohio State Univ., 1970.
Publications: Contributed to journals. Author, A Manual of
    Public Speaking, 1964; The Cry for Freedom, 1970.
Mailing Address: Oakwood College, Huntsville, Ala. 35806.

HALEY, ALEX, Author
Born: Ithaca, N.Y., August 11, 1921.
Education: High sch., Normal, Ala.; Alcorn AM&N; Elizabeth
    City State Teacher's Coll.; D. Litt (hon.), Simpson Coll.,
    Indianola, Iowa.
Professional Experience: U.S. Coast Guard, 1939-59.
Publications: The Autobiography of Malcolm X, 1965.
Mailing Address: Box 2907, San Francisco, Calif. 94126.

HALL, JAMES C., JR., Educator
Born: New York, N.Y., Aug. 10, 1932.
Education: B.S., New York Univ., 1954-57; M.A., ibid., 1959-
    62; Ed. D., ibid., 1962-66.
Family: d. Marie-Elena.
Professional Experience: Class Instr., life guard, court re-
    corder, U.S. Marine Corps, 1951-54; tchr. elementary
    grades 5 and 6, 1957-62; instr. science and mathematics,
    Mills Coll. of Ed., N.Y.C., summer 1962; elementary re-

source tchr., adminstrv. intern, supt.'s office, Mamaroneck, N.Y., 1962-63; elementary prin., Mamaroneck Ave. Sch., 1963-65; supr., student tchrs., Mamaroneck Ave. Sch., for New York Univ., 1963-64; coordinator of demonstration sch., New York Univ. project in Virgin Islands, 1965-66; asst. prof. tchr. ed., College of the Virgin Islands, St. Thomas, 1966-67; dir. interns and assoc. prof. tchr. ed., Antioch-Putney Graduate Sch. of Ed., Washington, D.C., Center, 1967-68; ed. specialist, Peace Corps, Office of Planning, Program Review and Research, Washington, D.C. 1968-69; dir. curriculum development, EDCOM Systems, Research and Development, Princeton, N.J., 1969; dean of students, New York Community Coll., Brooklyn, N.Y., 1970-; served as cons. for various programs, including Univ. of Maryland Model Sch. project, NEA publications, Peace Corps elementary tchr.-trainees and Vista trainees.
Memberships: Kappa Delta Pi; Phi Delta Kappa; NEA.
Publications: Contributed articles and book reviews to journals. Author, Damn Reading: A Case Against Literacy, 1969 (with James M. Gibson).
Mailing Address: Harbor View South, Staten Island, New York, N.Y.10301.

HALL, NATHANIEL B., Teacher
Born: Brevard, N.C., Jan. 17, 1916.
Education: B.S., Miner Tchrs. Coll., 1947; M.A., Catholic Univ. of America, 1953; Harvard Univ., 1966-67.
Family: m. Catherine W.; children, Winston Nathaniel, Bernard Alvin.
Professional Experience: Warrant officer, j.g., armed forces, 1941-45; clerk typist, Freedmens' Hospital, 1947-49; statistical clerk, Census Bureau, 1949-52; tchr. social studies, pub. schs., Washington, D.C., 1952-; asst. prin., Eastern High Sch., summer 1969.
Memberships: D.C. Assn. for Classroom Tchrs.; NEA.
Awards: Twenty Year Award for Government Service.
Publications: They've Been Neglected Too Long, 1969.
Mailing Address: 425 9 St., N.E., Washington, D.C. 20002.

HALLIBURTON, WARREN J., Author
Born: New York, N.Y., April 2, 1924.
Education: B.S., New York Univ., 1949.
Family: m. Marion; children, Cheryl, Stephanie, Warren, Jr.
Professional Experience: Instr., Prairie View A & M. Coll., 1949-51; assoc., Inst. of Internat. Ed., 1951-54; tchr., dean, coordinator, Bd. of Ed., N.Y.C., 1954-64; specialist, Bd. of Ed., N.Y., 1964-65; editor, McGraw-Hill Publishing Co., 1966-68.
Memberships: Alpha Phi Alpha.

Awards: Phi Beta Sigma; PTA; Community Track and Field.
Publications: Contributed to journals and newspapers.
   Author, The Heist, 1968; Cry Baby, 1968; Some Things
   That Glitter, 1969; edited, Year the Yankees Lost the
   Pennant, 1968; Minorities and Majorities: A Syllabus
   of United States History for Secondary Schools (with
   William L. Katz); Call of the Wild (by Jack London),
   1968.
Mailing Address: 19 Emery St., Hempstead, N.Y. 11550.

HAMER, MARTIN J., Marketing director
Born: New York, N.Y., Nov. 24, 1931; City Coll. of N.Y.,
   1959-64.
Family: m. Judith A.; children, three.
Professional Experience: Dir. of marketing, McGraw-Hill
   Book Co., 1967-.
Awards: Atlantic Monthly First, for "Sarah," 1964.
Publications: Timo the Draftsman, 1967; Sniper, 1970.
Mailing Address: 330 West 42 St., New York, N.Y. 10036.

HAMILTON, CHARLES V., Educator
Born: Muskogee, Okla., Oct. 19, 1929.
Education: B.A., Roosevelt Univ., 1948-51; J.D., Loyola
   Univ., 1951-54; M.A., Univ. of Chicago, 1955-57; Ph.D.,
   ibid., 1960-63.
Family: m. Dora L.; children, Carol, Valli.
Professional Experience: U.S. Army, 1948-49; asst. prof.,
   Tuskegee Inst., 1958-60; instr., Rutgers Univ., 1963-
   64; prof., Lincoln Univ., Pa., 1964-67; prof., Roosevelt
   Univ., 1967-69; prof., Columbia Univ., 1969-.
Memberships: Am. Political Science Assn.
Awards: Lindback Distinguished Teaching Award, 1965; Univ.
   of Chicago Alumni Award, 1970.
Publications: Contributed to journals. Author, Black Power:
   The Politics of Liberation in America (with Stokely
   Carmichael), 1967.
Mailing Address: Dept. of Political Science, Columbia Univer-
   sity, New York, N.Y. 10027.

HAMILTON, ROBERT (Bobb), Educator
Education: B.S., Ohio State Univ., 1950; New School 1954-57;
   Art Students League, 1959; New School, 1967; Queens
   Community Coll., Remedial Inst., summer 1970.
Professional Experience: Tchr. remedial English, ARCH
   Program, Harlem, 1969; tchr. art and writing, Dept. of
   Welfare, Bureau of Special Services, 1964-67; tchr.
   English (SEEK), Queens Coll., 1968-.

Awards: Writers' Fellowship, Fairleigh Dickinson, 1961; Citation in Sculpture, Afro Arts Theater, 1958; Harlem Cultural Council Grant, Creative Writing, 1969.
Publications: Contributed to journals. Poet and script writer, films for Jymie Productions' "Naifa," "Mo Militant," and "Home."
Mailing Address: 473 West 152 St., New York, N.Y. 10031.

HARDING, VINCENT, Educator
Born: New York, N.Y., July 25, 1931.
Education: B.A., City Coll. of N.Y., 1952; M.S., Columbia Univ., 1953; M.A., Univ. of Chicago, 1956; Ph.D. ibid., 1965.
Family: m. Rosemarie Freeney; children, Rachel Sojourner, Jonathan DuBois.
Professional Experience: U.S. Army, 1953-55; lay pastor (part-time), Seventh Day Adventist Mission Church, Chicago, 1955-57; lay pastor (part-time), Woodlawn Mennonite Church, Chicago, 1957-61; southern rep., Mennonite Service Com., Atlanta, Ga., acting as civil rights negotiator for various movement organizations, 1961-65; chmn., dept. of history and sociology, Spelman Coll., 1965-69; dir., Martin Luther King Library Project, 1968-70; dir., Inst. of the Black World, 1969-; chmn., Adv. Coordinating Com. for "Black Heritage," 108 TV programs on Afro-American History (CBS-TV), 1968-69.
Awards: Including research grants, Am. Council of Learned Societies, The Atlanta Univ. Center Research Com., Atlanta Univ. Center Non-Western Studies Com.
Publications: Contributed numerous articles and essays to journals and books. Author, Must Walls Divide? 1965; Black Radicalism in America (in preparation); editor (with John H. Clarke), 22 vol. series of Black Heritage Books, 1970; editor (with Wilfred Cartey and Hoyt Fuller), multi-volume series, Documents on the Black Experience (in preparation).
Mailing Address: 87 Chestnut St., Atlanta, Ga. 30314.

HARE, NATHAN, Educator, Publisher
Born: Slick, Okla., April 9, 1934.
Education: A.B., Langston Univ., 1954; M.A., Univ. of Chicago, 1957; Ph.D., Univ. of Chicago, 1962; Northwestern Univ., Medill Sch. of Journalism, 1959.
Family: m. Julia.
Professional Experience: Instr., Va. State Coll., 1957-58; interviewer (part-time), National Opinion Research Center, Youth Studies Center, Univ. of Chicago, 1959-61; research asst., Population Research and Training Center, Univ. of Chicago, 1960-61; asst. prof. sociology, Howard Univ.,

1964-67; chmn., Dept. of Black Studies, San Francisco
State Coll., 1968-69; dir., Black Studies Curriculum, San
Francisco State, Feb. - Sept., 1968; publisher, The Black
Scholar, Nov. 1969-; chmn., Task Force on Demographic
and Communal Characteristics, D.C. Pub. Schs., Colum-
bia Univ. Tchrs. College Study, 1966-67.
Memberships: Pres., Howard Univ. chapter of AAUP, 1967.
Awards: Including Best Tutor, Parents' Day Award, Langston
University, 1954; Omega Psi Phi Scholar of the Year
(Tex., La., Okla.), 1954; Favorite Professor, Howard
Univ., 1965-66, 1966-67; Black is Beautiful Citation,
United Black Artist, 1968; Black Power Award,
A.F.R.I.C.A., N.Y., 1968; elected to N.Y. Academy of
Sciences.
Publications: Contributed numerous articles and book reviews
to journals and magazines. Author, The Black Anglo
Saxons, 1965.
Mailing Address: The Black Scholar, Box 31245, San Francisco,
Calif. 94131.

HARPER, MICHAEL S., Educator
Born: Brooklyn, N.Y., Mar. 18, 1938.
Education: B.A., Calif. State, Los Angeles, 1959-61; M.A.,
ibid., 1962-63; M.A. (creative writing), Univ. of Iowa,
1961-62.
Family: m. Shirley; children, Roland Warren, Patrice Cuchu-
lain.
Professional Experience: Instr. English, Contra Costa Coll.,
1964-68; vis. prof., Lewis and Clark Coll., 1968-69;
vis. lectr., Reed Coll., 1968-69; assoc. prof., Calif.
State, Hayward; Brown Univ., 1969-; contributing editor,
the Black Scholar.
Memberships: Original founding mem., African Continuum, St.
Louis, Mo.
Awards: Post-doctoral fellow, Center for Advanced Study,
Univ. of Ill.
Publications: Contributed to magazines and anthologies.
Author, Dear John, Dear Coltrane, 1970; History Is
Your Own Heartbeat, 1971.
Mailing Address: Dept. of English, Brown University, Provi-
dence, R.I. 01912.

HARRIS, JANETTE HOSTON, Graduate student
Born: Monroe, La., Sept. 7, 1939.
Education: B.A., Central State Univ., 1962; M.A., Howard Univ.,
1972; Ph.D. candidate, history, Howard Univ.
Family: m. Rudolph; children, Rylan Rudolph, Junie Janette.
Professional Experience: Classification officer, Peace Corps,
Washington, D.C., April 1962 - April 1964; elementary
sch. tchr., D.C. Public Schs., Sept. 1964 - June 1970;

research asst., Assn. Study of Negro Life and History,
Washington, D.C., July 1970 - June 1972; research asst.
to Dr. Lorraine Williams, chmn., dept. of history,
Howard Univ., July 1972-; Blacks in Business project,
dept. of history, Howard Univ.; editor, Black Child Advocate newspaper; contract with Afro-American Bi-
Centennial on Blacks, Washington, D.C.; contract with
HEW, Office of Ed. on "Teacher Load."
Memberships: ASNLH; Organization of Am. Historians; Southern Historical Assn.; Phi Alpha Theta.
Awards: Ford Foundation grant; Roothbert Foundation grant.
Publications: Contributed articles to journals, encyclopedias,
book reviews and poetry to newspapers and magazines.
Publications: Black Crusaders in History, Congress and
Government, 1972; Directory of Black Historians, 1973.
Mailing Address: 18 Farragut Place, N.W., Washington, D.C.
20011.

HARRIS, MIDDLETON, Parole officer (ret.)
Born: Brooklyn, N.Y., Jan. 22, 1908.
Education: B.A., Howard Univ., 1927-31; M.S.W., Fordham
Univ., 1953-55.
Professional Experience: Boys worker, Hudson Ave. Boys
Club, Brooklyn, N.Y., 1931-35; senior parole officer,
N.Y. State Div. of Parole, 1935-69, ret.; Am. Red Cross
field dir., Southwest Pacific, World War II.
Memberships: Am. Academy of Political and Social Science;
NAACP; Nat. Assn. Social Workers; Nat. Council on
Crime and Delinquency; pres., Negro History Associates,
Inc.
Awards: Federation of Negro Civil Service Organization, 1965;
Plaque as founder of The Counseliers, an organization of
professional workers in field of parole, probation and re-
lated services.
Publications: A Negro History Tour of Manhattan, 1968; Case-
book #1: Uncle Spike, the Negro History Detective, 1967;
also filmstrips, "Early American Inventors," 1964;
"The Revolutionary Period: The Story of Lewis Lati-
mer," 1964; "The Doctor Is a Lady," 1967; "Anti-
Slavery Coins," 1967.
Mailing Address: 51 Herkimer St., Brooklyn, N.Y. 11216.

HASKETT, EDYTHE RANCE, Teacher
Born: Suffolk, Va.
Education: Lawrenceville Junior Coll., 1930-34; A.B., Shaw
Univ., 1938-39; M.A., New York Univ., 1946-49; Rutgers
Univ., 1958; Columbia Univ., 1966.
Family: s. John Oswald.
Professional Experience: Tchr., pub. schs., N.C., 1934-45;
elementary supr., Louisa County Schs., 1945-50; art

resource tchr., Norfolk City Schs., 1950; tchr.-prin.,
House of Bethany Episcopal High Sch., Robertsport,
Liberia, 1962-64.
Memberships: Alpha Kappa Alpha; Va. Ed. Assn., Norfolk Urban Coalition; Norfolk Chapter U.N.; Human Relations
Council; Women for Political Action; AAUW; NEA.
Awards: Outstanding Citizen, Radio Station WRAP citation,
1962; Distinguished Community Service Award by AKA;
Building Bridges of Understanding, citation by Commn.
on the Improvement of Ed., 1968.
Publications: Grains of Pepper (tales from Liberia), 1967;
Some Gold, A Little Ivory, 1971.
Mailing Address: 2741 Woodland Ave., Norfolk, Va. 23504.

HASKINS, JIM
Publications: Diary of a Harlem Schoolteacher, 1970.

HAWKINS, ODIE
Publications: Ghetto Sketches, 1972.

HAYDEN, ROBERT E., Poet
Born: Detroit, Mich., August 4, 1913.
Education: B.A., Wayne Univ.; M.A., Univ. of Mich.
Professional Experience: Teaching fellow, English, Univ. of
Mich., 1944-46; asst. prof., assoc. prof. English, Fisk
Univ., 1946-69; assoc. prof. English, Univ. of Mich.,
1969-.
Awards: Hopwood for poetry, 1938, 1942; creative writing fellowship, Special Services Com., Ann Arbor, 1946; Julius
Rosenwald Fellowship, creative writing, 1947; grand
prize, World Festival of Negro Arts, Dakar, Senegal, for
A Ballad of Remembrance; Ford Foundation fellow for
writing and travel in Mexico, 1954-55.
Publications: Contributed poetry to numerous magazines and
anthologies. Author, The Lion and the Archer (with Myron O'Higgins), 1948; A Ballad of Remembrance, 1963;
Selected Poems, 1966; Kaleidoscope: Poems by American
Negro Poets, 1968; editor, Afro-American Literature, An
Introduction (with David Burrows and Frederick Lapides),
1972.
Mailing Address: Department of English, University of Michigan, Ann Arbor, Mich. 48104.

HEARD, NATHAN C., Author
Born: Newark, N.J., Nov. 17, 1936.
Education: High sch. dropout.
Family: m. Nina; children, Melvin, Cliff, DeNina.

Professional Experience: Laborer, factory worker, musician; lectr., Fresno State Coll.; asst. prof. English, Rutgers Univ. (Livingston Coll.).
Awards: Author Award, N.J. Assn. of Tchrs. of English.
Publications: Howard Street, 1968; To Reach A Dream, 1970.
Mailing Address: 94 North 16 St., East Orange, N.J. 07017.

HERCULES, FRANK
Publications: Where the Hummingbird Flies, 1961; I Want a Black Doll, 1967; American Society and Black Revolution, 1972.

HERNTON, CALVIN C., Author, Educator
Born: Chattanooga, Tenn.
Education: B.A., Talladega Coll.; M.A., Fisk Univ.; Columbia Univ.
Professional Experience: Social worker, Leake and Watts Home for Children, Yonkers, N.Y., summer 1954; Youth House for Boys, Welfare Is., N.Y., 1956-57; social investigator, N.Y. Dept. of Welfare, 1961-62; instr. sociology and history, Southern Univ., Baton Rouge, La.; Edward Waters Coll., Jacksonville, Fla.; Alabama A & M Coll., Normal, Ala., 1957-61; technical typist, Chemical Bank New York Trust Co.; coding and research technician, Richard Manville Market Research; interviewer, National Opinion Research Center, N.Y.; writer-in-residence, Central State Univ., Wilberforce, Ohio, January-June 1970; assoc. prof., Afro-American Studies, Oberlin Coll.-; lectr., including West Indian Writers' Conf., Univ. of Kent, England, 1967, Columbia Univ., 1964; Clarte Soc., Stockholm, Sweden, 1967, New Sch. for Social Research, 1964, and others.
Awards: Fellow., Institute of Phenomenological Studies, London, 1965, 1968-69.
Publications: Contributed stories, poetry, and articles to numerous periodicals and anthologies; author, Sex and Racism in America, 1964; White Papers for White Americans, 1966; Coming Together, White Hate, Black Power and Sexual Hangups, 1971.
Mailing Address: 160 North Main St., Oberlin, Ohio 44074.

HIGGINS, CHESTER
Publications: Black Woman, 1970.

HILL, ADELAIDE CROMWELL
Publications: Apropos of Africa: Sentiments of Negro American Leaders on Africa from 1800's to the 1950's, 1969.

HIMES, CHESTER (Bomar), Author
Born: Jefferson City, Mo., July 29, 1909.
Education: Ohio State Univ., 1926-28.
Family: 1st m., Jean Lucinda Johnson; 2nd m., Lesley.
Professional Experience: Bellhop, Cleveland, O.; sentenced
    at age of nineteen to twenty years for armed robbery,
    served seven years in Ohio State Penitentiary where he
    began to write and contribute stories to magazines, re-
    leased, 1935; employed in various capacities as writer,
    WPA; worked on Louis Bromfield's farm, Malabar;
    shipyard and aircraft employee, World War II, Los
    Angeles and San Francisco; traveled abroad, 1953.
Awards: Rosenwald fellow, creative writing, 1944-45; Grand
    Prix Policier for writing, 1958.
Publications: Contributed numerous articles and short stories
    to magazines. Author of numerous books, including If
    He Hollers Let Him Go, 1945; Lonely Crusader, 1947;
    Cast the First Stone, 1952; The Third Generation, 1954;
    The Primitive, 1955; Pinktoes, 1965; Cotton Comes to
    Harlem, 1965; Blind Man with a Pistol, 1969; Hot Day
    Hot Night, 1970; Quality of Hurt, Vol. I, 1972.
Mailing Address: c/o Doubleday, Inc., 277 Park Ave., New
    York, N.Y. 10013.

HOAGLAND, ERIC
Publications: Black Velvet.

HOBSON, JULIUS
Publications: Black Pride (with Janet Harris), 1969.

HODGES, NORMAN EDWARD, Educator
Born: Detroit, Mich., Aug. 24, 1939.
Education: B.A., Fisk Univ.; M.SC., London Sch. of Economics;
    M.A., Yale Univ.; M.A., Columbia Univ.; Ed.M., Ph.D.,
    ibid.; Univ. of the West Indies, Certificate in Afro-
    Caribbean Studies.
Family: m. Alice Ruth Nzilani Menje; s. Wambua Ngotho.
Professional Experience: Lieutenant to captain, U.S. Air Force;
    asst. prof., Hampton Inst.; assoc. prof., Vassar Coll.-.
Memberships: Alpha Phi Alpha; The Goat's Club of London;
    London Sch. of Economics Soc.; CORE; Am. Assn. of
    Univ. Professors.
Awards: Fulbright Scholar; Ford Foundation Internat. Fellow;
    Heft Scholar.
Publications: Contributed articles to professional journals.
    Author, Black History, 1971; Breaking the Chains of
    Bondage, 1972; The Garveys: The Human Side of Two
    Black Nationalists (in press).
Mailing Address: Box 2473, GPO, New York, N.Y. 10001.

HOLDEN, MATTHEW, JR., Educator
Born: Mound Bayou, Miss., Sept. 12, 1931.
Education: Univ. of Chicago, 1946-50; B.A., Roosevelt Univ.,
    1950-52; M.A., Northwestern Univ., 1953-56; Ph.D.,
    ibid., 1958-61.
Family: m. Dorothy Amanda Howard; children, Paul Christo-
    pher Hendricks, John Matthew Alexander.
Professional Experience: Research assoc., Ohio Legislative
    Service Com., summers 1954-55; military service, U.S.
    Army, Korea, 1955-57; research asst., Cleveland Metro-
    politan Services Com., 1957-58; staff cons., Cuyahoga
    County Charter Commn., Jan.-Oct. 1959; research
    assoc., Inst. of Govt. and Pub. Affairs, 1959-61; lectr.
    (part-time) political science, evening division, North-
    western Univ., Feb.-June 1961; asst. prof. political
    science, Wayne State Univ., 1962-63; vis. asst. prof.
    political science, Univ. of Vermont, 1963; asst.
    prof. political science, Univ. of Pittsburgh, 1963-66;
    assoc. prof. political science, Wayne State Univ., 1966-
    68; prof. political science, Univ. of Wisconsin, 1969-;
    cons. for various projects, including Ford Foundation,
    social science analysis in urban conflict, U.S. Pub.
    Health Service, U.S. Senate Subcommittee on Employ-
    ment, Manpower, and Poverty.
Memberships: Am. Assn. for the Advancement of Science;
    AAUP; Am. Political Assn.; Am. Soc. for Pub. Admin-
    strn.; Law and Society Assn.; Midwest Political Science
    Assn.; Southwestern Social Science Assn.
Publications: Contributed to journals. Author, Pollution
    Control As a Bargaining Process, 1966; The Republican
    Crisis: Race and Politics in America, 1970.
Mailing Address: Dept. of Political Science, 322 North Hall,
    University of Wisconsin, Madison, Wis. 53706.

HOLT, LEN
Publications: An Act of Conscience, 1965.

HOOVER, DOROTHY ESTHERYNE McFADDEN, Operations Re-
    search analyst
Born: Hope, Ark., July 2, 1918.
Education: B.S., AM & N Coll., 1934-38; M.S., Atlanta Univ.,
    1939-42; M.A., Univ. of Ark., 1953-54.
Family: Children, Mrs. Viola Clementyne Clarke Brannan
    (deceased), Ricardo Allen (deceased).
Professional Experience: Tchr., Ark., Ga., Tenn., 1938-43;
    jr. mathematician, NACA, Langley Aeronautical Lab.;
    research scientist, NACA, Langley Aeronautical Lab.,
    1950-52; tchr. fellow, Univ. of Mich., 1955-56; mathe-
    matician, Joint Numerical Weather Prediction Unit Fleet,
    Weather Central, 1956-59; mathematician, NASA, 1959-

68; operations research analyst, Defense Communications Agency, Nat. Military Command System Support Center, 1968-.
Memberships: Campbell A.M.E. Church; NAACP; Washington Urban League, Inc.; Churchwomen United in Greater Washington, Sigma Pi Sigma, Physic Honor Soc., 1954; Pi Mu Epsilon, Math Honor Soc., 1954.
Awards: John Hay Whitney Foundation Fellowship, 1954; tchr. fellowship, Dept. of Mathematics, Univ. of Mich., 1955; Certificate for Twenty Years of Faithful Federal Service, 1968.
Publications: A Layman Looks With Love at Her Church, 1970.
Mailing Address: Wingate House, Apt. C 1009, 4660 Nichols Ave., S.W., Washington, D.C. 20032.

HORNSBY, ALTON
Publications: Editor, In the Cage: Eyewitness Accounts of the Freed Negro in Southern Society, 1877-1929, 1971; The Black Almanac, 1972.

HUDSON, HOSEA
Publications: Black Worker in the Deep South, 1972.

HUGGINS, NATHAN IRVIN, Educator
Born: Chicago, Ill., Jan. 14, 1927.
Education: A.B., Univ. of Calif. (Berkeley), 1954; M.A., ibid., 1955; A.M., Howard Univ., 1959; Ph.D., ibid., 1962.
Family: m. Brenda Carlota Smith.
Professional Experience: Tchr. fellow, Harvard Coll., 1960-62; asst. prof. history, Calif. State Coll., Long Beach, 1962-64; asst. prof., Lake Forest Coll., Ill., 1964-66; asst. prof., assoc. prof., Univ. of Mass., 1966-70; vis. assoc. prof., Univ. of Calif., Berkeley, 1969-70; prof. history, Columbia Univ., 1970-; dir., Upward Bound Project, Univ. of Mass.; Commissioner, Mass. Tchr. Corp. Com., 1967-69; cons., including Negro History program, Univ. of Calif. Extension, 1964, Brookline Mass. Public Schs., 1968, Educational Associates, Washington, D.C., 1969, Harcourt Brace Jovanovich.
Memberships: Including advisory bd., WGBH-TV program, "On Being Black," 1968-69; bd. of advisors, Children's TV Workshop ("Sesame Street"), 1970-; bd. of advisors, Danforth Foundation's Black Studies Project, 1970-.
Awards: John Hay Whitney Opportunity Fellow, 1955-56, 1959-60; Jessie Smith Noyes Fellow, 1959-60; Guggenheim Fellow, 1971-72; Ford Foundation Travel Study Fellowship, 1972.

Publications: Protestants Against Poverty, 1971; Key Issues
in the Afro-American Experience (edited with Martin
Kilson and Daniel Fox), 1971; Harlem Renaissance, 1971.
Mailing Address: 410 Riverside Dr., Apt. 122, New York, N.Y.
10025.

HULBERT, JAMES A., Librarian (ret.)
Born: Greenville, Miss., Mar. 16, 1906.
Education: B.A., Morehouse Coll., 1933; B.S.L.S., Hampton
Institute, 1932; M.S.L.S., Columbia Univ., 1939; Univ.
of Chicago, Grad. Lib. Sch., 1944; Columbia Univ.,
Sch. of Lib. Service, 1944, doctoral study, 1949-50.
Family: m. Jewel Gentry; children, Marilyn, Marguerite,
Monique.
Professional Experience: Branch libn., Houston Pub. Lib.,
1933-35; cataloging asst., Atlanta Univ., 1935-37, head
cataloger, ibid., 1938-39; faculty asst., Sch. of Lib.
Service, Columbia Univ., 1949-50; head libn. and prof.
of lib. science, Virginia State Coll., 1939-45; libn.,
USIS, 1951-53, dir. lib. service, USIS, Paris, 1953-55;
chief libn., Atlanta Univ., 1955-57; dir. lib. service,
USIS, Dacca, East Pakistan, 1957-64; prof. lib. science,
Univ. of Dacca.
Memberships: NAACP; ALA; Alpha Phi Alpha.
Awards: U.S. State Dept, retirement, 1967.
Publications: Contributed articles to professional journals.
Author, An Introduction to Library Service, 1972.
Mailing address: 1032 South Lauderdale, Memphis, Tenn.
38126.

HUNTER, KRISTIN, Author, Lecturer
Born: Philadelphia, Pa., Sept. 12, 1931.
Education: B.S., Univ. of Pa., 1947-51.
Family: m. John I. Lattany.
Professional Experience: Tchr., pub schs., Camden, N.J.,
1951-52; copywriter, Lavenson Bureau, Phila., Pa., 1952-
59; copywriter, Werman & Schorr, Phila., Pa., 1962-63;
information officer, city of Phila., 1963-66; lectr. English, Univ. of Pa., 1972-.
Awards: Fund for the Republic TV script prize, 1955; Philadelphia Athenaeum literary Award for God Bless the Child,
1964; Council Interracial Books for Children Award,
Lewis Carroll Shelf Award, and Nat. Conf. of Christians
and Jews Mass Media Award, all for The Soul Brothers
and Sister Lou; Sigma Theta Chi Best Magazine Reporting
of the Year Award, article, "Pray for Barbara's Baby,"
1968; Chicago Tribune Book World Book Fair Award for
Guests in the Promised Land, 1973.

Publications: God Bless the Child, 1964; The Landlords, 1966;
The Soul Brothers and Sister Lou, 1968; Boss Cat, 1971;
Guests in the Promised Land, 1973.
Mailing Address: Box 8371, Philadelphia, Pa. 19101.

HURST, CHARLES G., JR., College president
Education: B.S., Wayne State Univ., 1953; M.A., ibid., 1958;
Ph.D., ibid., 1961; Univ. of Florida, summer 1962; Ohio
State Univ., summer 1963; Univ. of Florida, summer
1964.
Professional Experience: Asst. dir., Univ. Remedial Program,
admissions officer and counselor and instr. speech,
Wayne State Univ., 1953-61; asst. prof., 1961-66, assoc.
prof., 1966-68, asst. dean, 1961-64, assoc. dean, 1966-
68, head, dept. of speech, dir., Communication Science
Research Center, prof., Howard Univ., 1961-69; pres.,
Malcolm X College, Chicago, 1969-; served as cons. for
such programs as Job Corps, Bd. of Ed., Berkeley,
Calif., Nat. Conf. of Christians and Jews; editor, Wash-
ington Linguistics Review, Communication Sciences Re-
search Newsletter; inventor of electronic intelligibility
trainer and programmed talking toys for pre-school and
elementary classrooms.
Memberships: Acoustical Soc. of America; Speech Assn. of
America; Am. Assn. of Mental Deficiency; Central State
Speech Assn.; CLA; Internat. Phonetics Assn.; Am.
Speech and Hearing Assn.; NCTE; Nat. Soc. for Pro-
grammed Instruction.
Awards: Numerous study grants and other awards, including
Certificate of Clinical Competence in Audiology, 1965;
Howard Univ. grant for research on learning and develop-
mental patterns of low socioeconomic students; Rehabili-
tation Service Adminstr., Office of Ed. grant.
Publications: Contributed over thirty articles to journals.
Author, Psychological Correlates in Dialectolalia, 1965;
Effective Expression, 1966.
Mailing Address: 1757 West Harrison St., Chicago, Ill. 60612.

IFETAYO, FEMI FUNNI
Publications: We the Black Woman, 1970.

JACKSON, CLYDE OWEN, Editor
Born: Galveston, Tex., April 7, 1928.
Education: B.S., Tuskegee Inst., 1945-49; B.Mus.Ed., Tex.
Southern Univ., 1956-60; M.Mus.Ed., ibid., 1962-64.
Professional Experience: 1st lt., U.S. Army, 1951-54; manag-
ing foreman, U.S. Posf Office, 1955; cons., Houston In-
former; editor, Office of Development, Tex. Southern
Univ., 1968-.

Memberships: Sponsor, Boy Scouts of America and YMCA;
founder, conductor, Tex. Southern Univ. Men's Glee
Club and Houston Post Office Chorale; sponsor, William
Dawson Scholarships, Tuskegee, and Clyde Jackson
Scholarships, Tex. Southern Univ.
Awards: Commendation Award for newswriting, U.S. Army,
1954; winner, NNPA Merit Award, 1955.
Publications: Contributed numerous articles to newspapers in
U.S. and Asia. Author, The Songs of Our Years, 1968;
Before the Darkness Covers Us, 1970.
Mailing Address: 10863 Fairland Dr., Houston, Tex. 77051.

JACKSON, JESSE, Author
Born: Columbus, Ohio
Education: Ohio State Univ.; Breadloaf Writers Conf., Bread-
loaf, Vt.
Professional Experience: Sewer inspector; laborer; postal
worker; journalist; editorial dept., Nat. Bureau of Eco-
nomic Research.
Publications: Call Me Charlie, 1945; Anchor Man, 1947; Room
for Randy, 1957; Tessie, 1968; Sickest Don't Always Die,
1971; Charlie Starts from Scratch, 1972; The Fourteenth
Cadillac, 1972.
Mailing Address: c/o Doubleday & Co., Inc. 501 Franklin Ave.,
Garden City, N.Y. 11530.

JACKSON, JOHN GLOVER, Author
Born: Ailen, South Carolina, April 1, 1907.
Education: Self-educated.
Professional Experience: Writer for the Truth Seeker, 1932-
52.
Memberships: District 65, Nat. Council of Distributive Work-
ers of America; Rationalist Press Assn., London, Eng-
land.
Publications: Introduction to American Civilizations, 1970.
Mailing Address: 388 Pearl St., Apt. 13-J, New York, N.Y.
10038.

JACKSON, MILES MERRILL, JR., Librarian, Educator
Born: Richmond, Va., April 28, 1929.
Education: A.B., Va. Union Univ., 1951-55; M.S.L.S., Drexel
Univ., 1955-56.
Family: m. Bernice; children, Miles III, Marsha, Muriel,
Melice.
Professional Experience: Branch libn., Free Lib. of Phila-
delphia, 1956-58; asst. prof. and head libn., Hampton
Inst., 1958-62; territorial libn., Govt. of Samoa, 1962-
64; chief libn., Atlanta Univ., 1964-69; vis. senior Ful-
bright prof., Univ. of Tehran, Iran, 1968-69; assoc.

prof., State Univ. of N.Y., 1969-; cons., Paine Coll.; Meredith Coll; Am. Assn. of Univ. Presses; Nat. Science Foundation; U.S. State Dept.
Memberships: ALA; ACRL.
Awards: Coll. Language Award, poetry and short stories, 1954-55; Am. Philosophical Soc. grant fellow for research on J.W. Johnson, 1966; U.S. Office of Ed. grant, 1965; Council on Lib. Resources Fellow, 1970.
Publications: Contributed to journals and magazines. Author, Bibliography of Negro History and Culture for Young Readers (with others), 1969; editor, Comparative and International Librarianship: Essays on Themes and Problems, 1970.
Mailing Address: State University of New York, School of Library Science, Genesco, N.Y. 14454.

JACKSON, NELL C., Educator
Born: Athens, Ga., July 1, 1929.
Education: B.S., Tuskegee Institute, 1947-51; M.S., Springfield Coll., 1952-53; Univ. of Oslo, summer 1955; Ph.D., Univ. of Iowa, 1960-62.
Professional Experience: Asst. prof., Tuskegee Inst., 1953-60; tchr. asst. and research asst., Univ. of Iowa, 1960-62; asst. prof., Tuskegee Inst., 1962-63; asst. prof., Illinois State Univ., 1963-65; asst. and assoc. prof., Univ. of Illinois, 1965-; liaison to U.S. Olympic Com., 1968; Bd. of Dirs., U.S. Olympic Com., 1969-72; chmn., U.S. Olympic Track and Field Com., 1969-71.
Memberships: A.A.H.P.E.R.; IAAPER; Am. Academy Sports Medicine; Kappa Delta Kamma.
Awards: Middle Atlantic Assn. of AAU, Philadelphia.
Publications: Contributed to athletic journals. Author, Track and Field for Girls and Women, 1965.
Mailing Address: Freer Gym, University of Illinois, Urbana, Ill. 61801.

JAMES, CHARLES L., Educator
Born: Poughkeepsie, N.Y., April 12, 1934.
Education: B.A., State Univ. Coll.; M.A., State Univ. of N.Y.
Family: m. Jane Fisher; children, Shelia Ellen, Terri Lynn.
Professional Experience: Sgt., U.S. Army, 1955-57; tchr. elementary, Spackenkill Schs., Poughkeepsie, N.Y.; tchr. English, Dutchess Community Coll., Poughkeepsie, N.Y., 1967-69; asst. prof. English, State Univ. Coll., Oneonta, N.Y., 1969-; chmn., Black-Hispanic Studies Program, Oneonta, N.Y.
Publications: Negro Literature in America: A Bibliography, 1968; editor, From the Roots: Short Stories by Black Americans, 1970.
Mailing Address: 27 Spencer Dr., Oneonta, N.Y. 13820.

JEFFERS, LANCE, Educator, Author
Born: Fremont, Neb., Nov. 28, 1919.
Education: B.S., Columbia Univ., 1951; M.A., ibid., 1951; Univ.
of Toronto, 1965-66.
Family: m. Trellie Lee James; children, Lance, Valjeanne,
Sidonie Colette, Honorée.
Professional Experience: 1st lt., Medical Adminstrv. Corps,
U.S. Army, World War II; prof. English, Florida A & M
Univ., 1964-65; tchr. fellow, English, Univ. of Toronto,
1965-66; lectr. English, Indiana Univ., 1966-68; prof.
creative writing and black lit., Calif. State Coll., Long
Beach, 1968-.
Awards: Franklin T. Baker Citation, Tchrs. Coll., Columbia
Univ.
Publications: Contributed poetry, fiction, essays to periodicals
and anthologies. Author, My Blackness Is the Beauty of
This Land, 1970.
Mailing Address: 15520 McKinley Ave., Compton, Calif. 90220.

JENKINS, CLARKE, Utility man, Inventor
Born: Chattanooga, Tenn., Feb. 26, 1917.
Education: Art and carving, Robert Treat Jr. High Sch.,
Newark, N.J.; Henry Bernard High Sch., history and
geography, Hartford, Conn., 1934.
Family: m. Erline E.; children, David E., Doris E. Booker.
Professional Experience: Amateur boxer, welterweight, 1934;
garment presser, Consolidated, Newark, N.J., 1934-35;
garment presser, La Measure, Detroit, Mich., 1936-42;
inspector, Ford Motor Co., 1942-45; utility man, Kelsey
Hayes and Chrysler, 1946-; inventor, explosive missile
for small arms use, 1940, snow dissolving concrete
1947, and other inventions.
Memberships: Unity of Judah and Israel, Spiritual Israel, Or-
thodox Church of Judah.
Awards: Citation, Ordinance Dept., U.S. Army, 1943.
Publications: The Black Hebrews, 1969.
Mailing Address: 10246 Cameron Dr., Detroit, Mich. 48211.

JOANS, TED
Publications: Black Pow-Wow, 1969; Afrodisia, 1971.

JOHNSON, ALICIA L., Educator, Author
Born: Chicago, Ill., Feb. 27, 1944.
Education: A.A., Wilson City Coll., 1962-66; certificate,
Cortez Peters Business, 1965-66; certificate, Univ. of
Ghana, July-August 1969; certificate, Univ. of the West
Indies, December 1969 - January 1970; Southern Ill.
Univ., 1966.

Professional Experience: Bankteller, Ill. Federal Savings
and Loan Assn.; lib. aide, Chicago Tchrs. Coll. and
Wilson City Coll; clerk, Ellis Bookstore; guest editor,
Grassroots Literary Magazine, 1969-70; co-instr.,
Black American Writers, Southern Ill. Univ., winter
1970; writer-in-residence and staff asst., Black American Studies Program, spring 1970, Southern Ill. Univ.;
instr. and English asst., Black American Writers, Southern Ill. Univ., 1970-; lectr., poetry readings, Univ. of
Chicago, Wilson City Coll., Roosevelt Univ., and others.
Publications: Contributed poetry and articles to journals and
newspapers. Author, Two Black Poems; Realities vs.
Spirits (a collection of privately published poetry).
Mailing Address: Southern Hills, Apt. 135-3, Carbondale, Ill.
62901.

JOHNSON, BERNARD H., JR., Educator
Born: Washington, D.C., Oct. 19, 1920.
Education: B.S., Howard Univ., 1942; M.S., ibid., 1944; Ph.D.,
Univ. of Pittsburgh, 1954.
Family: m. Eleanor; children Bernard, III, Lawrence Douglas,
Erich Myles.
Professional Experience: Grad. teaching asst., Sept. 1942 -
June 1944, instr. chemistry, Howard Univ., Sept. 1946 -
August 1948; assoc. prof., prof. chemistry, Central
State Univ. Oct. 1951-; chemistry specialist and cons.,
USAID, India/Education project, Univ. of Vikram, Ujjain,
India, training Indian univ. and coll. tchrs., summer 1966;
vis. scholar, Univ. of Utah, June-Sept. 1959; NSF Summer
Inst. in Inorganic Chemistry for coll. tchrs., Reed Coll.,
Portland, Ore., June-August 1963; research chemist,
Duriron Co., Dayton, Ohio, summers 1953 and 1955; re-
search chemist, Upjohn Pharmaceutical Co., Kalamazoo,
Mich., summers 1964 and 1965; research chemist, Dow
Chemical Co., Midland, Mich., May-Sept. 1969.
Memberships: Including Ohio Bd. of Regents, Master Plan Re-
view Com. on Allied Medical Professions, 1969-70; Ohio
Academy of Science, vice pres., chemistry section,
1971-72; Project Catalyst Com., Am. Chemical Soc.,
1969.
Awards: Research grant, Research and Development Command,
Air Force Office Scientific Research, 1956-59; Ful-
bright Scholar, lectr. and cons., in chemistry, Khon Kaen
Univ., Khon Kaen, Thailand, 1968-69.
Publications: Experimental Chemistry (with others), 1964.
Mailing Address: Dept. of Chemistry, Central State University,
Wilberforce, Ohio 45384.

JOHNSON, HARRY ALLEYN, Educator
Born: Norfolk, Va., Nov. 22, 1920.
Education: B.S., Virginia State Coll., 1942; M.S., Columbia
Univ. Tchrs. Coll., 1948; Ed.D. ibid., 1952.
Family: m. Mae Coleman; children, Sharon Lynne, Jeffrey
Alan.
Professional Experience: Capt., U.S. Army, 1942-45; Capt.,
U.S. Army Reserve (ret.); Assoc. dean. prof. ed.,
and dir., Learning Resources Center, Va. State Coll.,
1949-; Fulbright lectr. and research scholar, École
Normale Supérieure, Paris, 1958-59; vis. prof., Univ. of
Oslo, Norway, April 1959, Oct 1962, August-September
1965, August-September 1967; vis. prof. audiovisual ed.,
Univ. of Maine, summers 1955, 1956, 1959; vis. prof. ed.,
Calif. State Coll., Hayward, summer 1969; vis. prof. ed.,
Mich. State Univ., East Lansing, summer 1970; instr.
audiovisual ed., Columbia Univ., summer 1952; lectr.,
including Univ. of Puerto Rico, Univ. of North Caro-
lina, Univ. of Md., Fisk Univ.; cons., including Task
Force, Columbia Univ. NDEA Inst. for Ed. Media, sum-
mer 1965, Univ. of North Carolina, Univ. of Puerto
Rico.
Memberships: Including AAUP; Assoc. for Supervisors and
Curriculum Development; NEA; VEA; Kappa Alpha Psi;
Reserve Officers Assoc.
Awards: Two oak leaf clusters for Philippine Campaign,
World War II; Fulbright research scholar, Paris; South-
ern Ed. Foundation grant to direct action research pro-
ject.
Publications: Contributed articles to journals. Author,
Multimedia Materials for Afro-American Studies, 1971.
Mailing Address: Box 27, Virginia State College, Petersburg,
Va. 23803.

JOHNSON, JESSE J., Lieutenant colonel, AUS, (ret.)
Born: Hattiesburg, Miss., May 15, 1914.
Education: B.S., Tougaloo Coll.; LL.B., Am. Extension
Sch. of Law; M.A., Hampton Inst.; Officer Candidate
Sch., Fort Lee, Va., 1943.
Family: m. Elizabeth C.
Professional Experience: CCC camp adminstrv. suprv. and
tchr., Mich., 1937-42; writer, editor and interviewer,
Course Development Division, Transportation Sch.,
Fort Eustis, Va.; private, QM, Replacement Training
Center, Fort Lee, Va., Oct. 1942 - Jan. 1943; second
lt., QM Corps, April 1943; served in 92nd Infantry Div.,
QM Truck Co., Dec. 1943 - July 1944; asst. prof. mili-
tary science and tactics, Va. State Coll., ROTC Unit,
1951-53; battalion adjutant, QM Battalion Staff, Kwserslantern, Germany, 1953-54; command, QM Salvage

Co., Baumholder, Germany, 1954-55; QM supply officer, Kwserslantern, Germany, 1955-56; test officer and chief, mechanical engineering test service branch, QM Research and Engineering Center, Fort Lee, Va., 1956-60; supply, Hampton Inst., 1960-62; promoted to major, Reserve, 1954 and lt. col., Reserve, 1962; retired, Oct. 1962; personnel and general clerk, Hampton Inst., 1962-67.

Publications: Ebony Brass, 1967; The Black Soldier Documented (1619-1815), 1969; A Pictorial History of Black Soldiers in the U.S. in Peace and War, 1970.

Mailing Address: 41 Cornelius Dr., Hampton Institute, Hampton, Va. 23366.

JOHNSON, JOE, Educator
Born: New York, N.Y., Jan. 18, 1940.
Education: B.A., Columbia Univ.; M.A., ibid.
Professional Experience: Dir. tutorial centers, Harlem Ed. Project, N.Y.C., 1962-63; instr., dept. of special programs, City Coll. of N.Y., 1971-72; instr. (part-time), dept. of American studies, 1971-72, asst. prof., dept. of American studies, Ramapo Coll. of New Jersey, 1972-; coeditor, Umbra magazine; interviewer, radio-television, France; reporter, Harlem Daily, Newark Advance; coor. editor, Dues: Anthology of Earth Writing; poetry readings, including Sarah Lawrence Coll., Hofstra Univ., Umbra Arts Festival, radio stations WBAI and WPAT.
Memberships: Modern Language Assn.; Linguistic Soc. of Am.
Publications: Contributed poetry and short stories to magazines, journals, and anthologies.
Mailing Address: 215 West 92 St., Apt. 11E, New York, N.Y. 10025.

JOHNSON, WILLIAM MATTHEWS, Post office clerk
Born: Greenville, Tex., May 5, 1905.
Education: Wisconsin Univ., 1929-35; Indiana Univ., 1939-40, 1946.
Family: m. Catherine Mann.
Professional Experience: Recreation dir., Indianapolis, Ind., 1937-42; clerk, U.S. Civil Service, 1942-65; clerk, Post Office, Indianapolis, Ind., 1965-.
Memberships: NAACP; SCLC; ACLU; K. of P.; Federation of Postal Clerks.
Awards: Wisconsin Univ. Athenra Literary Soc. Award, 1931; Frankenburger Prize for Literature, 1934; Indiana Univ. Writers' Conf. Award, 1968.
Publications: Contributed to newspapers and magazines. Author, The House on Corbett Street, 1967.
Mailing Address: 1512 Bellefontaine St., Indianapolis, Ind. 46202.

JONES, LEROI, see BARAKA, IMAMU AMIRI

JONES, MAJOR J., Educator, Clergyman
Born: Rome, Ga.
Education: A.B., Clark Coll.; B.D., Gammon Theological Seminary; S.T.M., Oberlin Coll.; Th.D., Boston Univ.
Family: m. Mattie P.; d. Chandra J.
Professional Experience: Clergyman, prof., conf. dir., Christian ed. in the Methodist Church; supt., Knoxville district, East Tenn. Conf. of the Methodist Church; pres. and dir., Gammon Theological Seminary-.
Memberships: Including bd. of dir., Com. of Southern Churchmen; Am. Soc. of Christian Ethics; bd. of dir., Black Methodists for Church Renewal; Conf. of Christian and Jews.
Publications: Black Awareness, A Theology of Hope, 1971.
Mailing Address: Gammon Theological Seminary, Atlanta, Ga. 30314.

JONES, REGINALD L., Educator, Psychologist
Born: Clearwater, Fla., Jan. 21, 1931.
Education: A.B., Morehouse Coll., 1952; M.A., Wayne Univ., 1954; Ph.D., Ohio State Univ., 1959.
Family: m. Johnette; children, Juliette, Angela, Cynthia.
Professional Experience: Clinical psychologist, Logansport State Hospital, Indiana, summer 1953, spring 1956, summer 1957; clinical psychology specialist, U.S. Army hospitals, 1954-56; research asst., Dept. of Special Ed., Ohio State Univ., 1957; tchr. asst., Dept of Psychology, Ohio State Univ., 1957-59; research asst., Technical Planning Project, Am. Assn. on Mental Deficiency, 1958; research asst. prof., Instructional Research Service, Miami Univ., Oxford, Ohio, 1959-63; assoc. prof. psychology, Fisk Univ., 1963-64; asst. prof., Dept. of Ed., Univ. of Calif., Los Angeles, 1964-66; assoc. prof., Dept. of Psychology, Ohio State Univ., 1966-68; prof. psychology and ed., vice chmn., Dept. of Psychology, Ohio State Univ., 1968-69; prof. ed., Univ. of Calif., Riverside, Calif., 1969-; cons. for various programs, including Southeastern Ed. Laboratory.
Memberships: Am. Psychological Assn.; Am. Ed. Research Assn.; Council for Exceptional Children; Am. Assn. on Mental Deficiency; Midwestern Psychological Assn.; Handicapped Childrens Program.
Publications: Contributed numerous articles to journals, bulletins, and educational reports. Author, New Directions in Special Education, 1970; editor, Problems and Issues in the Education of Exceptional Children, 1971.
Mailing Address: Dept. of Education, University of California, Riverside, Calif. 92502.

JONES, ROSIE LEE LOGAN, Teacher
Born: Reagan, Tex., Oct. 23, 1924.
Education: B.S., Paul Quin Coll., 1952; Tex. Southern Univ.,
    1952-58; Prairie View Univ., 1963.
Family: m. Jake; stepchildren, Mrs. Elmirs Jones Pierre, Mrs.
    Jessie Lee Jones Hines, Mrs. Autholia Jones Payne,
    Mrs. Estella R. Jones Starks.
Professional Experience: Tchr., Falls County Schs., 1948-49;
    substitute tchr., pub. schs., Fort Worth, Ind., 1955-56;
    substitute tchr., pub. schs., Beaumont, Ind., 1956-.
Memberships: Piny Woods Writers Club.
Awards: Literary Award, Paul Quinn Coll., 1952.
Publications: Contributed to newspapers. Author, Treasures
    of Life, 1945; Raindrops and Pebbles, 1957.
Mailing Address: 3335 Pine St., Beaumont, Tex. 77703.

JORDAN, JUNE, Educator, Author
Born: Harlem, N.Y., July 9, 1936.
Education: Bernard Coll., Univ. of Chicago.
Family: s. Christopher.
Professional Experience: Tchr. English, Connecticut Coll.,
    1968; tchr., City Coll., City Univ. of N.Y.; tchr. English,
    Sarah Lawrence Coll., 1969-.
Awards: Rockefeller Foundation Fellowship in Creative Writ-
    ing, 1969-70; Rome Prize Fellowship in Environmental
    Design, 1970-71.
Publications: Contributed poetry and articles to various news-
    papers, journals and magazines. Author, Who Look at
    Me, 1969; Soulscript, 1970; Some Changes, 1970; Dry
    Victories, 1972.
Mailing Address: Wendy Weil, Literary Agent, 1301 Avenue
    of the Americas, New York, N.Y. 10019.

JORDAN, NORMAN, Author
Born: Ansted, W. Va., July 30, 1938.
Education: Ninth grade, Cleveland Pub. Schs.
Family: m. Brucella; children, Shirie, Eric.
Professional Experience: Seaman, U.S. Navy, 1955-59; dish-
    washer, laborer, stockboy, 1960-62; order filler, 1962-
    63; state highway inspector, 1963-65; youth leader,
    neighborhood center, 1965-66; out-reach worker, neigh-
    borhood center, 1966-67; dir., Hough Youth Center,
    Cleveland, Ohio, 1967-68; tech. writer, 1968-69; writer-
    in-residence, Karamu, Cleveland, Ohio, 1970-71; tech.
    advisor on film, Uptight.
Memberships: Exec. com., Hough Development Corp.; Ad-
    visory Com., Brotherman TV Show, Cleveland, Ohio.
Awards: Harriet Eells Performing Arts Fellowship, Karamu.

Publications: Contributed poetry to journals and anthologies.
Author, Destination: Ashes; Above Maya.
Mailing Address: Box 1852, Cleveland, Ohio 44106.

JOSEY, E. J. (Elonnie Junius), Library administrator
Born: Norfolk, Va., Jan. 20, 1924.
Education: A.B., Howard Univ., 1946-49; M.A., Columbia
    Univ., 1949-50; M.S.L.S., State Univ. of New York,
    1952-53.
Family: d. Elaine Jackqueline.
Professional Experience: Lib. I, Free Lib. of Philadelphia,
    1953-54; instr. social sciences, Savannah State Coll.,
    1954-55; libn., asst. prof., Delaware State Coll., 1955-
    59; libn., assoc. prof., Savannah State Coll., 1959-66;
    assoc., Academic and Research Libs., Division of Lib.
    Development, N.Y. State Ed. Dept., 1966-68; Chief,
    Bureau of Academic and Research Libs., Division of
    Lib. Development, N.Y. State Ed. Dept., Albany, N.Y.,
    1968-; participant, Evaluation Team for Evaluating Coll.
    and Univ. Libs., Bureau of Coll. Evaluation, N.Y. State;
    survey of Texas Southern Univ. Lib., 1967.
Memberships: ALA; AAUP; N.Y. Lib. Assn.; Kappa Phi
    Kappa; Alpha Phi Omega; NAACP; ACLU.
Awards: Savannah State Coll. Award for Distinguished Service
    to Librarianship, 1967; Journal of Library History
    Award for manuscript on Edward Christopher Williams,
    1970.
Publications: Contributed more than seventy-five articles to
    library and educational journals. Author, A Directory
    of College and University Libraries in New York State,
    1967; A Survey of Texas Southern University Library,
    1967; editor, A Directory of Reference and Research
    Library Resources Systems, 1967; The Black Librarian
    in America, 1970; What Black Librarians Are Saying,
    1973.
Mailing Address: 12-C Old Hickory Dr., Albany, N.Y. 12204.

KAISER, ERNEST, Library staff member, Editor
Born: Petersburg, Va., Dec. 5, 1915.
Education: City Coll. of N.Y., 1935-38.
Family: m. Mary Orford; children, Eric, Joan.
Professional Experience: Redcap, Erie Railroad, Jersey City,
    N.J., 1938-42; messenger, PM newspaper; clerk and
    messenger, art dealers galleries; editor, the Negro
    Quarterly; worker, Phelps Dodge (N.J.) war plant; stock
    clerk, Kress 5 and 10¢ store; lathe operator, N.Y.C.,
    Sept. 1942 - summer 1944; shipping clerk; CIO Political
    Action Com., summer 1944 - Jan. 1945; staff, Schomburg
    Center for Research in Black Culture, N.Y. Pub. Lib.,

Feb. 1945-; served as adv. and wrote introductions to
nine vols. of 141 vol. Arno Press series, The American
Negro: His History and Literature; editor and contributor, black biographies, McGraw-Hill and Crowell multi-
volume encyclopedias; reviewer, manuscripts on blacks,
McGraw-Hill; assisting documentation phase of Alex
Haley's Kinte genealogical lib. project; indexed all
magazines, Schomburg Center section, Index to Periodi-
cal Articles By and About Negroes, 1960-69; co-founder,
assoc. editor & contributor, Freedomways magazine,
published quarterly since 1961.
Memberships: Frederick Douglass Democratic Assn., Corona -
East Elmhurst, N.Y.; Am. Federation of State, County
and Municipal Employees Union; AFL-CIO, Am. Inst.
for Marxist Studies.
Awards: Honored (with Mary O. Kaiser) by the Corona-East
Elmhurst Friends of Freedomways, 1970.
Publications: Contributed numerous essays, reviews, bibliog-
raphies to journals, magazines and books. Author, In
Defense of the People's Black and White History and
Culture, 1970; editor, The Negro Almanac (with Harry
A. Ploski), 1971; Afro U.S.A.: A Reference Work on the
Black Experience (with Harry A. Ploski), 1971; Refer-
ence Library of Black America, 5 vols. (with Harry A.
Ploski and Otto J. Lindenmeyer), 1971.
Mailing Address: 31-37 95 St., East Elmhurst, N.Y. 11369.

KAUFMAN, BOB GARNELL, Poet
Born: New Orleans, La.; April 19, 1925.
Education: Self-educated.
Family: m. Eileen; children, Parker, 1st m., Tomi.
Professional Experience: Merchant marine at age 13.
Awards: Nominee, Guinness Poetry Award, England, 1960-61;
subject of a television show "Coming from Bob Kaufman,
Poet," NET, 1972-73; founder, Beatitude, magazine with
Allen Ginsberg, Bill Margolis and John Kelley, 1959.
Publications: Contributed to many journals and included in
fifteen anthologies. Author, Abomunist Manifesto, 1959;
Broadsides, 1959; Solitudes Crowded with Loneliness,
1965; The Golden Sardine, 1966; Does the Secret Mind
Whisper?; Watch My Tracks.
Mailing Address: 102 Mono Ave., Fairfax, Calif. 94930.

KELLEY, WILLIAM MELVIN, Author
Born: New York, N.Y., 1937.
Education: Fieldston Sch.; Harvard Coll.
Family: m. Karen Gibson; d. Jessica Gibson.
Professional Experience: Tchr., New School; author-in-resi-
dence, State Univ., Geneseo, N.Y.

Awards: Bread Loaf Scholar; John Hay Whitney; Rosenthal
 Foundation; National Institute of Arts and Letters.
Publications: Contributed to magazines. Author, A Different
 Drummer, 1962; Dancers on the Shore, 1964; A Drop of
 Patience, 1965; Dem, 1967; Dunfords Travels Every-
 wheres, 1970.
Mailing Address: c/o Doubleday and Co., Inc., 277 Park Ave.,
 New York, N.Y. 10017.

KELLY, ERNECE BEVERLY, Educator
Born: Chicago, Ill.
Education: A.B., Univ. of Chicago; M.A., ibid., 1954-59;
 Ph.D. candidate, Northwestern Univ., 1970.
Professional Experience: Coordinator coll. students, Civil
 Rights Coalition, Chicago, 1959-60; instr., Wilson Jr.
 Coll., Chicago, 1960-64; vis. lectr. Univ. of Chicago,
 1969-70; assoc. prof., Loop City Coll., Chicago, 1965-;
 cons., Ford Foundation Tchr. Training, summer 1969,
 Council for Bio-Medical Careers, 1968-.
Memberships: Exec. com., Conf. on Coll. Compostion and
 Communication, NCTE, 1969-71.
Awards: Training of Tchrs. Fellowship, Northwestern Univ.
Publications: Contributed to journals. Editor, Points of De-
 parture.
Mailing Address: 6022 Vernon Ave., Chicago, Ill. 60637.

KEMP, ARNOLD
Publications: Eat of Me, I am the Savior, 1972.

KENNEDY, ADRIENNE, Playwright
Born: Pittsburgh, Pa., 1931.
Education: Ohio State Univ.; Edward Albee's Workshop, 1962.
Professional Experience: Instr., lectr. playwriting, Yale
 Univ., 1972-73.
Memberships: Actor's Studio.
Awards: Obie Distinguished Play Award, for Funnyhouse of
 a Negro, 1964.
Publications: Contributed stories and poems to magazines.
 Plays, Funnyhouse of a Negro, 1962; The Owl Answers,
 1963, produced, White Barn Theater, Westport, Conn.;
 A Lesson in Dead Language, 1964; A Rat's Mass, 1965,
 produced by the Theater Co. of Boston, April, 1966; A
 Beast's Story, 1966; In His Own Write, adaptation of a
 book by John Lennon, given by the National Theatre in
 London, England.

KENNEDY, FLORYNCE R., Attorney, Lecturer
Born: Kansas City, Mo., Feb. 11, 1916.
Education: LL.B, Columbia General Studies, 1944-45; JS.D,
    Columbia Law Sch., 1948-51.
Family: m. Charles Dudley Dye (deceased).
Professional Experience: Dir., Media Workshop, Nat. Conf.
    on Black Power, Newark, N.J., 1968, Philadelphia, Pa.,
    1969, Atlanta, Ga., 1970; dir., Consumer Information
    Service, N.Y.C.; founder, Feminist Party, Nov. 3, 1971
    (125 chapters); special assignments, films, The Land-
    lord, Black Roots, 1973 Year of the Woman; campus
    lecturer, fall 1968-.
Memberships: Feminist Party.
Publications: Contributed to anthologies. Author, with Diane
    B. Schulder, Abortion Rap, 1971.
Mailing Address: Golden Gateway Center, Suite 607, 155 Jack-
    son St., San Francisco, Calif. 94111.

KENT, GEORGE EDWARD, Educator
Born: Columbus, Ga., May 31, 1920.
Education: B.A., Savannah State Coll., 1938-41; M.A., Boston
    Univ., 1945-49; Ph.D., ibid., 1953.
Family: m. Désire Ash; children, Sherald Anne, Edward
    Austin.
Professional Experience: Asst. prof. English, 1949-53, prof.
    English and chmn., dept. of languages and literature,
    1953-56, prof., dean, Delaware State Coll., 1957-60;
    prof. English and chmn., liberal arts div., Quinnipiac
    Coll., Hamden, Conn., 1960-69; prof. English, Univ. of
    Chicago, 1969-; vis. prof., Grambling State Coll., Gramb-
    ling, La., summer 1965; Florida A & M., Tallahassee,
    Fla., 1958; Univ. of Conn., Storrs, 1962-64; Wesleyan
    Univ., Middletown, Conn., 1965, 1969, 1970; advisory
    editor, CLA journal; literary cons., Univ. of Chicago
    Press, 1970, Macmillan Co., 1971; fellow, conf. on Afri-
    can and African-American Studies, Atlanta Univ.
Memberships: American Studies Assn.; CLA; MLA; NCTE.
Awards: Civic Leadership Plaque, state conference, NAACP,
    Delaware; Distinguished Lecturer, NCTE, 1972.
Publications: Contributed to professional journals. Author,
    Blackness and the Adventure of Western Culture, 1972.
Mailing Address: 1216 Madison Park, Chicago, Ill. 60615.

KILLEBROW, CARL
Publications: The Squared Circle.

KILLENS, JOHN OLIVER, Author
Born: Macon, Ga., Jan. 14, 1916.
Education: Edward Waters Coll.; Morris Brown Coll.; Atlanta
    Univ.; Howard Univ. (law); Terrell Law Sch.; Columbia
    Univ.; New York Univ.
Family: m. Grace W.; children, Jon C., Barbara E. Wynn.
Professional Experience: Tchr., creative writing, New York
    Sch. for Social Research; writer-in-residence, Fisk
    Univ.; adjunct prof., creative writing workshop, Colum-
    bia Univ.; writer-in-residence, Howard Univ., 1971-72;
    lectr., including Southern Univ., Cornell, Columbia,
    Howard, Rutgers, Brandeis, Springfield Coll., Univ. of
    Western Mich., Savannah State Coll., New Sch. for Social
    Research.
Memberships: Founder, and former chmn., Harlem Writers
    Guild; v.p., Black Academy of Arts and Letters; exec.
    bd., P.E.N.
Awards: Brooklyn branch, ASNLH; Empire State Federation
    of Women's Clubs; Afro Art Theatre; Waltann Sch. of
    Creative Arts, Climbers Business Club; Brooklyn
    NAACP; N.Y. State Fraternal Order of the Elks; Citizens
    of Macon, Ga.
Publications: Contributed numerous articles and essays to
    newspapers and journals. Author, films, Odds Against
    Tomorrow, Belafonte Productions, 1960; Slaves, Theatre
    Guild, 1969; drama, Lower Than the Angels, staged by
    American Place Theatre, N.Y.C., 1965; books, Young-
    blood, 1954, 1966; And Then We Heard the Thunder, 1963;
    Black Man's Burden, 1966; 'Sippi, 1967; Slaves, 1969; The
    Cotillion, 1971; Great Gitting Up Morning: A Biography of
    Denmark Vesey,1972.
Mailing Address: 1392 Union St., Brooklyn, N.Y. 11212.

KILSON, MARTIN L., Educator
Born: East Rutherford, N.J., Feb. 14, 1931.
Education: B.A., Lincoln Univ. (Pa.), 1953; M.A., Harvard
    Univ., 1958; Ph.D., ibid., 1959.
Family: m. Marion Dusser De Barenne; children, Peter,
    Jennie, Hannah.
Professional Experience: Research fellow, Harvard Center for
    Internat. Affairs, 1961; lectr. government, Harvard Univ.,
    1962-66; asst. prof., Harvard Univ., 1966-68; vis. prof.,
    Univ. of Ghana, 1964-65; prof. government, Harvard
    Univ., 1968-.
Awards: John Hay Whitney Opportunity Fellow, 1955-56,
    1957-58; Ford Foundation Foreign Area Grant, 1959-
    61.
Publications: Contributed to journals. Author, Political Change
    in a West African State, 1966; Political Awakening of
    Africa (co-edited with Rupert Emerson), 1965; Apropos

of Africa: Sentiments of Negro American Leaders on
Africa from the 1800's to the 1950's (co-edited with
Adelaide C. Hill), 1969; The Africa Reader (co-edited
with Wilfred Cartey), 1970.
Mailing Address: Dudley House, Harvard College, 16 Holyoke
St., Cambridge, Mass. 02138.

KING, CORETTA SCOTT (Mrs. Martin Luther King, Jr.),
    Lecturer, Author, Concert singer
Born: Marion, Ala., April 27, 1927.
Education: B.S., Antioch Coll., 1951; Mus.B., New England
    Conservatory of Music, 1954; L.H.D. (hon.), Boston
    Univ., 1969; L.H.D. (hon.), Marymount Manhattan Coll.,
    1969; L.H.D. (hon.), Brandeis Univ., 1969; LL.D. (hon.),
    Univ. of Bridgeport, 1970; L.H.D. (hon.), Wilberforce
    Univ., 1970; L.H.D. (hon.), Bethune-Cookman Coll.,
    1970; LL.D. (hon.), Morgan State Coll., 1970; L.H.D.
    (hon.), Morehouse Coll., 1970; L.H.D. (hon.), Princeton
    Univ., 1970; L.H.D. (hon.) Keuka Coll., 1970.
Family: m. Martin Luther King, Jr. (deceased); children,
    Yolanda Denise, Martin Luther III, Dexter Scott, Bernice
    Albertine.
Professional Experience: Concert singer debut, Springfield,
    Ohio, 1948; concerts throughout U.S.; instr. voice,
    Morris Brown Coll., Atlanta, Ga., 1962; lectr., first
    woman to deliver Class Day address, Harvard Univ.,
    1968; first woman to preach, Statutory service, St.
    Paul's Cathedral, London, Eng., 1969; pres., Martin
    Luther King, Jr. Memorial Center.
Memberships: Numerous civic and religious organizations,
    including Nat. Council of Negro Women; YWCA chmn.,
    Com. on Economic Justice for Women; Women's In-
    ternat. League for Peace and Freedom; Bd. of Dir.,
    SCLC; Martin Luther King, Jr., Foundation of Eng.;
    Links, Inc.; Alpha Kappa Alpha Sorority (hon.).
Awards: Numerous awards, including Annual Brotherhood
    Award, Nat. Council of Negro Women, 1957; Louise
    Waterman Wise Award, American Jewish Congress of
    Women's Auxiliary, 1963; Woman of Conscience Award,
    Nat. Council of Women, 1968; Academic Nazionale Del
    Lincei, Human Relations Award, Italy; Gallup Poll, Fifth
    Most Admired Woman in the World, 1968.
Publications: Contributed to journals. Author, My Life With
    Martin Luther King, Jr., 1969.
Mailing Address: 234 Sunset Ave., N.W., Atlanta, Ga. 30314.

KING, HELEN H., Author
Born: Clarksdale, Miss., Oct. 15, 1931.
Education: B.A., Univ. of Michigan, 1954.

Family: Children, Chad, Fenate.
Professional Experience: Children's librn., Chicago public libraries, 2 years; tchr., elementary and primary grades, Pontiac, Mich.; Chicago public schools; Roeper City and County School for the Gifted, Birmingham, Mich., 8 years; assoc. editor, Jet; assoc. editor, Ebony; assoc. editor and free-lance writer, Chicago Courier.
Awards: Christ United Methodist Church First Merit Award of Achievement for 1972.
Publications: Contributed to journals. Author, Willy, 1971; The Soul of Christmas, 1972.
Mailing Address: 2001 South Michigan, Chicago, Ill. 60616.

KING, WOODIE, JR.
Publications: Black Drama Anthology (with Ron Milner), 1972; Black Poets and Prophets (with Earl Anthony), 1972; editor, Black Short Story Anthology 1972; Blackspirits, 1972.

KIRKPATRICK, OLIVER AUSTIN, Librarian
Born: Jamaica, West Indies, June 12, 1911.
Education: B.S., New York Univ., 1944-50; New School for Social Research, 1951-52; M.S.L.S., Columbia Univ., 1951-53.
Family: m. Carol; children, Ian, Brian.
Professional Experience: Sports editor and columnist, Jamaica Standard, 1937-41; newscaster, radio Jamaica, ZQI, 1939-42; senior libn., New York Public Lib., supr., Brooklyn Public Lib., 1953-.
Memberships: ALA.
Awards: Joyce Kilmer, New York Univ., creative writing.
Publications: Contributed to journals. Author, Country Cousin, 1941; Naja the Snake and Mangus the Mongoose, 1970.
Mailing Address: 37 Tompkins Pl., Brooklyn, N.Y. 11231.

KITT, EARTHA MAE, Actress, Singer
Born: North, S.C., Jan. 26, 1928.
Education: High sch.
Family: d.
Professional Experience: Dancer, singer, Katherine Dunham Dance Group, 1948; night club singer, 1959-; singer, New Faces of 1952, N.Y.C., 1952; actress, Mrs. Patterson, N.Y.C., 1954; TV appearances; motion pictures, including New Faces 1953, Accused, 1957, Anna Lucasta, 1958.
Awards: Woman of the Year, Nat. Assn. Negro Musicians, 1968.
Publications: Thursday's Child, 1956.
Mailing Address: c/o Duell, Sloan & Pearce, Inc., 440 Park Ave., S., New York, N.Y. 10016.

KNIGHT, ETHERIDGE (Imamu Etheridge Knight Soa), Author
Born: Corinth, Miss., April 19, 1931.
Education: Public sch. through 8th grade, Paducah, Ky., 1936-
44.
Family: 2nd m. Mary Ellen McAnally; 1st m. Sonia San-
chez; children, 2nd m., Stephanie Tandiwe, James Bam-
bata.
Professional Experience: U.S. Army, 1947-51; prisoner in the
Indiana State Prison, 1962-68; instr., Univ. of Pitts-
burgh, 1969-70; instr., Univ. of Hartford, 1970-71; poet-
in-residence, Lincoln Univ., Mo., Dec. 1971 - Jan 1972.
Awards: $5,000 grant, National Endowment of the Arts, 1971.
Publications: Contributed poetry and articles to periodicals
and journals. Author, Poems from Prison, 1968; Black
Voices from Prison, 1969; Belly Song and Other Poems,
1972.
Mailing Address: 3955 N. College Blvd., Indianapolis, Ind.
46205.

KOINER, RICHARD B., Author, Artist, Speechwriter
Born: Atlantic City, N.J., Jan. 28, 1929; High Sch. of Music
and Art, 1942-46; Sch. of Visual Arts, 1947-49.
Family: m. Jacqueline Maria; children, Stacey-Jean, Richard
B., Eric B., Kyle B.
Professional Experience: Combat artist-correspondent, U.S.
Air Force, Korea, Japan, 1950-53; pub. relations
specialist, staff artist, Dept. of the Navy, Brooklyn
Navy Yard, 1960-63; speechwriter, pub. relations man
for Democratic Congressman John M. Murphy, N.Y.,
1969.
Memberships: Chmn. Steering Com., Sch. of Visual Arts
Alumni Assn.
Awards: Fellowship, 41st Annual Middlebury Coll. Bread Loaf
Writer's Conf., 1966.
Publications: Jack Be Quick, 1966.
Mailing Address: 96-08 57th Ave., Flushing, N.Y. 11368.

LACY, LESLIE ALEXANDER, Author, Lecturer
Born: Franklin, La., Aug. 8, 1937.
Education: M.A., Univ. of Southern Calif., 1959; M.A., Univ.
of Ghana, 1964.
Professional Experience: Tutor, Dept. of Political Science,
Univ. of Ghana, 1964-66; lectr., New York Univ., 1968-
70; lectr., Howard Univ., 1968-70; lectr., New School of
Social Research, 1969-70.
Publications: Contributed to journals and magazines. Author,
Black Africa on the Movè, 1969; The Rise and Fall of a
Proper Negro, 1970; Cheer the Lonesome Traveller,
1970.
Mailing Address: 3200 16 St., Washington, D.C. 20010.

LADNER, JOYCE A., Educator
Born: Waynesboro, Miss., October 12, 1943.
Education: B.A., Tougaloo Coll., 1964; M.A., Washington
Univ., 1966; Ph.D., ibid., 1968.
Professional Experience: Research assoc., Univ. of Dar es
Salaam, Tanzania, 1970-71; senior research fellow,
Institute of the Black World, Atlanta, Ga., 1969-71;
adjunct prof., Wesleyan Univ., Middletown, Conn., 1969-
70; curriculum specialist and asst. prof., sociology,
Southern Ill. Univ., Edwardsville, Ill., 1968-69; research
assoc., Social Science Institute; instr., sociology, Wash-
ington Univ., 1967-68; assoc. prof., sociology, Howard
Univ., 1969-; contributing and advisory editor, The Black
Scholar, and the Journal of Black Studies and Research.
Memberships: Bd. of dir., 21st Century Foundation; Am. Soc.
Assoc.; Soc. for the Study of Social Problems; ASNLH;
Caucus of Black Sociologists; Assoc. Institute of the
Black World; Ad Hoc Com., The Minority Center, Nat.
Inst. of Mental Health.
Awards: Grad. asst., Washington Univ., 1964-68; recipient,
1st fellowship, Black Women's Community Development
Foundation for study of the "Involvement of Tanzanian
Women in Nation Building," 1970-71; Russell Sage
Foundation grant, 1972.
Publications: Contributed articles to journals, newspapers and
anthologies. Author, Tomorrow's Tomorrow: The Black
Woman, 1971; ed., The Death of White Sociology (in
press).
Mailing Address: Department of Sociology-Anthropology,
Howard University, Washington, D.C. 20001.

LaGRONE, OLIVER, (Clarence Oliver), Teacher, Lecturer,
Sculptor, Poet
Born: McAlester, Okla.
Education: Harvard Univ., 1928-29; B.A., Univ. of New Mexico,
1931-38; Cranbrook Art Academy, 1939-41; Wayne State
Univ., 1956-61.
Family: d. Lotus Joy Johnson.
Professional Experience: Free-lance sculptor, artist, poet,
1940; internat. rep., U.A.W. and CIO, 1946-54; sales
rep., Frankemuth Brewing, 1954-56; tchr. special ed.,
pub. schs., Detroit-; poetry reading for "The Detroit
Adventures in Art," 1966; lectr. Afro-American history,
Marygrove Coll., 1969; tchr. Afro-American history,
Northwestern High Sch.; series of lectures, Internat.
Afro-American Museum, spring 1969; art exhibits,
Wayne State Univ.; Art Show for Nat. Black Unitarian,
Detroit, 1969; lectr., American Program Bureau; cons.,
Black Studies Dept. of Wayne State Univ., Univ. of De-
troit Black students, ASNLH, Hacomb County Commu-
nity Coll., pub. schs. of Detroit.

Memberships: NAACP; Mich. Poetry Soc.
Awards: Howard Univ. Alumni Award, 1965; first prize for
poem "The Limited," Mich. Poetry Soc., 1966.
Publications: Footfalls, They Speak of Dawns.
Mailing Address: 12787 Stoepel, Detroit, Mich. 48238.

LAMBIE, NAT, Free-lance photographer
Born: New York, N.Y., October 25, 1929.
Education: Brooklyn Community College, 1948-50; photography
certificate, N.Y. University.
Family: m. Constance; children, Kim, Kenyatta, Mathieu,
M'Balia.
Professional Experience: Free-lance photographer and camera-
man, U.S.I.S., Conakry, Guinea, Jan. 1959 - Nov. 1960;
chief, Services and Cinema Photography, Ministry of
Information & Tourism, Fria, Guinea, Jan. 1959 - Nov.
1960; chief, Service and Cinema Photography, Ministry of
Ed., Art, Youth, and Culture, Conakry, Guinea, West
Africa, Jan. 1961 - November 1962; general manager,
commercial radio and TV jingles, WNBS, Western Ni-
geria Broadcasting Station, Kim Limited, Lagos, Nigeria,
Jan. 1964 - Dec. 1965; photographer - laboratory technician, CBS-TV, Dec. 1965 - Dec. 1966; asst. photographer, Podell and Podell, N.Y.C., Dec. 1966 - Jan. 1967;
photographer, New Heritage Theater, Jan. 1967 - Jan.
1968, N.Y.C.; photographer Urban League of Greater
N.Y., Jan. 1968 - Feb. 1969; free-lance photographer,
Harcourt Brace Jovanovich, and Winston Burnett Con-
struction, N.Y.C.
Publications: Where Continents Meet, 1971.
Mailing Address: 332 East 93 St., New York, N.Y. 10028.

LATIMORE, JEWEL [AMINI, JOHARI]
Publications: Let's Go Somewhere, 1970.

LAWRENCE, HAROLD
Publications: Black Madonna.

LEE, DON L., Publisher, Lecturer
Education: Univ. of Ill., Chicago Circle campus.
Professional Experience: Publisher and editor, Third World
Press, Chicago, Ill; lectr. Afro-Am. Literature.
Publications: Several books of poetry, including Black Pride,
1968; Don't Cry, Scream, 1969; Think Black, 1969; We
Walk the Way of the New World, 1970.
Mailing Address: 7850 South Ellis Ave., Chicago, Ill. 60619.

LEE, IRVIN H., U.S. Air Force (ret.)
Born: Baltimore, Md., May 6, 1932.
Education: Morgan State Coll., 1951-52; Univ. of Md.
Family: m. Jacqueline Lee; d. Patricia.
Professional Experience: Public affairs, senior master
  sergeant, U.S. Air Force, 1952-72; President's Commit-
  tee, Jobs for Veterans.
Awards: Air Force Commendation Medal with 3 oak leaf
  clusters and Joint Services Commendation Medal.
Publications: Contributed to magazines. Author, Negro Medal
  of Honor Men, 1967.
Mailing Address: 2605 Hamlin St., N.E., Washington, D.C.
  20018.

LE MELLE, TILDEN J., Educator
Born: Feb. 6, 1929.
Education: A.B., Xavier Univ., 1953; M.A., ibid., 1958; Ph.D.,
  Univ. of Denver, 1965.
Family: m; children, 3.
Professional Experience: U.S. Army, 1953-56; instr. English,
  Xavier Univ., Xavier, La.; asst. prof. comparative litera-
  ture and foreign languages, Grambling Coll., Grambling,
  La.; research asst., Graduate Sch. of Internat. Studies,
  Univ. of Denver, 1964-65; asst. prof. internat. relations
  and African politics and government, Northern Illinois
  Univ., Dekalb, Ill., 1965-66; assoc. prof. internat. re-
  lations and African politics and government, Fordham
  Univ.; vis. assoc. prof. internat. relations, Graduate Sch.
  of Internat. Studies, Univ. of Denver; assoc. dir., Center
  on Internat. Race Relations, Graduate Sch. of Internat.
  Studies, Univ. of Denver; cons. for various programs,
  including Political Analyst to Nelson Research Assoc.,
  N.Y.C. on Pittsburgh Sch. System and Problems of De-
  centralization, summer 1968; First Nat. City Bank,
  N.Y.C.; Africanization Training Program at Bank of
  Monrovia, Liberia, summer-fall 1968; editor, Studies
  in Race and Nations and Africa Today.
Memberships: Alpha Mu Gamma Foreign Language Hon. Fra-
  ternity; hon. mem., Nat. Newman Foundation; Bd. of
  Dirs., Africa Today Associates, Inc., N.Y.C.; Exec. Bd.,
  African Heritage Studies Assn.; Editorial Bd., Pan-
  African Journal; Editorial Contributor's Bd., Africa
  Today.
Awards: Social Science Foundation Fellowship, 1963-65; John
  Hay Whitney Foundation Fellowship, 1964-65; Ford
  Foundation Ph.D. Research Grant, 1965; Hudson Insti-
  tute Seminar Scholarship, 1967; Social Science Founda-
  tion Travel-Research Grant in African Studies, summer
  1968.

Publications: Contributed to journals. Author, Comparison of
Two Methods of Teaching Remedial English to College
Freshmen, 1963; The Black College: A Strategy for
Achieving Relevancy, 1969; The Study of Race Among
Nations, 1970.
Mailing Address: 100 DeHaven Dr., Yonkers, N.Y. 10703.

LESTER, JULIUS, Author
Born: St. Louis, Mo., Jan 27, 1939.
Education: B.A., Fisk Univ., 1956-60.
Family: m. Joan Steinau; children, Jody Simone, Malcolm Col-
trane.
Professional Experience: Record store clerk; welfare investi-
gator; guitar tchr.; folk singer; dir. photography, SNICK,
1966-68; instr. black history, New School for Social Re-
search, 1968-70; radio producer, WBAI-FM, 1968-.
Awards: Nancy Bloch Award for To Be a Slave, 1969; runner-
up, Newbery Award for To Be a Slave, 1969.
Publications: Look Out, Whitey! Black Power's Gon' Get Your
Mama, 1968; Revolutionary Notes, 1969; Black Folktales, 1969; Search for the New Land, 1969; Seventh Son:
The Thoughts and Writings of W. E. B. Dubois, 1971;
The Knee-High Man and Other Tales, 1972; Long Journey
Home: Stories from Black History, 1972; Two Love Sto-
ries, 1972; Ain't No Ambulances for No Nigguhs Tonight,
1972.
Mailing Address: Chilmark, Mass. 02535.

LEWIS, DAVID LEVERING, Educator
Born: Little Rock, Ark., May 25, 1936.
Education: B.A., Fisk Univ., 1952-56; M.A., Columbia Univ.,
1957-58; Ph.D., London Sch. of Economics and Politi-
cal Science, 1958-62.
Family: m. Sharon; children, 2.
Professional Experience: Captain, U.S. Army, Landstuhl,
Germany; tchr., Univ. of Maryland Overseas Ed. Pro-
gram, 1960-62; lectr., Univ. of Ghana, 1963-64; lectr.,
Howard Univ., 1964-65; vis. asst. prof., European his-
tory, 1965-66; assoc. prof., European history, Morgan
State Coll., 1966-70; assoc. prof., history, Federal City
Coll., 1970-.
Awards: American Philosophical Soc. grant, summer 1967;
Social Science Research Council grant, summer 1967;
American Council of Learned Societies grant, 1971.
Publications: Contributed articles and reviews to journals and
newspapers. Author, King: A Critical Biography, 1970.
Mailing Address: Federal City College, Washington, D.C.
20001.

LEWIS, IDA, Publisher, Editor
Born: Morton, Pa.
Education: Grad., Boston Univ.
Professional Experience: Correspondent, Africa, Europe;
 journalist; U.S. correspondent, Jeune Afrique; first
 black woman editor-in-chief of a national magazine,
 Essence, 1970-71; first black woman publisher of national
 American magazine, founder, editor-in-chief, Encore,
 July, 1972-; panelist, NET, "Black Perspective on the
 News."
Publications: Contributed numerous articles to newspapers and
 periodicals.
Mailing Address: Encore, 572 Madison Ave., New York, N.Y.
 10022.

LEWIS, JAMES, JR., Public school administrator
Born: Newark, N.J.
Education: B.S., Hampton Inst., 1953; M.A., Columbia Univ.,
 1957; Ed.D., East Coast Univ., 1970.
Family: m.; children, 3.
Professional Experience: Tchr. industrial arts, Bd. of Ed.,
 Jersey City, N.J., 1956-57; tchr. special ed., Wyandanch
 Pub. Schs., N.Y., 1959-66; acting asst. high sch. prin.,
 Wyandanch Pub. Schs., N.Y., 1964-66; elementary prin.,
 Wyandanch Pub. Schs., 1966-67; district prin., Wyan-
 danch Pub. Schs., 1967-; major, U.S. Army Reserve,
 1955-57; cons., Center for Urban Ed., N.Y., 1968-71.
Memberships: Am. Assn. Sch. Adminstrs.; N.Y. State Council
 of Sch. District Adminstrs.; NEA; N.Y. State Tchrs.
 Assn.; Suffork County Sch. Executives Assn., Inc.;
 Schoolmen's Advisory Com. for Hofstra Univ., Sch. of
 Ed., 1969-70; Tchr. Ed. Program Advisory Council, 1969-
 70.
Awards: Alfred North Whitehead Fellow, Harvard Univ., 1970-
 71.
Publications: A Contemporary Approach to Nongraded Education, 1969; Administering the Individualized Instruction
 Program, 1970; The Tragedies in American Education,
 1970; A Systems Approach to Developing Behavioral Ob-
 jectives, 1970; Differentiating the Teaching Staff, 1971.
Mailing Address: Wyandanch Pub. Schs., U.F.S.D. 9, Wyandanch, N.Y. 11798.

LIGHTFOOT, CLAUDE M., Political activist, Author
Born: Lake Village, Ark., 1910.
Education: Va. Union Univ.
Professional Experience: Marxist historian and analyst.
Memberships: Active member of the Communist Party.

Publications: Black Power and Liberation; A Communist View, 1967; Ghetto Rebellion to Black Liberation, 1968; Black America and the World Revolution, 1970; Racism and Human Survival: The Lessons of Nazi Germany, 1972. Mailing Address: c/o International Publishers Co., Inc., 381 Park Ave. S., New York, N.Y. 10016.

LINCOLN, C. ERIC, Educator, Author
Born: Athens, Ala., June 23, 1924.
Education: A.B., LeMoyne Coll., 1947; M.A., Fisk Univ., 1954; B.D., Univ. of Chicago, 1956; M.Ed., Boston Univ., 1960; Ph.D., ibid., 1960; LL.D. (hon.), Carleton Coll., 1968; post baccalaureate, Univ. of Chicago Law Sch., 1948-49; post doctoral, Brown Univ., 1964-65.
Family: m. Lucy Cook; children, Cecil Eric, Joyce Elaine, Hilary Anne, Less Charles.
Professional Experience: Dir. pub. relations, LeMoyne Coll., 1950-51; asst. personnel dean, Fisk Univ., 1953-54; asst. personnel dean; asst. prof. religion and philosophy; adminstv. asst. to the pres.; prof. social philosophy; prof. social relations; dir., Institute of Social Relations, 1954-65, Clark Coll.; dir., Panel of Americans, Human Relations Center, 1958-60, Boston Univ.; adjunct prof., Boston Univ. Human Relations Center, 1963-65; lectr.-in-residence, Pub. Affairs Center, 1962, vis. prof. social relations, Pub. Affairs Center, Dartmouth Coll. 1963; post-doctoral intern, coll. adminstrn., resident fellow, Hope Coll., 1964-65; prof. sociology, Portland State Coll., 1965-67; vis. prof., Spelman Coll., summer 1966; adjunct prof., The San Francisco Theological Seminary, 1966-67; prof. sociology and religion, Union Theological Seminary, 1967-; adjunct prof. religion, Columbia Univ.; adjunct prof. sociology, Vassar Coll., 1969-; chmn. Dept. of Religion and Philosophy, Fisk Univ. June, 1973-; guest lectr., various colleges and universities; cons., numerous programs, including, Race Relations Inst., Fisk Univ. (1961), U.S. White House Conf.(1966), A.T. and T. (1968), Twentieth Century Fund (1968).
Memberships: Various organizations, including founding pres. of The Black Academy of Arts and Letters; The New York Academy of Arts and Sciences; Author's Guild; Author's League of America, Inc.; Nat. Assn. of Professors; ASNLH; NEA; Nat. Assn. of Inter-group Relations Officials.
Awards: John Hay Whitney Fellow, 1957-58; Crusade Fellow, Methodist Church, 1958-59; Human Relations Fellow, Boston Univ., 1968; Eli Lilly Fellow, 1959.
Publications: Contributed numerous articles to anthologies, journals and magazines. Author, numerous books, including The Black Muslims in America, 1961; My Face is Black, 1964; Sounds of the Struggle, 1967; Is Anybody

Listening, 1968; The Black Americans, 1969; The New
Blacks and the Black Estate, 1970; Martin Luther King,
Jr.: A Profile, 1970.
Mailing Address: Dept. of Religion and Philosophy, Fisk Uni-
versity, Nashville, Tenn. 37203.

LINDE, SHIRLEY MOTTER, Author, Publisher
Born: Cincinnati, Ohio, Mar. 22, 1929.
Education: B.S., Univ. of Cincinnati; M.S., Univ. of Mich. Medi-
cal Sch.; Univ. of Cincinnati; Northwestern Univ.; N.Y.
Univ.
Professional Experience: Assoc. editor, Together Magazine,
Methodist Pub. House; chief, information services,
Northwestern Univ. Medical and Dental Schs.; medical
copy editor, Year Book Publishers; asst. editor, Journal
of International Coll. Surgeons; research fellow, Univ.
of Mich. Medical Sch.; research asst., Univ. of Cincin-
nati Medical School; research chemist, Andrew Jergens
Co.; dir., Lake Lotawana Writers Conf.; Chicago bureau
chief, Medical News, Medical Tribune, Tele-Med, Inc.;
writer, editor, Collins Assoc. Publishing, Inc.; pres.,
Med-Assist., Inc., N.Y.C.; pres., Pavilion Publishing
Co., N.Y.C.-; newsletters editor, Medical Bulletin on
Tobacco, Stay Young, and Speaking Personally; films,
"Scientists in Outer Space," Sex Education Film Scripts;
public relations cons., including Ortho. Pharmaceutical
Co.; N.Y. Univ.; U.S. Dept., HEW; Am. Coll. of Cardiol-
ogy; Am. Airlines; Am. Coll. of Radiology; Am. Cancer
Soc.; news and features for various newspapers and
radio stations.
Memberships: Nat. Assn. of Science Writers, exec. com.;
Author's League; Medical Writers Assn; Chicago Press
Club; Am. Assn. for the Advancement of Science.
Awards: Outstanding Service Award, Am. Medical Writers
Assn., 1972.
Publications: Contributed numerous articles to scientific,
professional journals and magazines. Editor, Radio-
activity in Man, 1961; editor, Science and the Public,
1962; editor, Response of the Nervous System to Ionizing
Radiation, 1962; The Big Ditch: Story of the Suez Canal,
1962; Total Rehabilitation of Epileptics, 1962; editor,
Medical Science in the News, 1965; Heart Attacks That
Aren't, 1966; Airline Stewardess Handbook, 1968; Modern
Woman's Medical Dictionary, 1968; Cosmetic Surgery:
What It Can Do for You, 1971; Emergency Family First
Aid Guide, 1971; The Complete Allergy Guide (with
Howard G. Rapaport, M.D.), 1971; Orthotherapy (with
Arthur Michele, M.D.), 1971; Sickle Cell: A Complete
Guide to Prevention and Treatment, 1972.
Mailing Address: Pavilion Publishing Co., 520 East 77 St., New
York, N.Y. 10021.

LONG, CHARLES HOUSTON, Educator
Born: Little Rock, Ark.
Education: Dunbar Junior Coll.; B.D. Univ. of Chicago Divinity
  School; Ph.D. ibid.
Family: m. Alice Freeman; children, John Freeman, Carolyn
  Louise, Christopher Charles, Daniel Mark.
Professional Experience: U.S. Army Air Force, 1944-46;
  instr. religion and advisor to students, Divinity Sch.,
  Univ. of Chicago, 1956; Dean of Students, asst. prof.,
  prof. history of religions, and chmn., com. on African
  studies, Univ. of Chicago-; vis. prof., history of religions,
  Princeton Univ.; St. Xavier's Coll.; Florida Presbyterian
  Univ.; editor, History of Religions journal.
Memberships: International Assn. of Historians of Religion;
  Nat. Soc. for Religion in Higher Ed.; Am. Soc. for the
  Study of Religion; Soc. for the Study of Black Religion;
  pres., Am. Academy of Religion.
Publications: Contributed to journals. Author, Alpha, The
  Myths of Creation, 1963; editor, The History of Religions:
  Essays in Understanding (with Joseph Kitagawa), 1967;
  editor, Myths and Symbols: Essays in Honor of Mircea
  Eliade (with Joseph Kitagawa) 1969.
Mailing Address: Dept. of History of Religions, Swift Hall,
  University of Chicago, 1025-35 East 58 Street, Chicago,
  Ill. 60637.

LONG, DOUGHTRY
Publications: Black Love, Black Hope, 1971; Song for Nia, 1971.

LONG, R. CHARLES, Educator
Born: Norfolk, Va., Jan. 21, 1918.
Education: B.S., Hampton Inst., 1941-46; M.S., New York Univ.,
  1946-47; Ed.S., ibid., 1947-54; Ed.D., Univ. of North
  Dakota, 1965-67.
Family: m. Marguerite Selden; children, Robert, Marguerite,
  Sybille.
Professional Experience: Military, QM Truck Co. Commander,
  1941-45; chmn., Dept. of Business, Savannah State Coll.,
  1947-57; prof. and chmn., Dept. Business Technology,
  Washington Tech. Inst., 1969; graduate advisor and prof.
  Business Ed., Va. State Coll., 1957-; cons., State Supr.
  of Business Ed., State Bd. of Ed., Va.
Memberships: NEA; Va. Tchrs. Assn.; Pi Omega Pi Honor
  Soc.; Delta Pi Epsilon Honorary Graduate Soc.
Awards: Outstanding Service to Tchrs. of Va.
Publications: Contributed to journals. Co-author, Modern
  Communications.
Mailing Addrsss: 4100 Connecticut Ave., Washington Technical
  Institute, Washington, D.C. 20008.

LONG, RICHARD A., Educator
Born: Philadelphia, Pa., Feb. 9, 1927.
Education: A.B., Temple Univ., 1947; M.A., ibid., 1948; Univ.
of Pa., 1948-49; Oxford Univ., summer 1950; Univ. of
Paris, 1954; Doctorate (D. es. L.), Univ. of Poitiers,
1965.
Professional Experience: Instr., assoc. prof. English and
speech, Morgan State Coll., 1951-66; prof. English and
French, dir. Coll. Museum, Hampton Institute, 1966-68;
lecteur d'Anglais, Univ. of Poitiers, 1964-65; lectr.,
Afro-American studies, Harvard Univ., 1969-71; prof.
English and coordinator, Afro-American Studies, Atlanta
Univ., 1968-; spl. projects, including Symposium on Hai-
tian Art and Culture, Morgan State Coll, 1956, Exhibi-
tion of Primitive Art, Union Carbide Bldg., N.Y.C, 1967,
Conferences on African and African-American Studies,
Atlanta Univ, 1968-72, Symposium on African Art, Har-
vard Univ, 1971, editorial bds., Phylon, Black Books
Bulletin and Papers in Linguistics.
Memberships: Including past pres., CLA; pres., Southeastern
Conf. on Linguistics; Manpower Com., Linguistic Soc.
of Am.; MLA; MHRA; AAM.
Awards: Fulbright Scholar, Univ. of Paris, 1958-59.
Publications: Contributed articles to magazines and journals.
Co-editor, Negritude: Essays and Stories, 1967; editor,
Afro-American Writing: An Anthology of Prose and
Poetry (with Eugenia Collier), 1972.
Mailing Address: Atlanta University, Atlanta, Ga. 30314.

LORDE, AUDRE (Mrs. Edwin Ashley Rollins), Lecturer,
Author
Born: New York, N.Y., Feb. 18, 1934.
Education: B.A., Hunter Coll., 1951-59; M.L.S., Columbia
Univ., 1960-61; Univ. of Mexico, 1954-55.
Family: m. Edwin Ashley Rollins; children, Elizabeth, Jonno.
Professional Experience: Nurses's aide, Bellevue, 1951-52;
factory worker, Crystal Ribbon Factory, 1952-54; lib.
clerk, N.Y. Pub. Lib., 1955-58; arts and crafts supr.,
Police Athletic League, 1958-59; social investigator,
Bureau of Child Welfare, 1959-60; young adult libn.,
Mt Vernon Pub. Lib., 1960-62; self-employed, 1962-
65; head libn., Town Sch., 1965-68; poet-in-residence,
Tougaloo Coll., summer 1968; lectr., CCNY, 1968-69;
lectr., Lehman Coll., CCNY, 1968-70; lectr., John Jay
Coll., CCNY, 1970-.
Awards: National Endowment for the Arts grant, 1968.
Publications: Contributed to magazines and anthologies.
Author, The First Cities, 1968; Cable to Rage, 1970.
Mailing Address: 626 Riverside Dr., New York, N.Y. 10031.

LOVELL, JOHN, JR.
Publications: Black Song: The Forge and the Flame, 1972.

LUCAS, LAWRENCE EDWARD, Catholic priest
Born: New York, N.Y., July 8, 1933.
Education: Cathedral Coll., N.Y., 1947-53; St. Joseph's Semi-
    nary, Yonkers Coll., 1953-59; ordained N.Y. Archdio-
    cese, 1959.
Professional Experience: St. Joseph's Church, Croton Falls,
    N.Y., 1959; St. Peter's Church, Barclay St., N.Y., 1959-
    61; Resurrection Church, N.Y.C., 1961-; writer, nation-
    ally syndicated column entitled The Black Voice; lectr.
Memberships: Chmn., Eastern Region of National Black Catho-
    lic Clergy Caucus; bd. dir., Nat. Conf. Black Churchmen;
    Steering Com., Black Economic Development Council;
    Mayor's Com. of Religious Leaders.
Publications: Contributed numerous articles to newspapers
    and magazines. Author, Black Priest, White Church:
    Catholics and Racism, 1970.
Mailing Address: 276 West 151 St., New York, N.Y. 10039.

LYONS, W. T., Manpower analyst, Technical writer
Born: Griffin, Ga., Aug. 10, 1919.
Education: B.A., Howard Univ., 1949; M.A., ibid., 1952; Univ.
    of Pa.
Professional Experience: Housing clerk, Federal and Pub.
    Housing Adminstrn.; postal clerk, U.S. Post Office;
    clerk/messenger, ICC; congressional clerk-typist,
    Office of Dependency Benefits; substitute tchr.; office
    clerk, vocational high sch.; clerk chief, CCC; manpower
    analyst, Manpower Programs Support Division, April,
    1968-; manpower analyst, Manpower Analysis Staff,
    1968-; asst. for Manpower Management & Utilization,
    Naval Personnel Research Laboratory; cons., Naval
    Bureaus, officer, and Systems Commands, program ad-
    minstr., program improvement, project manager; first
    and only black man to date to serve on Management
    Analysis Staff, Chief of Naval Operations, Pentagon;
    technical writer of books & manuals published for and by
    U.S. Fed. Gov.
Memberships: NAACP; Armed Forces Management Assn.
Awards: Numerous awards for outstanding work performance
    in the U.S. Fed. Gov., including Letter of Commendation,
    Commanding Officer, U.S. Naval Air Station, Anacostia,
    D.C.
Publications: Soul in Solitude, 1970.
Mailing Address: 4208 East Capitol St., N.W., #204, Washing-
    ton, D.C. 20019.

McKISSACK, FLOYD B., Lawyer, Organization executive
Born: Asheville, N.C., Mar. 9, 1922.
Education: A.B., N.C. Coll., 1951; LL.B., ibid., 1952.
Family: m. Evelyn Williams; children, Joycelyn D., Andrée
    Y., Floyd Bixler, Stephanie, Charmaine.
Professional Experience: Attorney, 1952-; sr. partner,
    McKissack & Burt, Durham, N.C.; counsel, CORE, 1960-
    68; pres., Floyd B. McKissack Enterprises, Inc., 1968-;
    developer, new town, Soul City, 1969; columnist, N.Y.
    Amsterdam News, 1965; vis. prof., State Univ. of N.Y.,
    Binghamton, 1970.
Memberships: Bd., Nat. Southeastern Bar Assns.; bd., Am.
    Vets; Alpha Phi Alpha; Elk.
Awards: Man of Year, Durham Business and Prof. Chain,
    1959, 1960, 1961; Ike Small's Civil Rights NAACP Award,
    1962; conf. award, Civil Rights, A.M.E. Church, 1964.
Publications: Three-fifths of a Man, 1968; Black Power and
    the World Revolution (with W. Worthy), 1971.
Mailing Address: 414 West 149 St., New York, N.Y. 10031.

McLEMORE, WILLIAM P., Educator
Born: Savannah, Ga., March 30, 1931.
Education: B.S., Kent State Univ., 1954-57; M.Ed., ibid., 1957-
    63; Northwestern Univ., 1969.
Professional Experience: Cpl., USMC, 1950-52; ward sec., U.S.
    Veterans Administrn. Hospital, 1952-53; tchr., Cleveland
    pub. schs., 1957-62; tchr., Toledo pub. schs., 1963-65;
    tchr., Joliet Jr. Coll., 1965-69; tchr., Northwestern
    Univ., summer 1970; instr., Ill. State Coll., 1970-.
Memberships: Ill. Sociol. Assn.; Nat. Council for the Social
    Studies.
Awards: Pi Gamma Mu Nat. Social Science Soc.; TTT Fellow-
    ship, 1969-70; Univ. Fellowship, 1970-71.
Publications: Poems included in Negro History Bulletin.
Mailing Address: 1570 Oak Ave., Evanston, Ill. 60201.

McPHERSON, JAMES A., Author
Born: Savannah, Ga., Sept, 16, 1943.
Education: B.A., Morgan State Coll., 1965; LL.B., Harvard Law
    Sch., 1965-68; M.F.A., Univ. of Iowa, 1968-69.
Professional Experience: Waiter, janitor, research asst.,
    writer, tchr., contributing editor, Atlantic Monthly.
Awards: Atlantic First Award; Atlantic Grant; Rockefeller
    Grant; Nat. Inst. of Arts and Letters.
Publications: Stories selected for inclusion in O'Henry Prize
    Stories and Best American Short Stories. Author, Hue
    and Cry, 1969.
Mailing Address: 143 Stephen Road, Aptos, Calif. 95003.

MADGETT, NAOMI LONG, Educator, Author
Born: Norfolk, Va., July 5, 1923.
Education: B.A., Va. State Coll., 1941-45; M.Ed., Wayne State
    Univ., 1951-52, 1954-55; Univ. of Detroit, 1962-63;
    Wayne State Univ., 1966-67.
Family: d. Jill Annette Witherspoon, step-children, William
    H. and Gerald Madgett, Jr.
Professional Experience: Staff writer, Michigan Chronicle,
    1946-47; service representative, Michigan Bell Telephone
    Co., 1948-54; tchr., Northwestern High Sch., Detroit,
    1955-68; assoc. prof. English, Eastern Mich. Univ.,
    Ypsilanti, 1968-.
Memberships: Delta Kappa Gamma Soc.; Alpha Kappa Alpha;
    MLA; NCTE; Council of Tchrs. of English.
Awards: 1st recipient, $10,000 Mott Fellowship in English,
    Oakland Univ., 1965-66; Distinguished English Tchr. of
    the Year, Metropolitan Detroit English Club, 1967; Soror
    of the Year, Alpha Kappa Alpha.
Publications: Contributed to newspapers, journals, and maga-
    zines. Author, Songs to a Phantom Nightingale, 1941
    (Naomi Cornelia Long); One and the Many, 1956; Star
    by Star, 1965.
Mailing Address: 18080 Santa Barbara Dr., Detroit, Mich.
    48221.

MAHONE, BARBARA
Publications: Sugarfields, 1970.

MAJOR, CLARENCE, Editor, Author
Born: Atlanta, Ga., Dec. 31, 1936.
Education: Pub. schs., Chicago, Ill.
Professional Experience: Tchr., Harlem Ed. Program, 1967;
    tchr., Columbia Univ. Tchrs. and Writers Collaboration,
    1967; tchr., Academy of Am. Poets, Bd. of Ed. project,
    May 1968; tchr., Pa. Advancement Sch., 1968-69; tchr.,
    Brooklyn Coll., 1968-69; tchr., Center for Urban Ed.,
    Crisis Workshop, 1967; tchr., Cazenovia Coll., summer
    inst., 1969; tchr., Univ. of Wisconsin, Dept. of English,
    Dec. 1969; tchr., Community Coll., Dept. of English,
    1970; assoc. editor, Proof, 1960; editor, Coercion Re-
    view, 1958-63; bk. review editor, Anagogic and Paideumic
    Review, 1960-61; assoc. editor, Journal of Black Poetry,
    1967-70; assoc. editor, Caw, 1967-68; bd. dir., What's
    Happening, 1969-; assoc. editor, Umbra, 1969-; poetry
    readings and talks presented at various institutions,
    including Bowdoin Coll., Afro-American Soc., New Sch.
    for Social Research, Guggenheim Museum, Internat.
    Poetry Forum, Carnegie Lib., Pittsburgh.

Memberships: Advisory Com., A Reading Program for Jr.
High Schs., Sch. District #5, Manhattan; The Academy of
Am. Poets, 1970-.
Publications: Contributed to anthologies, magazines, and news-
papers. Author, All-Night Visitors, 1969; Dictionary of
Afro-American Slang, 1970; Swallow the Lake, 1970; edi-
tor, The New Black Poetry, 1969; privately printed col-
lections of poems, The Fires That Burn in Heaven, 1954;
Human Juices, 1965; television script, "Africa Speaks
to New York," 1970; No, 1973.
Mailing Address: 94 St. Marks Pl., New York, N.Y. 10009.

MAJOR, REGINALD, Author
Born: New York, N.Y.
Education: Univ. of Chicago, 1946-50.
Professional Experience: Driver's license examiner, Calif.;
driver improvement analyst; dir., Educational Oppor-
tunity Program, San Francisco State Coll.
Publications: A Panther Is a Black Cat, 1971.
Mailing Address: c/o William Morrow & Co., Inc., 425
Park Ave. S., New York, N.Y. 10016.

MANDEL, BERNARD, Author
Publications: Labor, Free and Slave: Workingmen and the
Anti-slavery Movement in the United States, 1955; Samuel
Gompers, 1963; Young People's History of the United
States, 1968. Author of numerous articles and reviews.
Mailing Address: 1575 East Blvd., #717, Cleveland, Ohio
44106.

MAPP, EDWARD CHARLES, Library administrator
Born: New York, N.Y.
Education: B.A., City College of N.Y., 1953; M.S., Columbia
Univ., 1956; Ph.D., New York Univ., 1970.
Family: s. Andrew.
Professional Experience: Lib. asst., reference dept., N.Y.
Pub. Lib., 1948-55; asst. libn., N.Y.C. Community
Coll., 1956-57; tchr. libn., Bd. of Ed., N.Y.C., 1957-64;
chief libn., N.Y.C. Community Coll., 1964-; reviewer,
Library Journal; served, Middle States Assn. Evaluation
Teams.
Memberships: ALA; AAUP; N.Y.C. Lib. Assn.; N.Y. Lib. Club.
Awards: N.Y. Univ. Founders Day Award.
Publications: Contributed to professional journals and antholo-
gies. Author, Books for Occupational Education Pro-
grams: A List for Community Colleges, Technical In-
stitutes, and Vocational Schools, 1971.
Mailing Address: 950 East 14 St., Brooklyn, N.Y. 11230.

MARSHALL, PAULE, Author
Born: Brooklyn, N.Y., April 9, 1929.
Education: B.A., Brooklyn Coll., 1953; Hunter Coll., 1955.
Family: s. Evan.
Professional Experience: Staff writer, Our World magazine,
    1953-56; lectr. black literature, numerous colleges and
    universities, including Cercle Cultural de Royaumont
    (Paris), Oxford Univ. (England), Columbia Univ., Cornell
    Univ., Michigan State, Fisk Univ., Wesleyan, Lake For-
    rest.
Awards: Guggenheim Fellowship, 1960; Rosenthal Award, Am.
    Academy of Arts and Letters, 1961; Ford Foundation
    Grant for Poets and Fiction Writers, 1964-65; Nat. En-
    dowment on Arts and Humanities, 1967-68.
Publications: Contributed short stories to magazines and an-
    thologies. Author, Brown Girl, Brownstones, 1959; Soul
    Clap Hands and Sing, 1961; The Chosen Place, The Time-
    less People, 1969.
Mailing Address: 407 Central Park West, New York, N.Y.
    10025.

MARTIN, HERBERT WOODWARD, Educator
Born: Birmingham, Ala., Oct. 4, 1933.
Education: B.A., Univ. of Toledo.
Professional Experience: Teaching assistantship, State Univ. of
    N.Y., Buffalo, 1964-67; instr., asst. prof., poet-in-resi-
    dence, Aquinas Coll., 1967-70; Univ. of Dayton, 1970-;
    poetry reading, colleges and universities, including
    Bread Loaf, Mich. State Apple Blossom Festival, The
    Enjoyment of Poetry, WEVD radio.
Memberships: AAUP.
Awards: Scholarships in poetry, Antioch Coll., Univ. of Colo-
    rado, Bread Loaf of Middlebury Coll.; fellowship in
    Drama, Wagner Coll.; fellowship in English, S.U.N.Y.;
    scholarship in English, Bread Loaf Sch. of English.
Publications: Contributed to journals and magazines. Author,
    New York the Nine Million and Other Poems, 1969; Three
    Garbage Cans, a play, produced 1969.
Mailing Address: 1834 Glenwood Ave., Toledo, Ohio 43620.

MARVIN X
Publications: Black Man Listen, 1969.

MASON, B. J., Author, Editor
Born: Shreveport, La., April 5, 1944.
Education: B.S., Grambling Coll., 1959-63; M.A., Colorado
    State Univ., 1964-65.

Professional Experience: Tchr., Jackson High Sch., Corsicana,
Tex., 1963-64; civil rights worker, lectr., and writer,
Miss., La., Ala., Ga., 1965-69; professional actor and
writer, Hollywood, Calif., 1969-72; editor, Ebony maga-
zine, Johnson Publishing Co., 1972-.
Memberships: Writer's Guild of America; Screen Actors
Guild; NAACP; pres., CORE branch; SCLC; SNCC.
Publications: The Jerusalem Freedom Manufacturing Company,
1971; Sleep in the Meantime, 1973; Cry Like a Man, 1973.
Mailing Address: 820 South Michigan Ave., Chicago, Ill. 60605.

MATHIS, SHARON BELL, Teacher
Born: Atlantic City, N.J., Feb. 26, 1937.
Education: B.A., Morgan State Coll., 1954-58; D.C. Tchrs.
Coll.
Family: m. Leroy Franklin Mathis; children, Sherie, Stacy,
Stephanie.
Professional Experience: Caseworker, Children's Hosp.,
Washington, D.C., 1958-59; substitute tchr., pub. schs.,
Washington, D.C., 1959-60; tchr., Holy Redeemer Catho-
lic Sch., 1960-65; tchr., Charles Hart Jr. High Sch.,
1965-; writer-in-residence, Howard Univ., 1972-.
Awards: 1957 Benjamin F. Jackson Prize; Emmanuel Chambers
Memorial Sociology Award, 1958; Eliza Jane Cummings
Medal, 1958; Council on Interracial Books for Children
Award for Sidewalk Story, 1970; Weekly Reader Chil-
dren's Book Club Fellowship, 1970.
Publications: Contributed short stories to magazines and
several confessions to Tan. Author, Brooklyn Story,
1970; Sammy's Baby, 1970; Sidewalk Story, 1971; Teacup
Full of Roses, 1972.
Mailing Address: 131 Elmira St., S.W., Washington, D.C.
20032.

MATTHEWS, JOHN L., Postal clerk (ret.)
Born: Montgomery, Ala., May 30, 1899.
Education: State Normal Sch., Montgomery, Ala.; Oakwood
Coll., Huntsville, Ala.
Family: m. Julia Goss; s. John L., Jr.
Professional Experience: Various jobs; post office, 1937-68.
Publications: A Layman Looks at the Gods of the Bible, 1970.
Mailing Address: 3235 Lucerne St., Bronx, N.Y. 10465.

MAYFIELD, JULIAN, Author
Born: Greer, S.C., June 6, 1928.
Education: Lincoln Univ. (Pa.).
Family: m. Dr. Ana Livia Cordero; children, Rafael, Emiliane
Kwasi.

Professional Experience: Aide to President Kwame Nkrumah,
1962-66; founding editor, The African Review; instr.,
Schweitzer Program in the Humanities, New York Univ.
Awards: Fellow of the Society for the Humanities, Cornell
Univ., 1967-68; W.E.B. DuBois Distinguished Visiting
Fellow, Africana Studies and Research Center, Cornell
Univ.
Publications: Contributed articles, essays, reviews and short
stories to newspapers, magazines and anthologies.
Author, The Hit, 1957; The Long Night, 1958; The Grand
Parade, 1961; editor, The World Without the Bomb: The
Papers of the Accra Assembly, 1963.
Mailing Address: Chaka Farm, RFD 2, Spencer, N.Y. 14883.

MAYS, BENJAMIN E., Author, College president (ret.)
Born: Epworth, S.C., Aug. 1, 1895.
Education: A.B., Bates Coll., 1920; M.A., Univ. of Chicago,
1925; Ph.D., ibid., 1935; LL.D. (hon.) Denison Univ.,
1945; D.D. (hon.) Howard Univ., 1945; LL.D. (hon.)
Va. Union Univ., 1945; Litt.D. (hon.) South Carolina State
Coll., 1946; D.D. (hon.) Bates Coll., 1947; L.H.D. (hon.)
Boston Univ., 1950; D.D. (hon.) Bucknell Univ., 1954;
D.D. (hon.) Berea Coll., 1955; D.D. (hon.) Kalamazoo
Coll., 1959; LL.D. (hon.) Univ. of Liberia, 1960; L.H.D.
(hon.) Kenka Coll., 1962; LL.D. (hon.) St. Augustine's
Coll., 1963; D.Ed. (hon.) St. Vincent Coll., 1964; LL.D.
(hon.) Lincoln Univ., 1965; D.D. (hon.) Morris Coll.,
1966; D.D. (hon.) Ricker Coll., 1966; L.H.D. (hon.) Shaw
Univ., 1966; L.H.D. (hon.) Morehouse Coll., 1967;
LL.D. (hon.) Harvard Univ., 1967; LL.D. (hon.) Morgan
Coll., 1967; Litt.D. (hon.) Grinnell Coll., 1967; LL.D.
(hon.) Michigan State Univ., 1968; L.H.D. (hon.) New
York Univ., 1968; J.D.D. (hon.) Middlebury Coll., 1969;
L.H.D. (hon.) Emory Univ., 1970; L.H.D. (hon.) Brandeis
Univ., 1970; LL.D. (hon.) Centre Coll. of Kentucky, 1970;
L.H.D. (hon.) Benedict Coll., 1970.
Family: m. Sadie G. (deceased).
Professional Experience: Tchr. higher mathematics, More-
house Coll., 1921-24; pastor, Shiloh Baptist Church,
Atlanta, Ga., 1921-24; instr. English, State Coll., Orangeburg, S.C., 1925-26; exec. sec., Tampa Urban League,
1926-28; nat. student sec., YMCA, 1928-30; dir., study
of Negro Churches, Inst. of Social and Religious Research, 1930-32; dean, Sch. of Religion, Howard Univ.,
1934-40; pres., Morehouse Coll., 1940-67; pres. emeritus, Morehouse Coll., 1967; vis. prof., and advisor to
pres., Mich. State Univ., East Lansing, 1968-69; cons.,
Office of Ed., HEW, Washington, 1969; cons., Ford Foundation, 1970; contributing editor, Journal of Negro Education; weekly columnist for the Pittsburgh Courier,
1946-.

Memberships: Numerous organizations, including pres.,
Atlanta Bd. of Ed., 1970; Bd. of Southern Ed. Foundation;
Delta Sigma Rho; Delta Theta Chi; Omega Psi Phi; Phi
Beta Kappa Society; central com., World Council of
Churches, 1949-53; trustee, Danforth Foundation.
Awards: Numerous, including Schomberg Honor Roll of Race
Relations, 1944; Alumnus of the Year, Divinity Sch.,
Univ. of Chicago, 1949; Amistad Award, Am. Missionary
Assn., 1968; Russwurm Award, NNPA, 1970; Award of
Achievement, Black Educational Services, Chicago,
1970.
Publications: Contributed numerous articles to books, journals,
magazines, and newspapers. Author of books, including
The Negro's Church (with Joseph W. Nicholson), 1933,
republished, 1969; The Negro's God as Reflected in His
Literature, 1968; Seeking to be Christian in Race Rela-
tions, 1957; Disturbed About Man, 1969; Born to Rebel,
1970.
Mailing Address: 3316 Pamlico Dr., S.W., Atlanta, Ga. 30311.

MENCHAN, W. McKINLEY, Educator
Born: Marion County, Fla., Nov. 2, 1898.
Education: A. B., Howard Univ., 1924; A.M., Univ. of Pa.,
1928; Ed.D., ibid., 1950.
Family: m. Aponte R. Brown; children, Aponte Elizabeth
(deceased), Dillard B.
Professional Experience: Tchr., pub. schs., Coatesville, Pa.,
1925-28; prof., Alabama State Coll., 1928-31, 1934-38;
instr., Howard Univ., 1931-33; parent ed. leader, Philip's
P.E. Church, N.Y., 1933-34; dean of academic affairs,
Cheyney State Coll., Pa., 1938-67; vis. grad. prof.,
Prairie View Coll., summer 1947; vis. grad. prof., A & T
State Univ., N.C., summers 1951, 1953, 1954.
Memberships: High Sch. and Coll. Evaluation Team, Middle
States Assn. Colleges and Secondary Schs.; NEA; PSEA;
Assn. of Pa. State Coll. Faculties; Nat. Assn. for Nur-
sery Ed.; Nat. Assn. of Spelman Fellows; Am. Tchrs.
Assn.; Nat. Congress of Colored Parents and Tchrs.; Am.
Academy of Political and Social Science.
Publications: Contributed to journals and magazines. Author,
Introduction to Child Development and Parent Education,
1969.
Mailing Address: 5712 Nassau Road, Philadelphia, Pa. 19131.

MEREDITH, JAMES
Publications: Three Years in Mississippi, 1966.

MERIWETHER, LOUISE M., Author, Free-lance writer
Born: Haverstraw, N.Y.
Education: B.A., New York Univ.; M.S. Univ. of Calif., Los
Angeles, 1965.
Professional Experience: Legal sec., N.Y. and Calif., 1950-61;
reporter, Los Angeles Sentinel, 1961-64; story analyst,
Universal Studios, Universal City, Calif., 1965-67; free
lance writer-.
Memberships: Watts Writers' Workshop; Harlem Writers'
Guild; Author's Guild.
Publications: Articles and short stories in magazines. Author,
Daddy Was a Number Runner, 1970; The Freedom Ship
of Robert Small, 1971; Don't Ride the Bus on Monday:
The Rosa Parks Story, 1973.
Mailing Address: 1691 E. 174 St., #7D, Bronx, N.Y. 10472.

MILLER, ADAM DAVID, Educator
Born: Orangeburg, S.C., Oct. 8, 1922.
Education: M.A., Univ. of Calif.
Family: m. Lois Grene; children, Carmen, Robin, Pemba.
Professional Experience: Instr. English, languages, Commu-
nity Coll., Oakland, Calif.; theater dir., actor, Aldridge
Players West; TV producer; radio program of poetry,
"The Imaged Word," KPFA-FM.
Awards: Award of merit for film, Dices on Black Bones,
Calif., Assn. of Tchrs. of English, 1973.
Publications: Contributed articles on black poetry, drama,
literature, film and esthetics. Author, Dices on Black
Bones, 1970.
Mailing Address: Box 162, Berkeley, Calif. 94701.

MILLICAN, ARTHENIA JACKSON BATES, Educator
Born: Sumpter, S.C., June 1, 1920.
Education: B.A., Morris Coll., 1941; M.A., Atlanta Univ., 1948;
Ph.D., Louisiana State Univ., 1942.
Family: m. 1st Calvin Shepherd Jackson; 2nd Wilbert Millican;
children, stepson, Wilbert James Millican.
Professional Experience: Instr. English, Westside High, Ker-
shaw, N.C., 1942-45; instr. English, civics, Butler High
Sch., 1945-46; dept. chmn. English, Morris Coll., Sum-
ter, S.C., 1947-49; instr. English, history, Mary Bethune
High Sch., Halifax, Va., 1949-55; instr. English, Mississippi Valley State Coll., 1955-56; instr. English, Southern
Univ., Baton Rouge, La., 1956-59; asst. prof. English,
1959-63; assoc. prof. English, 1963-72; prof. English,
creative writing, 1972-; instr. creative writing, Camp
Miniwauca, Stony Lake, Michigan, summer, 1962, 1963;
recruiter, The American Youth Foundation; coordinator
of creative writing, Southern Univ., Baton Rouge.

Memberships: CLA; Delta Sigma Theta; Gamma Sigma Sigma; YWCA, Baton Rouge.
Publications: Contributed short stories, poetry, and book reviews to magazines and journals. Author, Seeds Beneath the Snow, 1969.
Mailing Address: Rt. 2, Box 284, Baker, La. 70714.

MILNER, RONALD
Publications: Black Drama Anthology (with Woodie King), 1972.

MITCHELL, LOFTEN, Playwright
Born: New York, N.Y.
Education: City Coll. of N.Y., studied playwriting; grad., Talladega Coll., 1943; Columbia Univ., playwriting.
Professional Experience: U.S. Navy; social investigator, Dept. of Welfare, N.Y.C.; plays produced, The Cellar and Bancroft Dynasty, Harlem Showcase; plays written, Blood in the Night and A Land Beyond the River, Greenwich Mews Theatre, N.Y.C., March 28, 1957; Star in the Morning (story of black entertainer, Bert Williams); wrote musical with Irving Burgie, Ballad for Bimshire, produced on Broadway, 1963-64.
Awards: Guggenheim for creative writing, 1958-59; Rockefeller Foundation grant, 1961.
Publications: Contributed radio scripts, screenplays and articles on the theatre to magazines and newspapers. Author, Black Drama: The Story of the American Negro in the Theater, 1970.
Mailing Address: c/o Hawthorne Books, Inc. 70 Fifth Ave., New York, N.Y. 10011.

MONROE, REGINALD, Advertising
Born: Brooklyn, N.Y., Jan. 30, 1938.
Education: Central Brooklyn Neighborhood Coll.
Family: m. Carol Foy.
Professional Experience: VISTA; Central Brooklyn Neighborhood Coll.; Abe Chizner Roofing Co.; advertising, Young and Rubicam, 1970-.
Publications: Poetry Book, 1970.
Mailing Address: 131-31, 142 St., Queens, N.Y. 11436.

MOODY, ANNE (Mrs. Austin Straus), Author
Born: Centreville, Miss., Sept. 15, 1940.
Education: Natchez Jr. Coll., 1958-60; B.S., Tougaloo Coll., 1960-63.
Family: m. Austin Straus.

Professional Experience: Civil rights worker for NAACP,
    CORE, SNCC, 1960-64; fund raiser, pub. speaker, nat.
    CORE, 1964; civil rights project coordinator, Cornell
    Univ., 1964-65; full-time writer, 1965-.
Memberships: P.E.N.
Awards: All for the book, Coming of Age in Mississippi: ALA,
    One of Best Books of the Year, Gold Medal NCCJ, Made-
    moiselle.
Publications: Coming of Age in Mississippi, 1968.
Mailing Address: 1 Vanderbilt Ave., New York, N.Y. 10017.

MOORE, CARMAN LEROY, Educator, Author
Born: Lorain, Ohio, Oct. 8, 1936.
Education: B.Mus., Ohio State Univ., 1954-58; M.Mus., Julliard
    Sch. of Music, 1965.
Family: m. Susan K.; s. Martin Douglass.
Professional Experience: Tech. asst., N.Y. Pub. Lib., 1958-63;
    tchr. music, Dalton Sch., N.Y. C., 1963-67; music critic,
    Village Voice, 1964-; lectr., Manhattanville Coll., 1969;
    record reviewer and occasional columnist, The New York
    Times (Sunday); columnist for Vogue and Essence maga-
    zines; asst. prof., Yale Univ., 1970-.
Memberships: Founder and sec.-treas., Soc. of Black Com-
    posers; Am. Music Center.
Publications: Contributed to magazines and newspapers.
    Author, Somebody's Angel Child: The Story of Bessie
    Smith, 1970.
Mailing Address: 148 Columbus Ave., New York, N.Y. 10023.

MORRISON, C. T. (Charles Theodore), Social worker
Born: Webster Groves, Mo., June 29, 1936.
Education: B.J., Lincoln Univ., Mo., 1954-58.
Professional Experience: Caseworker, St. Louis City Welfare,
    1967-70; social worker, St. Louis County, 1970-.
Publications: The Flame in the Icebox, 1968.
Mailing Address: 311 Eldridge Ave., Rock Hill, Mo. 63119.

MORRISON, TONI (Chloe Anthony Wofford), Author, Editor
Born: Lorain, Ohio, Feb. 18, 1931.
Education: B.A., Howard Univ., 1949-53; M.A., Cornell Univ.,
    1953-55.
Family: Children, Harold Ford, Slade Kevin.
Professional Experience: Instr. English, Tex. Southern Univ.,
    1955-57; instr. English, Howard Univ., 1957-64; senior
    editor, Random House, 1965-; assoc prof., S.U.N.Y. at
    Purchase, 1971-72.
Memberships: Authors Guild Council; Nat. Council Endowment
    of the Arts.

Publications: Contributed numerous articles and book reviews
to magazines and newspapers. Author, The Bluest Eye,
1970.
Mailing Address: Random House, Inc., 201 East 50 St., New
York, N.Y. 10022.

MORROW, E. FREDERIC, Banker
Born: Hackensack, N.J., April 20, 1909.
Education: A.B., Bowdoin Coll., 1926-30; LL.B., Rutgers Univ.
Law Sch., 1946-48; Jur.D., ibid., 1958; LL.D. (hon.)
Bowdoin Coll., 1970.
Family: m. Catherine Gordon.
Professional Experience: Business manager for Opportunity
Magazine, Nat. Urban League, 1933-37; coordinator of
NAACP branches, 1937-42; major of artillery, U.S.
Army, 1942-46; pub. affairs staff, Columbia Broadcasting
System, 1946-52; adminstrv. asst., Sec. of Commerce,
Washington, D.C., 1953-55; adminstrv. asst., President
of the U.S., 1955-61; vice pres., African-American
Inst., 1961-64; vice pres., Bank of America, 1964-.
Memberships: Alpha Phi Alpha; trustee, N.Y.C. Pub Develop-
ment Corp.; dir., U.S. Com. for Refugees; dir., Nat.
Safety Council.
Publications: Black Man in the White House, 1963; Way Down
South Up North, 1973.
Mailing Address: 1270 Fifth Ave., New York, N.Y. 10029.

MORSE, EVANGELINE F., Social worker
Born: Augusta, Ga., Feb. 1, 1914.
Education: A.B., Talladega Coll., 1933-37; M.A., Chicago
Theological Seminary, 1939-41.
Family: d. Corine Morse Williams (adopted).
Professional Experience: Dir., religious ed., Lincoln Memorial
Congregational Church, Chicago, 1937-41; tchr., South-
ern Christian Inst., Edwards, Miss., 1942-43; program
dir., Campbell Friendship Settlement House, Gary, Ind.,
1943-57; social worker, Gary, Ind., 1957-.
Memberships: AKA.
Publications: Brown Rabbit, 1967.
Mailing Address: 2162 Vermont St., Gary, Ind. 46407.

MOSES, HENRY ARCHIE, Educator
Born: Gastonia, N.C., Sept. 8, 1939.
Education: B.S., Livingstone Coll., 1955-59; M.S., Purdue
Univ., 1959-62; Ph.D., ibid., 1962-64; teaching asst.,
freshman chemistry, Livingstone Coll., 1957-59;
research asst., Purdue Univ., 1959-64; asst. prof. biochemistry, Meharry Medical Coll., Nashville, Tenn.,

1964-; asst. prof. biochemistry, Tennessee A & I State
Univ., Inservice Inst., 1965-66; vis. prof. biochemistry,
Fisk Univ., Nashville, 1967-; prof. biochemistry, Tennessee State Univ., 1967-.
Memberships: AAAS; ACS; Alpha Chi Sigma, fraternity for
chemists; AAUP; N.Y. Academy of Science; Tenn. Academy of Science; Beta Kappa Chi Scientific Honor Soc.;
dir., Central Region, Nat. Inst. of Science, 1968-.
Awards: Golden Apple Award (teaching recognition), 1968.
Publications: Contributed to journals. Author, Experimental
Biochemistry of Medical Science Students, 1970.
Mailing Address: 1902 Salem Mason Dr., Nashville, Tenn.
37208.

MUMFORD, SAMUEL T., Mail express handler
Born: Greensboro, Ga., Dec. 8, 1906.
Education: Ninth grade, Maxey High Sch., Greensboro, Ga.
Professional Experience: Farmer; shop laborer; Seaboard
Railroad, 1923-43; cpl., U.S. Army, 1943-46; mail
express handler, C & O Railroad, 1943-.
Memberships: Internat. Masons; Crusade of Voters; NAACP.
Publications: Jack Betrayed His Buddy, 1969.
Mailing Address: 2925 Hawthorne Ave., Richmond, Va. 23222.

MURPHY, BEATRICE (Beatrice Murphy Campbell), Editor,
Author
Born: Monessen, Pa., June 25, 1908.
Education: Dunbar High Sch., 1928.
Family: s.
Professional Experience: Contributed column, "Think It Over,"
1933-35; feature and children's page editor, Washington
Tribune, 1935-37; book review columnist, Afro-American newspapers; sec. to head, sociology dept., Catholic
Univ.; stenographer, Office of Price Adminstrn.; writer
of poetry and special feature column, Associated Negro
Press; book reviewer, Pulse magazine, New York-San
Antonio Register and other media; founder and managing
editor-director, Negro Bibliographic and Research Center, Inc., and its publications, Washington, D.C.
Awards: Several for short stories, poetry and articles.
Publications: Contributed numerous articles, poetry and short
stories to magazines and journals. Author, Catching the
Editors' Eye, 1947; editor, Negro Voices, 1938; Love Is
a Terrible Thing, 1945; Ebony Rhythm, 1947; The Rocks
Cry Out (with Nancy Arnez), 1969; Today's Negro Voices,
1970.
Mailing Address: 117 R Street, N.E., Washington, D.C. 20002.

MURRAY, ALBERT, USAF major (ret.), Author
Born: Nokomis, Ala., 1916.
Education: B.S., Tuskegee Inst., 1939; M.A., New York Univ.,
    1948; Univ. of Mich.; Northwestern Univ.; Univ. of Paris;
    Air Force Univ.; Ohio State.
Professional Experience: Instr. composition and literature and
    dir., College Little Theatre, Tuskegee Inst., 1940-43,
    1946-51; instr., Graduate Sch. of Journalism, Columbia
    Univ., 1968; O'Connor Prof. of Lit., Colgate, 1970; vis.
    prof. lit., Univ. of Mass., 1971; base level plans and
    training officer, World War II; tchr. geopolitics and
    AFROTC subjects; staff training officer, command level,
    Southern Air Material Area, North Africa and Middle
    East; personnel services officer (education, recreation,
    family services, casualty assistance), Los Angeles,
    Calif.; major, USAF, ret.; lectr., including jazz and
    American Arts, American consul, Morocco, New School,
    Brandeis Univ., Peace Corps Training Center, Puerto
    Rico.
Publications: Contributed numerous articles, reviews and fic-
    tion to anthologies, newspapers and journals. Author,
    The Omni-Americans, 1970; South to a Very Old Place,
    1972; The Hero and the Blues, 1973.
Mailing Address: 45 West 132 St., New York, N.Y. 10037.

MURRAY, JAMES PATRICK, Free-lance author, Editor, Film
    critic
Born: New York, N.Y., Oct. 16, 1946.
Education: A.B., Syracuse Univ., 1964-68.
Professional Experience: Copy editor, White Plains Reporter
    Dispatch, July-Aug. 1968; lt., military police, AUS,
    Oct. 1968 - July 1970; news trainee, ABC-TV News,
    Aug. 1970 - April, 1971; public relations assoc., West-
    ern Electric Co., May 1971 - Sept. 1972; free-lance
    writer, critic, publicist, N.Y.C., Oct. 1972-; managing
    editor, Black Creation; contributing arts columnist,
    Amsterdam News; contributing film columnist, Encore;
    contributing arts columnist, Community News Services;
    free-lance publicity writer for promotion campaign,
    Stax Film/Wolper Pictures production, Wattstax; promo-
    tion writer, The Urban Center Lecture Series, Columbia
    Univ.; announcer, WNYC radio "Focus on the Commu-
    nity," Oct. 1970; cons. WNET, "Free Time" program on
    black films, Nov. 1971; guest lectr. Roslyn Jr. High Sch.,
    Roslyn, N.Y., Nyack Coll., Nyack, N.Y.; guest host,
    "Vibrations New York" Cable TV Show, Mar. 1973.
Memberships: 1st black, N.Y. Film Critics Circle; Sigma
    Delta Chi; Omega Psi Phi; Program Corp. of Amer.;
    Speaker Bureau, Hartsdale, N.Y.; Writers Workshop,
    Countee Cullen Lib., N.Y.C.

Awards: Bronze Star Medal and Army Commendation Medal,
U.S. Army.
Publications: Contributed articles and film reviews to maga-
zines and journals. Author, To Find an Image, 1973.
Mailing Address: 56 Dobbs Ferry Road, White Plains, N.Y.
10607.

MURRAY, JOAN, Television news correspondent, Advertising
executive
Born: Ithaca, N.Y., Nov. 6, 1941.
Education: Ithaca Coll.; Hunter Coll.; New School for Social
Research; the French Inst.
Professional Experience: Sec., CBS-TV Network Press In-
formation Dept., 1960; production asst. and script writer,
"Candid Camera" series; hostess, writer, producer,
NBC's radio program, "Women On The Move," 1964; 1st
black woman TV news correspondent, WCBS-TV, April
1965; co-hostess, WCBS-TV news correspondent with
Jim Jensen, "Opportunity Line," presented with N.Y.
State and N.J. State Employment Services; hostess-
coordinator, series of high sch. equivalency examination
preparatory broadcasts, ed. TV; interviewer syndicated
radio program, "The Joan Murray Show . . . And There
Are Women"; co-owner and exec. vice pres., Zebra
Associates, Inc.; 1st black to enter transcontinental
Women Air Race.
Memberships: NAACP; YWCA; Nat. Assoc of Media Women;
Nat. Urban League; TV Academy of Arts and Science;
Am. Women in Radio and TV; Nat. Council of Negro
Women; Am. Fed. of TV and Radio Artists.
Awards: Foremost Women in Communications, 1969-70; Made-
moiselle Award for Outstanding Achievement, 1969;
Media Woman of the Year; N.Y. Urban League's Certi-
ficate of Merit; John Russwurm Award; Mary McLeod
Bethune Achievement Award, Nat. Council of Negro
Women; Links Distinguished Service Award in the Field
of Communications; Reporter in the Field of Communi-
cations; Beta Phi Omega; Award of Excellence Citation,
City Hall.
Publications: A Week With the News, 1968.
Mailing Address: 536 East 79 St., New York, N.Y. 10021.

MURRAY, WALTER I., Educator
Born: New Orleans, La., May 22, 1910.
Education: Ph.D., Univ. of Chicago, 1947.
Family: m. Barbara W.; children, Walter, Jr., Daniel Andrew.
Professional Experience: Tchr., elementary sch., Robbins,
Ill.; tchr. mathematics, Gary Pub. Schs., Ind., 1934-47;
prin., Dunbar Elementary Sch., Phoenix, Ariz., 1947-53;

research asst., Univ. of Chicago, 1944-47; instr., South-
ern Univ., 1953-54; instr., A & T Coll., N.C., 1955-56;
Brooklyn Coll., 1956, prof. of ed., 1969-; cons., Human
Affairs Research Center, U.S. Office of Ed.
Memberships: Including Yearbook Com., Assoc. Supervision
and Curriculum Development, 1963-64; Com., Intergroup
Understanding, 1962-64; Civilian Police Review Bd.,
N.Y.C., 1966; bd. of dir., Opportunities Industrialization
Center, 1968.
Awards: Service Key Award, Phi Delta Kappa; Citizen of the
Year, Omega Psi Phi, 1962; Beta Tau, plaque for service
as faculty advisor, Brooklyn Coll., 1961; Tau Alpha
Omega, plaque for service as faculty advisor, Brooklyn,
Coll., 1958.
Publications: Contributed articles to journals. Author, Mate-
rials and Methods in Elementary Education: A Book of
Readings (with L. Crow and A. Crow), 1961; Educating
the Culturally Disadvantaged (with Crow and Smythe),
1966; Teaching the Language Arts in the Elementary
School (with Crow and Bloom), 1968.
Mailing Address: 143-15, 170 St., Springfield Gardens, N.Y.
11434.

MYERS, WALTER DEAN, Author, Editor
Born: West Virginia, Aug. 12, 1937.
Education: New York City College.
Family: Children, Karen, Michael Dean.
Professional Experience: AUS, 1954-57; various other employ-
ment, 1957-70; senior trade book editor, Bobbs-Merrill
Pub. Co., Jan. 1970-.
Publications: Where Does the Day Go?, 1969; The Dancers,
1972; The Dragon Takes a Wife, 1972.
Mailing Address: 150 West 225 St., Sec. 10, Bronx, N.Y.
10463.

NEAL, LARRY, Author
Born: Atlanta, Ga., Sept. 5, 1937.
Education: B.A., Lincoln Univ., 1957-61; M.A., Univ. of Pa.,
1961-63.
Family: m. Evelyn.
Professional Experience: Editor of arts, Liberator magazine,
1964-66; instr. English, City Coll. of N.Y., 1968-69;
writer-in-residence, Wesleyan Univ., 1969-70; fellow,
Yale Univ., 1970-75.
Awards: Yale Fellow; Guggenheim Fellow.
Publications: Contributed to journals. Author, Hoodoo Hollerin'
Bebop Ghosts, 1971; editor, Black Fire (with LeRoi
Jones), 1971; Analytical Study of Afro-American Culture,
1972.
Mailing Address: 12 Jumel Terrace, New York, N.Y. 10032.

NELSON, SOPHIA
Publications: The Black Man and the Promise of America (with
Lettie J. Austin and Lewis H. Fenderson), 1970.

NEWTON, HUEY
Publications: To Die for the People, 1972; Revolutionary
Suicide, 1973.

NICHOLS, CHARLES H., Educator
Born: Brooklyn, N.Y., July 6, 1919.
Education: B.A., Brooklyn Coll., 1938-42; Ph.D., Brown Univ.,
1944-48.
Family: m. Mildred; children, David, Keith, Brian.
Professional Experience: Assoc. prof. English, Morgan State
Coll., 1948-49; prof. English, Hampton Inst., 1949-59;
prof. language and literature, Free Univ., Berlin, 1959-
69; prof. English and chmn., Afro-American Studies
Program, Brown Univ., 1969-; contributing editor, Lexi-
kon Der Philosophie, Munich.
Memberships: German Assn. for American Studies; MLA.
Awards: Rachel Herstein Scholarship; N.Y. State Regents
Scholarship; Brown Univ. Graduate Scholar; Rosenwald
Fellow; Fulbright Prof.
Publications: Contributed numerous articles and book reviews
to journals. Author, Many Thousand Gone: the Ex-
Slaves' Account of Their Bondage, 1963; Black Men in
Chains: An Anthology of Slave Narratives, 1970; A
Guide Through American Literature, 1970.
Mailing Address: 56 Fosdyke St., Providence, R.I. 02906.

NKRUMAH, BAHALA T.
Publications: Black Unity.

NOBLE, JEANNE, Educator
Born: Palm Beach, Fla., July 18, 1926.
Education: B.A., Howard Univ., 1946; M.A., Columbia, 1948;
Ed.D., ibid., 1955.
Professional Experience: Asst. prof., Albany State Coll.,
1948-50; dean of women, Langston Univ., 1950-52; re-
search asst., grad. training and counseling, Municipal
Colleges, N.Y.C., 1954-55; guidance counselor, City
Coll. of N.Y., 1955-; prof. ed., N.Y. Univ., 1957-; exec.
pres., Nat. Council of Negro Women, 1972-73; bd. com.
Girls Job Corps, 1964; served on such commissions as
Status of Women, Presidential Scholars, Study the Draft,
All-Volunteer Armed Force; dir., Women's Job Corps;
Nat. Bd. of Girl Scouts; U.S. Advisory Com. on UNESCO.

Memberships: Bd. of Trustees, Lincoln Univ., Marymount Man-
hattan Coll., and Internat. House; past pres., Delta Sigma
Theta; vice pres., NCNW, 1965-69; AAUW; NAACP.
Awards: Jessie Smith Noyes research grant, 1954; Pi Lambda
Theta research award for The Negro Woman's College
Education; named Ebony magazine's "100 Most Influential
Negroes of the Emancipation Centennial Year," 1963;
Bethune-Roosevelt Award, 1965; local Emmy Award for
WCBS-TV program, "The Learning Experience,"
N.Y.C., 1970.
Publications: Contributed articles to professional journals.
Author, The Negro Woman's College Education, 1956;
College Education as Personal Development (with
Margaret Barrow Fisher), 1960.
Mailing Address: National Council of Negro Women, 815 Second
Ave., New York, N.Y. 10017.

O'DANIEL, THERMAN BENJAMIN, Educator
Born: Wilson, N.C., 1908.
Education: B.A., Lincoln Univ., Pa., 1930; M.A., Univ. of
Pennsylvania, 1932; Ph.D., Univ. of Ottawa, 1956.
Family: m. Lillian Davis.
Professional Experience: Instr., head, English dept., 1933-34,
prof. English, and chmn., div. of languages and liter-
ature, 1934-37, dean of the Liberal Arts Coll., 1937-40,
acting pres., March-July 1939, Allen Univ., Columbia,
S.C.; pres., Allen-Benedict Summer Sch., 1939; assoc.
prof. English, Fort Valley State Coll., 1940-43; prof.
English, ibid., 1944-55; acting adminstrv. dean and
acting registrar, ibid., 1945-46; dir., summer sch., ibid.,
1946; head, English dept., ibid., 1946-52; registrar and
dir. summer sch., ibid., 1952-55; assoc. prof. English,
Dillard Univ., New Orleans, 1955-56; asst. prof. English,
Morgan State Coll., 1956-63; dir., summer sch., ibid.,
1962, 1963; assoc. prof. English, ibid., 1963-67; prof.
English, ibid., 1967-; editor, CLA Bulletin, 1950, 1951;
founder and editor, CLA Journal, 1957-; dir., Special
Teacher-Training Sch. for qualified soldiers as prospec-
tive tchrs. of illiterate soldiers, Fort Benning, Ga.,
August 26 - Sept. 14, 1946; cons., including EPDA, Insti-
tute on Negro Lit. and History, North Carolina Central
Univ., 1969.
Memberships: Including MLA; NCTA; CEA; NEA, life member;
the Melville Society; Md. Council of Eng. Tchrs.;
ASNLH; Soc. for Study of Southern Lit.
Awards: General Ed. Bd. Fellowship, 1936-37; Ford Founda-
tion Fellowship, 1951-52; for the CLA Journal, the
Black Academy of Arts and Letters Special Alice E.
Johnson Memorial Fund Award, 1972.

Publications: Contributed numerous articles to journals.
Editor, Langston Hughes, Black Genius: A Critical
Evaluation, 1971; James Baldwin: A Critical Evaluation
(in press).
Mailing Address: 4920 Ivanhoe Ave., Baltimore, Md. 21212.

ODELL, ALBERT CHARLES, Teacher
Born: Baton Rouge, La., June 13, 1922.
Education: B.A., Grambling Coll., 1949; State Univ. of Iowa,
summer 1951.
Family: Children, Reginald C., Mrs.Yivette Louisa Thomas.
Professional Experience:Sgt. AUS, 1942-45; tchr., E.B.R. Par-
rish Sch. Bd., 1951-68; tchr. drama,West High Sch., Tor-
rance, Calif., 1968-; chmn., speech and drama, LA Ed.
Assn., 1962-64; dir., Ebony Community Players.
Memberships: LA Ed. Assn.; CTA.
Awards: Alumnus of the Year, Grambling Coll., 1965.
Publications: Contributed to journals. Author, A River
Divided, a play, 1963.
Mailing Address: 6818 South Denver Ave., Los Angeles,
Calif. 90044.

ODEN, GLORIA C., Educator, Poet
Born: Yonkers, N.Y., Oct. 30, 1923.
Education: B.A., Howard Univ., 1944; J.D., ibid., 1948; New
York Univ., 1969-71.
Professional Experience: Vis. lectr., State Univ of N.Y.,
Stony Brook; lectr., New Sch., for Social Research,
N.Y.; senior project editor, mathematics and science
and project dir., secondary language arts, Holt, Rine-
hart and Winston, N.Y.; senior editor, Inst. of Electrical
and Electronic Engineers, and the Am. Inst. of Physics;
asst. prof. English, Univ. of Md., 1971-; poetry readings,
including Syracuse Univ., Univ. of Maine, Catonsville
Community Coll., City Univ. of N.Y., N.Y. Community
Coll.; one of three poets subject of an educational film,
Poetry Is Alive and Well and Living in America, dis-
tributed overseas by U.S. State Dept.
Awards: Two awards, John Hay Whitney Foundation for crea-
tive writing; fellowship, Yaddo, Saratoga Springs, N.Y.;
fellowship, Bread Loaf Writers Conf., Middlebury Coll.
Publications: Contributed poetry to the following anthologies:
American Negro Poetry; New Negro Poets: USA; La
Poésie Negro-Américaine; The Angry Black; Schwarzer
Orpheus; The Poetry of the Negro:1746-1970; Black-
american Literature; Invitation to Poetry; Kaleidoscope;
Modern and Contemporary Poetry.
Mailing Address: 1518 Park Ave., Baltimore, Md. 21217.

O'DONNELL, LORENA, School principal
Born: Cincinnati, Ohio, May 1, 1929.
Education: B.S., Univ. of Cincinnati, 1949-51; M.Ed., Miami
    Univ., 1960.
Professional Experience: Clerk, Univ. of Cincinnati, 1949-51;
    tchr., pub. sch., Bd. of Ed., Cin., O., 1951-61; asst.
    prin., ibid., 1961-64; assoc. personnel supr., ibid., 1964-
    69; prin., ibid., 1969-; cons., Nat. Adv. Commn. for
    Programs, ESEA; instr., Cin. Bible Seminary.
Memberships: Com. of Management, YMCA; St. John's Chapter
    125; OES; Delta Sigma Theta.
Awards: WCIN Award for best citizen contributing to ed., 1968.
Publications: God in the Inner City, 1970.
Mailing Address: 139½ Huntington Pl., Cincinnati, Ohio 45219.

OFARI, EARL, Author
Born: Chicago, Ill., Oct. 8, 1945.
Education: A.A., Los Angeles City Coll., 1963-66; B.A., Cali-
    fornia State Coll., Los Angeles, 1966-68; M.A. (sociol-
    ogy), ibid.; M.A. (Afro Studies), Cornell Univ., 1970-
    71.
Family: m. Yvonne; d. Sikivu Fanon.
Professional Experience: Social worker, LA County, 1969;
    staff writer, LA Free Press, 1968; tutorial cons., Calif.
    State Black Community Relations Center, June-Aug.
    1967.
Memberships: SNCC; Black Student Union; Afro-American Cul-
    tural Assn.
Publications: Contributed to magazines. Author, The Black
    Book, 1969; The Myth of Black Capitalism, 1970.
Mailing Address: 116 West 14 St., New York, N.Y. 10011.

OLIVER, CLARENCE, see LAGRONE, OLIVER

PARKS, GORDON ALEXANDER BUCHANAN, Photographer,
    Author, Composer
Born: Ft. Scott, Kan., Nov. 30, 1912.
Education: Pub. schs., St. Paul; A.F.D. (hon.), Md. Institute.
Family: Children, 1st m., Gordon Roger, Toni, David; 2nd m.,
    Leslie.
Professional Experience: Photographer, Fed. Security Agency,
    1942-43; OWI, 1944; Standard Oil Co., N.J., 1945-48;
    Life magazine, 1948-72; writer, producer and dir. of
    film, The Learning Tree, 1969; composer, piano sonatas,
    concerto.
Memberships: Urban League; NAACP; Newspaper Guild; Assn.
    Composers and Dirs.; Am. Soc. Magazine Photographers;
    Kappa Alpha Mu.

Awards: Including Rosenwald fellow, 1942-43; NCCJ, 1962;
     Phil. Club, 1963-64; Am. Soc. Magazine Photographers,
     1963; Frederick W. Brehm award, 1962; Mo. Sch. Jour-
     nalism, 1964.
Publications: Contributed to periodicals. Author, The Learning
     Tree, 1963; A Choice of Weapons, 1966; Gordon Parks:
     A Poet and His Camera, 1968; Gordon Parks: Whispers
     of Intimate Things, 1971; In Love, 1971; Born Black, 1971.
Mailing Address: 15 Adams Pl., White Plains, N.Y. 10603.

PASCHAL, ANDREW G.
Born: Grady, Ark., Jan. 22, 1907.
Education: Wendell Phillips High Sch., 1928; Richard T.
     Crane Jr. Coll., 1931; Ph.B., Northwestern Univ.,
     1949; ibid., 1951; Medill School of Journalism.
Family: m. Luetta Austell-Paschal (deceased); children,
     Beverly Jean, Andrew G., Jr.
Professional Experience: Instr., Bd. of Ed., Chicago, 1934-
     37; writer and reporter, Ill. Writers' Project, 1937-40;
     interviewer, Ill. Dept. of Labor Employment Service,
     1941-42; T/sgt., U.S. Air Force, 1942-45; ed. dir. and
     counselor, U.S. Air Force, 1945; employment rep., Ill.
     State Employment Service, 1945-67; lectr.
Memberships: Collegiate Club; Negro History Club; German
     Club; Writer's Club.
Awards: Soldiers' Good Conduct Medal; Athlete Track Medals.
Publications: Contributed articles to journals and newspapers.
     Editor, A W.E.B. DuBois Reader.
Mailing Address: 1322 West 109 Pl., Chicago, Ill. 60643.

PATTERSON, LINDSAY
Publications: Editor, Anthology of the American Negro in the
     Theatre; A Critical Approach, 1968; editor, Black
     Theater: A Twentieth Century Collection of the Works of
     Its Best Playwrights, 1971.

PATTERSON, RAYMOND R., Lecturer, Poet
Born: New York, N.Y., Dec. 14, 1929.
Education: A.B., Lincoln Univ. (Pa.), 1947-51; M.A., New York
     Univ., 1954-56.
Family: m. Boydie Cooke; d. Ama.
Professional Experience: Children's supr., Youth House for
     Boys, Bronx, N.Y., 1956-58; instr. English, Benedict
     Coll., Columbia, S.C., 1958-59; tchr. English, Bd. of
     Ed., N.Y.C., 1958-68; lectr. English, City College of N.Y.,
     1968-.
Memberships: Dir., Black Poets Reading, Inc.

Awards: Borestone Mountain Poetry Awards, 1950; Nat. Endowment for the Arts Discovery Award, 1970.
Publications: Poetry published in magazines. Author, Get Caught: A Photographic Essay, 1964; Twenty-six Ways of Looking at a Black and Other Poems, 1969; At That Moment, 1970.
Mailing Address: 2 Lee Court, Merrick, N.Y. 11566.

PAWLEY, THOMAS D., Educator
Born: Jackson, Miss., Aug. 5, 1917.
Education: A.B., Virginia State, 1933-37; A.M., Univ. of Iowa, 1937-39; Ph.D., ibid., 1947-49; post-graduate studies, television, ibid., 1957.
Family: m. Ethel Louise McPeters; children, Thomas IV, Lawrence Austin.
Professional Experience: Instr., Prairie View State Coll., 1939-40; instr., Atlanta Univ., summers 1939, 1940, 1941, 1943, 1944; asst. prof., assoc. prof., prof., head, Dept. of English and Speech, and chmn., Division of Humanities and Fine Arts, Lincoln Univ. Mo., 1940-; vis. prof. dramatic art, Univ. of Calif., Santa Barbara.
Memberships: AETA; NADSA; AAUP; Alpha Phi Alpha.
Awards: Nat. Theatre Conf. Fellow, 1948; playwriting Contest Award, Jamestown, Va., 1954.
Publications: Contributed to journals. Author, Judgement Day, one-act play in The Negro Caravan, 1941; The Black Teacher and the Dramatic Arts (with William Reardon), 1970.
Mailing Address: 1014 Lafayette, Jefferson City, Mo. 65101.

PEEKS, EDWARD
Publications: Long Struggle for Black Power, 1971.

PERRY, MARGARET, Librarian
Born: Cincinnati, Ohio, Nov. 15, 1933.
Education: A.B., Western Mich. Univ., 1950-54; City Coll. of N.Y., 1957-58; M.S.L.S., Catholic Univ.
Professional Experience: Young adult and ref. libn., N.Y. Pub Lib., 1954-55, 1957-58; libn., Dept. of Army, Europe, 1959-67; ref. libn., U.S. Military Academy, 1967-70; head, Ed. Dept., Univ. of Rochester Lib., 1970-.
Memberships: ALA.
Awards: Scholarship to the seminar, "American Writing and Publishing," Schloss Leopoldskron, Salzburg, Austria, Feb.-Mar. 1956; honorable mention, Armed Forces Writers League Short Story Contest, 1965; 1st Prize, Armed Forces Writers League Short Story Contest,

1966; Certificate of Merit, Writers Digest Short Story
Competition, 1968; 2nd Prize, Francis Steloff Fiction
Prize, 1968.
Publications: Contributed poems, short stories and articles
to journals and magazines. Author, Bio-Bibliography
of Countee P. Cullen, 1903-1946, 1970.
Mailing Address: c/o E.A. Perry, 1005 Mace's Lane, Cam-
bridge, Md. 21613.

PETERS, JAMES S., Vocational rehabilitation administrator
Born: Ashdown, Ark., May 11, 1917.
Education: B.S., Southern Univ., 1935-39; M.A., Hartford
Seminary Foundation, 1940-42; M.S., Illinois Inst. of
Technology, Chicago, 1950-52; Ph.D., Purdue Univ.,
1953-55.
Family: m. Marie F.; children, Donna Marie, Kimberly Cordell, James S.
Professional Experience: Clinical counseling psychologist,
Veterans Administration Hospital, Kines, Ill., 1952-53;
asst. prof. and dir. of graduate program in vocational
rehabilitation, Springfield Coll., Springfield, Mass.,
1955-56; assoc. commr., Division of Vocational Rehabilitation, Conn. Dept. of Ed.
Memberships: Am. Personnel and Guidance Assn.; Am. Psychological Assn.; Conn. Ed. Assn.; Conn. State Psychological Assn.; Council of Administrators of State Vocational Rehabilitation Assn.; Nat. Vocational Guidance
Assn.; New England Psychological Assn.
Publications: Contributed to journals. Author, A Guide to
Vocational Rehabilitation, 1967.
Mailing Address: 328 Huckleberry Hill Rd., Avon, Conn.
06001.

PETRY, ANN, Author
Born: Old Saybrook, Conn., Oct. 12, 1912.
Education: Connecticut Coll. of Pharmacy (Univ. of Conn.),
1931; Columbia Univ., 1943-44.
Family: m. George D.; d.
Professional Experience: Pharmacist, 1931-38; advertising de-
partment, N.Y. Amsterdam News, N.Y., 1938-41; editor,
women's pages, People's Voice, N.Y., 1941-44.
Memberships: Authors Guild; Authors League; P.E.N.
Awards: Houghton Mifflin Fellowship, 1945.
Publications: The Street, 1946; The Drugstore Cat, 1949; The
Narrows, 1953; Harriet Tubman: Conductor on the Under-
ground Railroad, 1953; Tituba of Salem Village, 1946;
Legends of the Saints, 1970; Miss Muriel and Other
Stories, 1971.
Mailing Address: c/o Russell and Volkening, Inc., 551 Fifth
Ave., New York, N.Y. 10017.

PHARR, ROBERT DEANE, Author
Born: Richmond, Va., July 5, 1916.
Education: B.A., Virginia Union Univ., 1936-39; Fisk Univ.
Family: d. Lorelle R. Jones.
Memberships: Distinguished Alumnus, Va. Union; Omega
Psi Phi.
Publications: Contributed to P.E.N. Author, Book of Numbers,
1969; S.R.O., 1971; The Welfare Bitch, 1973.
Mailing Address: 435 West 118 St., New York, N.Y. 10027.

PHILLIPS, BILLIE ANN McKINDRA, Teacher
Born: St. Louis, Mo., July 1, 1925.
Education: B.A., Stowe Teachers Coll., 1942-47; Harris
Teachers Coll., 1962-65; Washington Univ., 1966-68;
Indianapolis Univ., summer 1968.
Family: s. La Monte Hamilton Mays.
Professional Experience: Postal clerk, U.S. Govt., 1946-47;
G.S. III, government, 1950-52; primary tchr., 1952-
65; conducted art workshop, summer 1969, St. Louis,
Mo.; tchr. art, summer sch., St. Louis, Mo., 1969; con-
ducted reading workshop, St. Louis, Mo., 1968; special
tchr. art ed., 1965-; lectr.; writer of tracts for Con-
cordia Publishing Co.: Christmas is When, A Birthday,
Easter Eggs.
Memberships: St. Louis State Tchrs. Assn.; NEA; Mo. Art Ed.
Assn.; Mo. State Tchrs. Assn.
Publications: Contributed to Grade Teacher magazine. Author,
The Skyline Reading Series: Out Jumped Abraham, 1967;
Watch Out for C, 1965; The Hidden Lookout, 1965; Who
Cares, 1965.
Mailing Address: 4658 Pope, St.Louis, Mo. 63115.

PHILLIPS, JANE
Publications: Mojo Hand, 1966.

PINKNEY, ALPHONSO, Educator
Born: Tampa, Fla., Dec. 15, 1929.
Education: B.A., Florida A & M Univ., 1947-51; M.A., New
York Univ., 1951-52; Ph.D., Cornell Univ., 1957-61.
Professional Experience: Dir., evaluation research, HARYOU-
ACT (OEO), Project Uplift, Harlem; instr., prof., Hunter
Coll., N.Y.C., 1961-69; prof. sociology, Univ. of Chicago,
1969-.
Memberships: Am. Assn. for the Advancement of Science; Am.
Sociol. Assn.; Eastern Sociol. Soc.
Awards: Ford Foundation Fellowship; Soc. for Psychological
Study of Social Issues Grant.

Publications: Contributed to journals. Author, The Committed:
White Activists in the Civil Rights Movement, 1968;
Black Americans, 1969; The American Tradition of Vio-
lence, 1971; co-author, Poverty and Politics in Harlem,
1970.
Mailing Address: Dept. of Sociology, University of Chicago,
Chicago, Ill. 60637.

PINSON, IRA DAVID, Author
Born: Philadelphia, Pa., Sept. 22, 1922.
Education: Morris Coll., 1938-39; B.S., South Carolina State
Coll., 1939-41, 1946-48; A.B., Tenn. State Univ., 1949-
50.
Professional Experience: Cpl., U.S. Army, 1941-42; 2nd lt.,
U.S. Army, 1942-45; sleeping car attendant, Canadian
Pacific Railway, 1950-70.
Memberships: Kappa Alpha Psi.
Publications: Poetry published in magazines. Author, Studies
in Black and White, 1966.
Mailing Address: 1430 Stanley St., Montreal 110, Quebec,
Canada.

PITTMAN, SAMPLE NOEL, Educational director
Born: Caldwell, Tex., April 22, 1925.
Education: B.A., Samuel Houston Coll., 1946-49; M.A., Texas
Southern Univ., 1950-52; New York Univ., 1964.
Family: m. Vivian Jo; children, Sample, Jr., Ava, Nicholas.
Professional Experience: Child guidance cons., St. Charles
State Training Sch. for Boys, St. Charles, Ill., 1954-56;
Juvenile Parole Agency, Ill. Youth Commn., Chicago,
1956-57; asst. dir., Migration Service, Chicago Comm.
on Human Relations, 1957-59; instr. sociology, Woodrow
Wilson Branch, Chicago City Jr. Coll., 1959-62; dean of
students and assoc. prof. sociology, Dillard Univ., 1963-
64; asst. dir., N.Y.C. Housing and Redevelopment Bd.,
Hudson Conservation Project, Feb. 1964; acting dir.,
ibid., March 1965-66; research assoc., Inst. of Strategic
Studies, Bd. of National Missions of the United Presby-
terian Church, U.S.A., Oct. 1966; dir., Ed. Dept., Train-
ing Resources for Youth, Brooklyn, N.Y., 1968-69; dir.,
Harlem Inst. for Tchrs., April 1969-; cons., lectr., In-
tercollegiate Conf. on Human Relations, NCCJ, 1960-62;
Institutional Rep., Boy Scouts of America, Chicago, 1960-
62.
Memberships: NAIRO; NAACP; NEA; Chicago Urban League;
Urban League of Greater N.Y.; Alpha Phi Alpha; Phi
Delta Kappa.
Awards: Schwartzhaupt Foundation grant, 1962.

POLITE / 127

Publications: In Essence, Epigrams and Quotable Quotes in
Race Relations from the Writings of Dr. Dan W. Dobson,
1966.
Mailing Address: 290 Convent Ave., New York, N.Y. 10031.

PLUMP, STERLING D., Editor, Educator
Born: Clinton, Miss., Jan 30, 1940.
Education: St. Benedict's Coll., 1960-62; B.A., Roosevelt
Univ., 1966-70.
Family: m. Falvia DeGracia.
Professional Experience: Clerk, U.S. Post Office, 1962-69;
military policeman, U.S. Army, 1964-66; counselor,
North Park Coll., 1969-71; instr., Univ. of Illinois,
Chicago Circle, 1970-; editor, Third World Press.
Publications: Contributed poems, reviews and articles to
journals and Black Books Bulletin. Author, Portable
Soul, 1969; Half Black, Half Blacker, 1970; Black Rituals,
1972.
Mailing Address: 7258 East End Ave., Chicago, Ill. 60649.

POINSETT, ALEX, Editor
Born: Chicago, Ill., Jan. 27, 1926.
Education: B.S., Univ. of Ill., 1947-52; M.A., ibid., 1952-53;
Univ. of Chicago, 1956-57.
Family: m. Norma R.; children, Pierrette, Pierre.
Professional Experience: Yeoman 3/c, U.S. Navy, 1944-47;
asst. ed., assoc. ed., senior staff ed., Johnson Pub. Co.
Memberships: Institute of the Black World, Atlanta, Ga.
Awards: J.C. Penney, Univ. of Missouri Journalism Award
($1,000) for Aug. 1967 Ebony article, "Ghetto Schools:
An Educational Wasteland."
Publications: Common Folk in an Uncommon Cause, 1972;
Black Power: Gary Style, 1970.
Mailing Address: 8532 South Wabash, Chicago, Ill. 60619.

POLITE, CARLENE HATCHER, Author
Born: Detroit, Mich., Aug. 28, 1932.
Education: Detroit Pub. Schs.; Martha Graham School of Con-
temporary Dance.
Family: Children, Glynda, Lila.
Professional Experience: Dancer, Concert Dance Theatre,
N.Y.C., 1956-59; actress and dancer, Equity Theatre,
Detroit, 1960-62; guest instr., YWCA, 1960-62; organizer,
Girl Friday, Michigan Democratic Party, 1962; elected
Mich. Democratic State Central Com., 1962-63; coordi-
nator, Detroit Council for Human Rights, 1963; partici-
pated, "Walk to Freedom" with Martin Luther King, Jr.,
June 23, 1963.

Awards: Nat. Foundation on Arts and Humanities.
Publications: The Flagellants, 1966.
Mailing Address: Farrar, Straus and Giroux, 19 Union Sq.
West, New York, N.Y. 10003.

PORTER, DOROTHY BURNETT, Librarian
Born: Washington, D.C., May 25, 1905.
Education: A.B., Howard Univ., 1928; B.S., Columbia Univ.,
1931; M.S. (library science), Columbia Univ., 1932;
American Univ., Certificate, Preservation and Admini-
stration of Archives, 1957; D.Litt. (hon.), Susquehanna
Univ., 1971.
Family: m. James A. Porter (deceased); d. Constance
Uzalac.
Professional Experience: Supr., The Moorland-Spingarn Col-
lection of Negro Life and History, Howard Univ., 1930-73;
cons., Ford Foundation Nat. Lib., Lagos, Nigeria; Kraus
Publications; lectr. Afro-Am. Studies Seminars.
Memberships: Including exec. Council, ASNLH; editorial bd.,
Journal of Negro Education; bd. of editorial advisors,
The Booker T. Washington Papers; advisory bd., Arno
Press Negro History project; Bibliographical Soc. of
Am.; Soc. of Am. Archivists; African Studies Assn.;
Nigerian Historical Soc.; Am. Soc. of African Culture;
Phi Beta Kappa; Black Academy of Arts and Letters;
Am. Antiquarian Soc.
Awards: Julius Rosenwald scholarship for study toward M.S.
degree, 1931-32; Julius Rosenwald Fellowship for re-
search in Latin American Lit., 1944-45; award for second
best article of the year, Journal of Negro History, 1943;
Distinguished Achievement Award, D.C. chapter, Nat.
Barristers Wives, Inc., for outstanding service, human
relations, 1968; Distinguished Service to Howard Univ.,
by students of Coll. of Liberal Arts, 1970; honors, Nat.
Council of Negro Women, Delta Sigma Theta.
Publications: Contributed numerous articles and book reviews
to journals. Editor, Catalogue of Books in the Moorland
Foundation Collection, 1939; North American Negro
Poets: A Bibliographical Checklist of Their Writings,
1760-1944, 1945; Catalogue of the African Collection at
Howard University, 1958; The Negro in American Cities,
1967; A Working Bibliography on the Negro in the United
States, 1969; The Negro in the United States, A Selected
Bibliography, 1970; Early Negro Writing, 1760-1837,
1971.
Mailing Address: 7632 17 St., N.W., Washington, D.C. 20012.

POUSSIANT, ALVIN FRANCIS, Psychiatrist
Born: New York, N.Y., May 15, 1934.
Education: B.A., Columbia Univ., 1956; M.D., Cornell Univ.,
1960; M.S., Univ. of Calif., Los Angeles, 1964; intern,
Univ. of Calif., Los Angeles Center Health Science, 1960-
61; resident psychiatry, Neuro. Psychiatric Institute,
1961-64; chief resident, 1964-65; Southern field dir.,
Medical Com. Human Rights, Jackson, Miss., 1965-66;
asst. prof. psychiatry, Tufts Univ. Medical Sch., 1966-
69; assoc. prof. psychiatry, Harvard Medical School,
1969-.
Memberships: Am. Psychiatric Assn.; Nat. Medical Assn.;
Black Academy of Arts and Letters; Medical Com.
Human Rights.
Awards: Michael Schwerner, 1968.
Publications: Contributed numerous articles to magazines and
journals. Author, Why Blacks Kill Blacks, 1972.
Mailing Address: 25 Shattuck St., Boston, Mass. 02115.

PRESTWIDGE, KATHLEEN J., Educator
Born: New York, N.Y., Jan. 1, 1927.
Education: B.A., Hunter Coll., 1949; M.A., Brooklyn Coll.,
1957; Ph.D., St. John's Univ., 1970.
Professional Experience: Medical laboratory technician,
1949-50; technician in hematology, enzymology, 1951-
56; tchr., junior high sch., N.Y.C., 1956-59; prof. biology
and medical laboratory technology, Bronx Community
Coll., 1959-.
Memberships: Am. Assn. for the Advancement of Science; Am.
Institute of Biological Sciences; Soc. of Nuclear Medi-
cine; N.Y. Academy of Sciences, AAUP.
Publications: Wisdom Teeth, 1973.
Mailing Address: 76-11 160 St., Flushing, N.Y. 11366.

PRITCHARD, NORMAN HENRY, II, Author, Poet.
Born: New York, N.Y., Oct. 22, 1939.
Education: B.A., Washington Square Coll., New York Univer-
sity, 1957-61; Inst. of Fine Arts, New York Univ., 1961-
63; Columbia Univ., 1962.
Professional Experience: Co-chairman of the Nat. Standing
Com. on Poetry for the Am. Festival of Negro Arts,
1963-64; poet-in-residence, Friends Seminary, 1968-;
instr., poetry workshop, New School for Social Research,
1969-; poetry read for record albums, Destinations:
Four Contemporary American Poets, 1964-65, New Jazz
Poets, 1967.
Memberships: St. George's Society of N.Y.; Audubon Society;
Asia Society.

Publications: Contributed poems and prose to journals,
magazines and anthologies. Author, The Matrix: Poems
1960-1970; EECCHHOOEESS, 1971.
Mailing Address: 131 East 70 Street, New York, N.Y. 10021.

PROCTOR, SAMUEL DEWITT, Educator, Clergyman
Born: Norfolk, Va., July 13, 1921.
Education: B.A., Va. Union Univ., 1942; Divinity Sch., Yale
Univ., 1945-46; Th.D., Boston Univ., 1950.
Family: m. Bessie Louise Tate; children, Herbert, Timothy,
Samuel, Steven.
Professional Experience: Pastor, Pond St. Baptist Church,
Providence, R.I., 1945-49; prof. religion and ethics and
dean, Sch. of Religion, Va. Union Univ., 1949-50; vice-
pres., ibid., 1953-55; pres., ibid., 1955-60; pres., A&T,
North Carolina, 1960-64; assoc. dir., Peace Corps,
1963-64; assoc. general sec., Nat. Council Churches,
1964-65; dir., Northeast region, spl. asst., nat. dir.,
OEO, 1965-66; pres., Inst. for Services Ed., 1966-68;
dean, special projects, Univ. of Wisconsin, Madison,
1968-69; prof. ed., Graduate Sch. of Ed., Rutgers Univ.,
New Brunswick, N.J.-; lectr., including Emory Univ.,
Atlanta Univ., Am. Baptist Assembly.
Memberships: N.E.A.; Kappa Alpha Psi; Sigma Pi Phi.
Awards: Outstanding Alumnus, Boston Univ., 1964; Distin-
guished Service Award, State Univ. of N.Y., Platts-
burgh, 1966.
Publications: The Young Negro in America, 1960-1980, 1966.
Mailing Address: 63 MacAfee, Somerset, N.J. 08873.

QUARLES, BENJAMIN ARTHUR, Educator
Born: Boston, Mass., Jan. 23, 1904.
Education: A.B., Shaw Univ., 1927-31; M.A., Univ. of Wiscon-
sin, 1933; Ph.D., ibid., 1940; Litt.D. (hon.), Shaw Univ.,
1966; hon. degrees: Towson State Coll., Kenyon Coll.
Family: 2nd m. Ruth Brett; children, 2nd m., Pamela Ann; 1st
m., Roberta Alain Knowles.
Professional Experience: Instr. history, Shaw Univ., Raleigh,
N.C., 1935-39; prof. history, Dillard Univ., New Orleans,
La., 1939-53; prof. history, Morgan State Coll., 1953-.
Memberships: Including Com. on Professional Register; Am.
Historical Assn.; Bd. of Trustees, U.S. Capital Historical
Soc.; editorial bd., Journal of Negro History; bd. of edi-
tors, Maryland Historical Magazine; founding mem.,
Black Academy of Arts and Letters; advisory council,
Inst. of Afro-American Studies, Martin Luther King, Jr.
Center; ASNL; Phi Alpha Theta; chmn., Md. Commn. on
Negro History and Culture; adv. bd., Frederick Douglass
Inst. of Negro History and Culture.

Awards: Social Science Research Council; John Simon Guggenheim Fellow, 1959; Am. Council of Learned Societies,
grant-in-aid, 1967.
Publications: Contributed numerous articles and book reviews
to journals;chapters and introductions to books. Author,
Frederick Douglass, 1948; The Negro in the Civil War,
1953; The Negro in the American Revolution, 1961; Lincoln and the Negro, 1962; The Negro in the Making of
America, 1964; Black Abolitionists, 1969; The Black
American: A Documentary (with Leslie H. Fishel, Jr.),
1970.
Mailing Address: 2205 Southern Ave., Baltimore, Md. 21214.

QUIGLESS, HELEN GORDON, Media specialist
Born: Washington, D.C., July 16, 1944.
Education: Bard Coll., 1962-64; A.B., Fisk Univ., 1964-66;
M.L.S., Atlanta Univ., 1967-68.
Professional Experience: Media specialist, Federal City Coll.,
1968; head, Urbania Collection; Afro-American bibliog-
rapher.
Awards: Rockefeller grant, Atlanta Univ., 1967-68.
Publications: Poems included in For Malcolm, 1967, The New
Black Poetry, 1968, New Negro Poets, 1970.
Mailing Address: 1884 Columbia Rd., Washington, D.C. 20009.

RANDALL, DUDLEY FELKER, Librarian, Poet, Publisher
Born: Washington, D.C., Jan. 14, 1914.
Education: B.A., Wayne Univ., 1946-49; M.A.L.S., Univ. of
Mich., 1949-51.
Family: m. Vivian Barnett Spencer; d. Phyllis Ada Randall
Sherron.
Professional Experience: Laborer, Ford Motor Co., 1932-37;
letter carrier and clerk, U.S. Post Office, 1937-51;
reference libn., 1951-54, cataloger, 1952-53, instr. lib.
science, reference books, 1952-54, Lincoln Univ., Mo.;
assoc. libn., tech. services, 1954-55, assoc. libn., pub-
lic services, 1955-56, Morgan State Coll.; hospital
libn., Wayne County Federated Lib. System, Wayne,
Mich., 1956-63; head, reference interloan, Wayne County
Fed. Lib. System, 1963-69; reference libn., Univ. of
Detroit, 1969-; poet-in-residence, Univ. of Detroit,
1969-; vis. lectr., Afro-American Literature, Univ. of
Mich., 1969-; instr. black poetry, Univ. of Detroit,
1970-; founder of Broadside Press which specializes
in publishing black poetry, 1965.
Memberships: Kappa Alpha Psi; Arts Extended Gallery; Detroit Soc. for the Advancement of Culture and Educa-
tion; Mich. Lib. Assn.; ALA; Mich. Council for the
Arts, Literature Com.

Awards: Tompkins Award, Poetry and Fiction, 1962; Tompkins
Award, Poetry, 1966; grant, Coordinating Council of
Literary Magazines for Broadside Press, 1970.
Publications: Contributed poetry, essays and book reviews to
journals and magazines. Author, Poem Counterpoint
(with Margaret Danner), 1966; For Malcolm (with
Margaret J. Burroughs), 1967; Cities Burning, 1968; edi-
tor, Black Poetry, 1969; Love You, 1970; More to Re-
member, 1970; editor, The Black Poets, 1971.
Mailing Address: 12651 Old Mill Pl., Detroit, Mich. 48238.

RAVEN, JOHN
Publications: Blues for Mama.

REDDING, JAY SAUNDERS, Director, research and publica-
tions
Born: Wilmington, Del., Oct. 13, 1906.
Education: Lincoln Univ., 1923-24; Ph.B., Brown Univ., 1928;
M.A., ibid., 1931-33; D.Litt., ibid., 1963; H.H.D. (hon.)
Hobart Coll., 1964.
Family: m. Esther Elizabeth James; children, Conway Holmes,
Lewis Alfred.
Professional Experience: Instr., Morehouse Coll., 1928-31;
instr., Louisville Municipal Coll., 1933-35; prof. and
chmn., Southern Univ., 1936-38; prof. and chmn., State
Tchrs. Coll., Elizabeth City, N.C., 1943-66; prof. Eng-
lish, 1943-66 (Johnson Prof. Creative Literature until
1966); dir., div. research and publ., Nat. Endowment
for Humanities, Washington, D.C., 1966-; state dept.
lectr., India, 1952; lectr., Am. Society African Culture,
1962.
Memberships: Fiction Award Com., Nat. Book Award, 1955;
Sigma Pi Phi; ASNLH; Folklore Soc.; English Assn.;
exec. bd., Am. Soc African Culture; editorial bd., Am.
Scholar, 1954-62.
Awards: Phi Beta Kappa; Rockefeller Foundation Fellow,
1940-41; Guggenheim Fellow, 1944-45, 1959-60; May-
flower Award, N.C. Historical Soc., 1944.
Publications: Contributed to journals. Author, To Make a
Poet Black, 1939; No Day of Triumph, 1942; Stranger
and Alone, 1950; They Came in Chains, 1951; On Being
Negro in America, 1952; The Lonesome Road, 1958;
The Negro, 1967.
Mailing Address: 310 Winthrop Dr., Ithaca, N.Y. 14850.

REDMOND, EUGENE, Educator, Poet
Born: St. Louis, Mo., 1938.
Education: A.B., Southern Ill. Univ.; M.A., Washington Univ.

Professional Experience: Writer-in-residence, Oberlin Coll.,
1969-70; senior cons., Katherine Dunham Performing
Arts Training Center, East St. Louis, Ill.; writer, dir.,
actor, The Ode to Taylor Jones; dir., Black Arts Workshop; vis. writer-in-residence, Southern Univ., Baton
Rouge, La.; prof. English and poet-in-residence, Ethnic
Studies, Sacramento State Coll., Sacramento, Calif.;
lectr., part-time, Sch. of Afro-American Thought; contributing editor, East St. Louis Monitor and Confrontation: A Journal of Third World Literature.
Publications: Sentry of the Four Golden Pillars, 1970; River
of Bones and Flesh and Blood, 1972.
Mailing Address: Sacramento State College, Sacramento,
Calif.

REED, ISHMAEL, Author
Born: Chattanooga, Tenn., Feb. 22, 1938.
Education: Univ. of Buffalo, 1956-60.
Family: m. Carla Blank; d. Timothy Brett.
Professional Experience: Instr., Univ. of Seattle, Jan.-Mar.
1968; instr., Univ. of California, Berkeley, Spring 1968,
1969.
Memberships: Author's League of Am.; P.E.N.
Awards: Univ. of Calif., Berkeley, Outstanding Instr. of the
Year, Unit. #2, Assn., 1968.
Publications: The Free-Lance Pallbearers, 1967; Yellow
Back Radio Broke Down, 1969; Nineteen Necromancers
from Now, 1970.
Mailing Address: 6 Bret Harte Way, Berkeley, Calif. 94708.

REESE, CAROLYN
Publications: Letter from a Wife.

REEVES, DONALD
Publications: Notes of a Processed Brother, 1971.

REID, INEZ SMITH, Educator
Born: New Orleans, La.
Education: B.A., Tufts Univ., 1959; LL.B., Yale Univ., 1962;
M.A., Univ. of Calif., Los Angeles, 1963; Ph.D., Colum-
bia Univ., 1968.
Family: m. Frantz F-J.
Professional Experience: Ecole Nationale de Droit et d'Admini-
stration, Congo-Kinshasa (Zaire), 1963-64; NAACP Legal
Defense Fund, summers 1962-64; asst. prof. African
studies and political science, 1964-65; lectr. political
science, Hunter Coll., 1966-; exec. dir., Black Women's

Community Development Foundation, 1971-; assoc. prof.
political science, Barnard Coll., 1972-; cons., Ford
Foundation Fellowship Program for Afro-Americans;
Selection Com., Foreign Area Training Fellowship.
Memberships: Including Calif. and N.Y. Bars; African Law
Assn.; African Heritage Studies Assn.; Am. Political
Science Assn.; Nat. Conf. of Black Lawyers; Nat. Conf.
of Black Political Scientists; bd. of trustees, Antioch
Coll.
Publications: Contributed articles and book reviews to pro-
fessional journals. Author, "Together" Black Women,
1972.
Mailing Address: Black Women's Community Development
Foundation, 1028 Connecticut Ave., N.W., Suite 1010,
Washington, D.C. 20036.

RENDER, SYLVIA LYONS, Educator
Born: Atlanta, Ga.
Education: B.A., Tennessee A & I State Coll., 1931-34; Univ.
of Chicago, 1934-35; M.A., Ohio State Univ., 1951-52;
Ph.D., George Peabody Coll., 1959-62.
Family: m. Frank Wyatt (deceased); s. Frank Wyatt.
Professional Experience: Clerical and professional posts in
state and federal agencies, Columbus, Ohio, newspaper
reporter, columnist, editor, 1939-50; dir., out-of-state
scholarship aid program; instr., asst. prof., assoc. prof.,
prof. English, Florida A & M Univ., 1950-64; prof. English, North Carolina Central Univ., Durham, N.C., 1964-;
cons., Ford Foundation, 1970-71.
Memberships: Urban League; Alpha Kappa Alpha; Am. Red
Cross (Gray Lady); United Nations Assn.; Durham Council on Human Relations; MLA; NCTE; CLA; North Carolina Tchrs. Assn.; North Carolina Folklore Soc.; South
Atlantic Modern Language Assn.; Kappa Delta Pi.
Awards: Am. Philosophical Soc., summer 1964; North Carolina College Research Com. grants, 1964-65, 1969;
fellow, Cooperative Program in the Humanities, Duke
Univ. and Univ. of North Carolina, 1967-68; Ford Foun-
dation grant, 1971.
Publications: Contributed "Charles W. Chesnutt," Encyclo-
paedia Britannica, 1969 edition; introduction to the book,
Charles W. Chesnutt, The Morrow of Tradition, 1969.
Articles on Chesnutt to other journals. To be published,
a biography of Charles W. Chesnutt in preparation,
Twayne Author Series; editor, The Short Fiction of
Charles W. Chesnutt (in press).
Mailing Address: 101 Oakmont Circle, Durham, N.C. 27707.

RIVERS, CLARENCE
Publications: Celebration, 1969.

ROBERSON, ED
Publications: When Thy King Is a Boy, 1970.

ROBERTS, J. DEOTIS, SR., Theologian
Born: North Carolina, July 12, 1927.
Education: A.B., Johnson C. Smith Univ., 1947; B.D., Shaw
    Univ., 1950; B.D., and S.T.M., Hartford Seminary Foun-
    dation, 1951-52; Ph.D., Univ. of Edinburgh, 1957; pro-
    fessional study, Univ. of Cambridge, spring 1958.
Family: m. Elizabeth Caldwell; children, Carlita, Kristina,
    Charmaine, J.
Professional Experience: Pastor, Union Baptist Church, Tar-
    boro, N.C.; asst. pastor, Union Baptist Church, Hart-
    ford, Conn.; minister, migrant workers comm., N.Y.,
    Del.; pastor-ad-interim, Radnor Park Congregational
    Church, Clyde Bank, Glasgow, Scotland; dean of religion,
    Georgia Baptist Coll., Macon, Ga.; prof. philosophy and
    religion and dir., religious activities, Shaw Univ.; prof.
    religious philosophy and theology, Sch. of Religion,
    Howard Univ.; vis. prof. religion, Swarthmore Coll.,
    1969-70.
Memberships: Academy of Religion; Biblical Theologians;
    Assn. of Asian Studies; Assn. of Coll. and Univ. Pro-
    fessors; Internat. Congress of the History of Religions;
    Internat. Congress of Orientalists.
Awards: Including Lily Foundation Fellow, Christianity and
    Politics, Duke Univ., summer 1960; Study-Travel
    Fellow in Asian Religions of the Soc. of Religion in
    Higher Ed., 1964-65; Fellow, Am. Assn. of Theological
    Schs., Harvard Divinity Sch., spring 1965.
Publications: Contributed to journals. Author, A Comparative
    Study of Faith and Reason in Pascal, Bergson and James,
    1962; From Puritanism to Platonism in Seventeenth
    Century England, 1968; Liberation and Reconciliation,
    1971; co-editor, Quest for a Black Theology, 1971.
Mailing Address: 1428 Whittier Pl., N.W., Washington, D.C.
    22212.

ROBINSON, ARMSTEAD
Publications: Editor, Black Studies in the University, A
    Symposium (with Donald Ogilive and Craig C. Foster),
    1969.

ROBINSON, FLORINE, Educator
Born: Pittsburgh, Pa., Sept. 14, 1920.
Education: B.E., Univ. of Pittsburgh, 1938-42; M.Ed., ibid.,
    1946-48.

Professional Experience: Tchr., 1948-69, asst. principal,
Pittsburgh Bd. of Ed. 1969-70; principal, ibid., 1970-;
tchr. remedial reading.
Memberships: Alpha Kappa Alpha Sorority.
Publications: Ed and Ted, 1965; Friends Together: Ned and
Ed, 1967.
Mailing Address: 331 Michigan St., Pittsburgh, Pa. 15210.

ROBINSON, LEWIS GREEN, Civil rights organizer
Born: Decatur, Ala., Jan. 5, 1929.
Education: Calvin Coolidge Coll., 1948-49; LL.B., Portia
Law Sch., 1956.
Family: Children, M. Bruce, Malcolm Ari.
Professional Experience: Farmworker, shipyard worker,
handyman, porter, busboy, steelworker, Decatur, Ala.;
agent, Internal Revenue, 1957; housing inspector, Cleve-
land, 1960-64; asst. dir., Economic Development, Hough
Area Development Corp., 1968-; pres. and organizer,
Freedom Fighters, Inc., 1960; organizer, Cleveland
United Freedom Movement, 1963; organizer, Medgar
Evers Civil Rights Rifle Club, 1964; co-dir., J.F.K.
House Nationalist, 1964; chmn. and state vice chmn.,
New Democratic Coalition, 1971-72.
Publications: The Making of a Man, 1970.
Mailing Add: 1242 East 89 St., Cleveland, Ohio 44108.

ROBINSON, LOUIE
Publications: Arthur Ashe, Tennis Champion, 1970; The Black
Millionaires, 1972.

ROBINSON, ROSE, Author
Born: Chicago, Ill.; B.A., art education, Sch. of the Art In-
stitute, Chicago, Ill.; Univ. of Chicago; DePaul Univ.;
Western Reserve Univ.; Univ. of Washington.
Awards:Guest of honor, Friends of the Free Library, Phila-
delphia, Pa.; invitation to Author's Guild.
Publications: Contributed articles to periodicals. Author,
Eagle in the Air, 1969.
Mailing Address: Crown Publishers, Inc., 419 Park Ave. S.,
New York, N.Y. 10016.

ROBINSON, WILLIAM H., Educator
Born: Newport, R.I.
Education: B.A., New York Univ., 1951; M.A., Boston Univ.,
1957; Ph.D., Harvard Univ., 1964.
Family: m. Doris Carol Johnson.

Professional Experience: Instr., Prairie View Coll., Texas;
A & T State Univ., Greensboro, N.C.; Howard Univ.;
Boston Univ.; Univ. of Mass.; teaching fellow, humanities, Harvard Univ.; prof. English and Afro-American
literature, Rhode Island Coll., 1970-; teaches Negro
and Black American literature, Harvard Univ. Exten-
sion; writer, ed. TV, radio, stage; lectr. Black litera-
ture; vis. scholar, North Carolina Central Univ., Dur-
ham.
Awards: Intercollegiate script-writing contests.
Publications: Early Black American Poets, 1969; Early Black
American Prose (1734-1930), 1970; Nommo: A Modern
Anthology of Black African and Black American Literature, 1971; Major Black American Literature (in press).
Contributed to journals.
Mailing Address: 42 Stephen Hopkins Court, University
Heights, Providence, R.I. 02906.

ROGERS, CAROLYN M., Author
Born: Chicago, Ill.
Education: Univ. of Ill., 1960-61; B.A., Roosevelt Univ., 1961-
65.
Professional Experience: Social worker, poverty program,
1965-68; tchr., Afro-American lit., Columbia Coll.,
1969; instr. Afro-American literature, Univ. of Washing-
ton, Seattle, 1971; writer-in-residence, Albany State
Coll., Ga., and Malcolm X. Coll., Chicago, 1972; colum-
nist, Milwaukee Courier; book reviewer, Chicago Daily
News.
Memberships: OBAC; Gwendolyn Brooks Writers Workshop;
Delta Sigma Theta.
Awards: 1st Conrad Kent Rivers, 1969; Nat. Endowment of
Arts, 1970; Soc. of Midland Authors, 1970.
Publications: Contributed numerous articles and poetry to
anthologies, magazines and journals. Author, Paper
Soul, 1968; I Love Raps, 1969; Songs of a Blackbird,
1970.
Mailing Address: 5463 South Cornell, Chicago, Ill. 60615.

ROLLINS, BRYANT, Academic administrator
Born: New York, N.Y., Dec. 13, 1937.
Education: B.A., Northeastern Univ., 1955-60.
Family: m.; children 2.
Professional Experience: Newspaper reporter, Boston Globe,
Jan. 1962 - Aug. 1965; co-founder and editor, Bay State
Banner, Boston, Mass., Sept. 1965 - June 1966; coordi-
nator, Afro-American History Curriculum Working
Party, Educational Development Centers, Cambridge
and Waltham, Mass, June 1966 - June 1967; dir., Com-

munity Development; dir., Boston Coll. Urban League
Joint Center for Inner City Change; dir., Small Business
Development Center, June 1967 - Feb. 1969; vice-pres.,
H. Carl McCall & Associates, Consultants in Urban Af-
fairs, Feb. 1969 - October 1971; exec. editor, N.Y.
Amsterdam News, Oct. 1971 - Oct. 1972; adminstr.,
summer program, minority journalists, Columbia Univ.
Graduate Sch. of Journalism, Jan. 1973-; stringer,
Time and Newsweek magazines, 1963-66; lectr., colleges
and universities, civil rights organizations.
Memberships: Including Nat. Training Labs Institute for Ap-
plied Behavioral Sciences; editorial bd., N.Y. Amsterdam
News; bd. of dir., Boston Urban League.
Awards: Annual Poet of the Year, Northeastern Univ., 1959;
wrote script for Riot, winner of 1969 OBIE, produced
by the OM Theatre Workshops of Boston.
Publications: Danger Song, 1967; Goin Down Slow (in press).
Mailing Address: 10 West 135 Street, New York, N.Y. 10037.

ROLLINS, CHARLEMAE, Librarian (ret.)
Born: Yazoo, Miss., June 20, 1897.
Education: Special work, Univ. of Chicago; special courses,
lib. science, Columbia Univ.
Family: m. Joseph W.; s. Joseph W., Jr.
Professional Experience: Children's libn., George C. Hall
Branch, Chicago Pub. Lib., 1927-63 (now retired); tchr.,
children's literature, Roosevelt Univ., Chicago, 1946-60;
tchr., Fisk Univ., Nashville, Tenn.; Human Relations
Workshop, San Francisco State Coll.; Dept. of Lib. Sci-
ence, Rosary Coll., River Forest, Ill.; presented Jane
Addams Book Award to Norwegian author in Oslo, Nor-
way, 1962.
Memberships: Pres., Children's Services Division, ALA,
1957-58; chmn., Children's Section of Ill. Lib. Assn.,
1953-54; chmn., Newbery-Caldecott Awards Com., ALA,
1956-57; chmn., Elementary Section of Ill. Unit of
Catholic Lib. Assn., 1953-54; honorable member, Phi
Delta Kappa (tchrs. Sorority), 1959.
Awards: Am. Brotherhood Award, NCCJ, 1952; Lib. Letter
Award, ALA, 1953; Crolier Soc. Award, ALA, 1955; Good
Am. Award, Chicago Com. of One Hundred, 1962; Negro
Centennial awards in three areas, 1963; Children's
Reading Round Table Award, 1963.
Publications: Contributed to journals. Author, We Build To-
gether, 1941, 1966; Christmas Gif', 1964; They Showed
the Way, 1964; Famous Negro Poets, 1965; Famous
Negro Entertainers, 1967; Langston Hughes, 1970.
Mailing Address: 500 East 33 St., Chicago, Ill. 60616.

ROWAN, CARL T., Author, Syndicated columnist, Journalist
Born: Ravenscroft, Tenn., Aug. 11, 1925.
Education: A.B., Oberlin Coll., 1947; M.A., Univ. of Minnesota,
    1948; D.Litt. (hon.), Simpson Coll., 1957; Hamline Univ.,
    1958; L.H.D. (hon.), Washburn Univ., 1964; Talladega
    Coll., 1965; St. Olaf Coll., 1966; Knoxville Coll., 1966;
    LL.D. (hon.), Howard Univ., 1964; Alfred Univ., 1964;
    Temple Univ., 1964; Atlanta Univ., 1965; Allegheny Coll.,
    1966; D.Pub. Adminstrn., Morgan State Coll., 1964.
Family: m. Vivien Louise Murphy; children, Barbara, Carl
    Thomas, Geoffrey.
Professional Experience: U.S. Navy, 1943, commissioned en-
    sign in Naval Reserve; copywriter, 1948-50; staff-
    writer, Minneapolis Tribune, 1950-61; Dep. Asst. to Sec.
    State for Public Affairs, Dept. of State, 1961-63; U.S.
    Ambassador to Finland, 1963-64; dir., USIA, Washington,
    1964-65; columnist, Chicago Daily News, 1965-; syndi-
    cated columnist.
Memberships: Gridiron Club.
Awards: Including Sidney Hillman Award, best newspaper
    reporting, 1952; ALA annual list of best books, South
    of Freedom, 1953; Am. Teamwork Award, Nat. Urban
    League, 1955; foreign corr. medallion for articles on
    India, 1955, and on South East Asia, coverage of Bandung
    Conf., 1956; ALA annual list of best books, The Pitiful
    and the Proud, 1956; Philadelphia Fellowship Com.,
    1961; Communications Award, Human Relations, Anti-
    Defamation League B'nai B'rith, 1964; Distinguished
    Service Award, Capital Press Club, 1964; Nat. Brother-
    hood Award, NCCJ, 1964; Am. Southern Regional Press
    Inst. Award, 1965.
Publications: South of Freedom, 1953; The Pitiful and the
    Proud, 1956; Go South to Sorrow, 1957; Wait till New
    Year, 1960.
Mailing Address: 3116 Fessenden St., N.W., Washington, D.C.
    20008.

ROYSTER, PHILIP M., Educator
Born: Chicago, Ill., July 31, 1943.
Education: Univ. of Illinois, 1960-62; A.B., DePaul Univ.,
    1963-65; M.A., ibid., 1965-67; Loyola Univ., 1967.
Family: m. Sandra; children, Rebecca Suzanne, Francesca
    Therese.
Professional Experience: Janitor's asst., 1954-62; porter
    and clerk, Jax Drug Co., 1958-62; govt. clerk, Internal
    Revenue Service and Social Section, 1962-63; postal
    clerk, U.S. Post Office, 1963-66; tchr., St. Mec High
    Sch., Chicago, 1966-67; bus driver, Chicago Transit
    Authority, summer 1967; teaching asst., 1967-68; instr.,
    Loyola Univ., 1969-70; instr. English, Fisk Univ., 1970-.

Memberships: Organization of Black American Culture Writers' Workshop; pres., Loyola Graduate English Club; pres., Univ. of Ill., Navy Pier Jazz Club.
Awards: Arthur J. Schmitt scholarship; Loyola Univ. assistant-ship; Loyola Univ. fellowship.
Publications: Contributed poems to Cadence and Liberator. Author, Suggestions for Instructors to Accompany Contexts for Composition, 1969; The Back Door, 1971.
Mailing Address: 1809 Morena St., Apt. C-3, Nashville, Tenn. 37208.

ROYSTER, SANDRA HOWE, Poet, Library coordinator
Born: Chicago, Ill., Sept. 11, 1942.
Education: Univ. of Illinois, 1960-63.
Family: m. Philip M.; children, Rebecca Suzanne, Francesca Therese.
Professional Experience: Clerk, B. H. Miller Toys, 1956-60; posting billing clerk, Metropolitan Mutual Assn., 1960-62; program coordinator, Nashville Pub. Lib., 1972-; TV shows, Reading and Rap program, Nashville Pub. Lib.; participated in poetry workshops, Ky. Arts Com.; poetry programs.
Memberships: Honorary Soc. of Ky. Colonels; Fisk Writer's workshop.
Awards: Broadside Press Award for Previously Published Poet, 1972.
Publications: Author, Woman Talk, 1973.
Mailing Address: 1809 Morena St., Apt. C-3, Nashville, Tenn. 37208.

RUSSELL, CHARLIE L., Lecturer
Born: Monroe, La., March 10, 1932.
Education: B.A., Univ. of San Francisco, 1956-59; M.S.W., New York Univ., Graduate Sch. of Social Work, 1964-66.
Family: d. Katheryn Kenyatta.
Professional Experience: Counselor, SEEK program, City Coll. of N.Y., 1967-; lectr. basic writing, Livingston Coll., Rutgers Univ.; founder, Onyx Publications; writer, jazz column, Manhattan Tribune, N.Y.C.; editor, leader of Ritual Workshop, Nat. Black Theater, N.Y.C.
Publications: Contributed to magazines. Wrote Nat. ABC-TV script "The Black Church"; and "A Man Is Not Made of Steel," for On Being Black, WGBH-TV (Boston). Author, A Birthday Present for Katheryn Kenyatta.
Mailing Address: Onyx Publications, Box 414, New York, N.Y. 10031.

RUSTIN, BAYARD, Civil rights organizer
Born: West Chester, Pa., March 10, 1910.
Education: Wilberforce Univ., 1930-31; City Coll. of N.Y.,
    1933-35; LL.D. (hon.), New Sch. for Social Research,
    1968; Litt. D. (hon.), Montclair State Coll., 1968.
Professional Experience: Race relations sec., Fellowship of
    Reconciliation, 1941-53; youth organizer, A. Philip
    Randolph's March on Washington, 1941; first field sec.,
    CORE, 1941; assisted in helping to protect property of
    Japanese Americans placed in work camps in Calif.,
    1942; imprisoned, Lewisburg Penitentiary, as conscie-
    tious objector, 1943-45; chmn., Free India Com., 1945;
    participated in first Freedom Ride, 1947, to test en-
    forcement of the 1946 Irene Morgan Case outlawing dis-
    crimination in interstate travel, arrested in North Caro-
    lina, served 30 days on a chain gang; organized Com. to
    support South African Resistance; worked with Azikewe
    and Nkrumah, West Africa, 1951; dir., Committee
    Against Discrimination in the Armed Forces, 1953,
    which secured Pres. Truman's executive order eliminat-
    ing segregation in the military; exec. sec., War Regis-
    ter's League, pacifist organization, 1953-55; spl. asst. to
    Dr. Martin Luther King, Jr., 1955-60; coordinated body
    of 35,000 on Prayer Pilgrimage to Washington for Civil
    Rights, 1957; dir., Youth Marchers for Integrated Schs.,
    1958-59; deputy dir., March on Washington, Aug. 28,
    1963; dir., N.Y. sch. boycott of Feb. 3, 1964; aided strik-
    ing Memphis sanitation workers in raising $100,000; or-
    ganized massive march following Dr. Martin Luther
    King's assassination, 1968; dir., A. Philip Randolph
    Institute, N.Y.C., 1964-.
Memberships: Soc. of Friends.
Awards: Eleanor Roosevelt Trade Union Leadership Council,
    1966; Man of Year, Pittsburgh branch, NAACP, 1965;
    Liberty Bell, Howard Univ. Law Sch., 1967; John Dewey,
    United Fed. Tchrs., 1968; Family of Man, Nat. Council
    Churches, 1969; John F. Kennedy, NCJW, 1971.
Publications: Contributed numerous articles to magazines and
    newspapers. Author, Down the Line, 1971.
Mailing Address: 340 West 28 St., New York, N.Y. 10001.

RUTHERFORD, TONY
Publications: Black and White.

RUTLAND, EVA, Housewife
Born: Atlanta, Ga.
Education: B.A., Spelman Coll., 1933-37.
Family: m. William G.; children, Elsie A., William, Patty Jo,
    Ginger.

Professional Experience: Bursar, Miles Coll., Birmingham,
Ala., 1937-41; sec., War Dept., Washington, D.C., 1941-
42; sec., Tuskegee Army Air Force, Tuskegee, Ala.,
1942-44; intermittent work, Calif. Legislature, 1957-65.
Publications: Contributed to magazines. Author, Trouble with
Being a Mama.
Mailing Address: 1261 35 Ave., Sacramento, Calif. 95822.

SANCHEZ, SONIA, Educator, Author
Born: Birmingham, Ala., Sept. 9, 1934.
Education: B.A., Hunter Coll., 1951-55.
Family: Children, Anita, Morani Neusi, Mungu Neusi.
Professional Experience: Tchr., Community Sch., 1965-67;
instr., San Francisco State Coll., 1967-69; instr., Univ.
of Pittsburgh, 1969-70; asst. prof., Rutgers Univ., 1970-
73; assoc. prof. literature and creative writing, Amherst
Coll., 1973-.
Awards: Grants from P.E.N.
Publications: Contributed to journals. Author, Homecoming,
1969; We a Baddddd People, 1970.
Mailing Address: 86 College St., Amherst, Mass. 01002.

SCOBIE, EDWARD
Publications: Black Britannia: A History of Blacks in Britain,
1972.

SCOTT, GLORI VAN
Publications: Baba and the Flea, 1973.

SCOTT, JOSEPH WALTER, Educator
Born: May 7, 1935.
Education: B.S., Central Mich. Univ., 1953-57; M.A., Indiana
Univ., 1957-59; Ph.D., ibid., 1959-63.
Family: m.; children, 3.
Professional Experience: Teaching asst., Indiana Univ., 1957-
58; research asst., Detroit Area Traffic Study, Wayne
State Univ., summer 1957, 1958; teaching asst., Indiana
Univ., 1958-60, June 1962 - Aug. 1962; teaching assoc.,
Indiana Univ., 1962-63; assoc. research scientist, U.S.
Army Infantry Human Research Unit (Div. of Human Re-
sources Research Organization), achieved rank of cap-
tain; lectr. social psychology, criminology, complex
organizations, Fort Benning Extension, American Univ.,
July 1963 - June 1965; asst. prof. sociology, Univ. of
Kentucky, 1965-67; Fulbright prof. social psychology,
Universidad del Litoral, Rosario, Argentina, summer
1967; assoc. prof. sociology, Univ. of Toledo, 1967-68;

vis. lectr. sociology, Mich. State Univ., summer 1968; assoc. prof. sociology and principal investigator, Crime and Delinquency Project, Model Cities Program, Toledo; Fulbright prof. sociology, La Universidad Nacional de Buenos Aires, Argentina, summer 1969.
Awards: Including Kentucky Research Foundation grant, 1966; 75th Anniversary Outstanding Achievement Award, Central Mich. Univ., 1967.
Publications: Numerous professional articles and papers.
Mailing Address: 2507 Glenwood, Toledo, Ohio. 43610.

SCOTT, NATHAN A., JR., Educator, Theologian
Born: Cleveland, Ohio, April 24, 1925.
Education: A.B., Univ. of Mich., 1944; B.D., Union Theology Seminary, 1946; Ph.D., Columbia Univ., 1949; Litt.D. (hon.), Ripon Coll., 1965; L.H.D. (hon.), Wittenberg Univ., 1965; D.D. (hon.), Philadelphia Divinity Sch., 1967; S.T.D. (hon.), General Theological Seminary, 1968; Litt.D. (hon.), Saint Mary's Coll., Notre Dame, 1969.
Family: m. Charlotte Hanley; children, Nathan A., III., Leslie Kristin.
Professional Experience: Dean of the chapel, Va. Union Univ., 1946-47; assoc. prof. humanities; dir., General Ed. Program in the Humanities, Howard Univ., 1948-55; prof. theology and lit. in the Divinity Sch., and prof., English dept., Univ. of Chicago, 1955-; priest of the Episcopal Church; Canon Theologian of the Cathedral of St. James, Chicago, 1967-; vis. prof. English, Univ. of Mich., 1969; co-editor, The Journal of Religion.
Memberships: MLA; Am. Philosophical Assn.
Awards: Kent Fellow, Soc. for Religion in Higher Ed.; Fellow, Sch. of Letters of Indiana Univ.
Publications: Contributed numerous essays to journals and symposia. Author of eighteen books, including latest: Ernest Hemingway, 1966; The Modern Vision of Death, 1967; Adversity and Grace: Studies in the Recent American Literature, 1968; Craters of the Spirit: Studies in the Modern Novel, 1968; Negative Capability: Studies in the New Literature and the Religious Situation, 1969; The Unquiet Vision: Mirrors of Man in Existentialism, 1969.
Mailing Address: The Divinity School, The University of Chicago, Chicago, Ill. 60637.

SCOTT-HERON, GIL, Educator, Musician, Author
Born: Chicago, Ill., April 1, 1949.
Education: Lincoln Univ. (Pa.), 1967-70; Johns Hopkins Univ., 1971-72.

Professional Experience: Composer, singer lyricist, Flying
   Dutchman Production, Washington, D.C., June 1970-
   June 1973; asst. prof. English, Federal City Coll., Wash-
   ington, D.C., Sept., 1972-; TV production concert series;
   lyricist, Midnight Band.
Memberships: ASCAP; Am. Federation of Musicians.
Awards: Langston Hughes Creative Writing Award, Lincoln
   Univ. (Pa.), 1968.
Publications: Small Talk at One Hundred Twenty Fifth &
   Lenox, 1970; Vulture, 1970; The Nigger Factory, 1972.
Mailing Address: 632 East Capitol, Apt. 8, Washington, D.C.
   20013.

SEALE, BOBBY
Publications: Seize the Time: The Story of the Black Panther
   Party, 1970.

SHARP, SAUNDRA, Actress, Singer
Born: Cleveland, Ohio, Dec. 2, 1942.
Education: B.S., Bowling Green State Univ., 1960-64.
Professional Experience: Copywriter, TV Guide; modeling;
   TV debut, special guest singer, "Captain Kangaroo,"
   CBS-TV, April 1965; substitute tchr. music and other
   areas, 1965-68; tchr., actress, study, HARYOU-Act
   Drama Workshop, 1965-68; model and spokeswoman for
   Buick, Seagram's 100 Piper's Scotch, Exquisite Nail,
   Robertson Games; prints for Avon Products, Am. Photo-
   graph Co., True Confessions and Elegant Teen; singer
   with Voices, Inc., all-black musical theatre group, 1966-
   67; female vocalist, Bill Barnes Calypso Combo; singer,
   "Hello Dolly" chorus, Pearl Baily Co., Oct., 1969;
   "Prissy" in The Learning Tree, 1968; instr. Afro-
   American Culture and contemporary Negro Heritage,
   N.Y.C. Title I Ed. program, Feb., 1968; TV commercials;
   off-Broadway performer, To Be Young, Gifted and Black;
   Poets and Performers; singer, Sammy Benskin Trio,
   Holiday Inn, Paramus, N.J.
Publications: From the Windows of My Mind, 1970.
Mailing Address: 308 West 103 St., Apt. 8D, New York, N.Y.
   10025.

SHOCKLEY, ANN ALLEN, Librarian, Author
Born: Louisville, Ky.
Education: B.A., Fisk Univ., 1948; M.S.L.S., Case Western
   Reserve Univ., 1959-60.
Family: Children, William Leslie, Jr., Tamara Ann.

Professional Experience: Staff writer, Louisville Defender newspaper; free-lance writer; columnist, Federalsburg Times and Bridgeville News; substitute tchr., Delaware and Maryland pub. schs.; asst. libn., Delaware State Coll., 1959-60; asst. libn., curator of Negro Coll., Univ. of Maryland, Eastern Shore Branch, Princess Anne, 1960-65; assoc. libn., 1966-69; Special Collections libn. and asst. prof., Fisk Univ., 1969-70; assoc. libn., head of Special Collections, and assoc. prof., Fisk Univ., 1970-; dir., Oral History Program, Fisk Univ., 1971-; lectr., Upward Bound students, Univ. of Md., 1968; instr., Inst. on the Selection, Organization, and Use of Materials By and About the Negro, Fisk Univ., summer 1970; instr., Institute in Black Studies Librarianship, Fisk Univ., summer 1971; cons., Black Collections; editor, ALA, Black Caucus, 1971-.
Memberships: ALA; ASNLH; Tenn. Lib. Assn.; Soc. of Am. Archivists; Oral History Assn.; Assn. of Recorded Sounds; Com. on Collecting of Personal Papers and Manuscripts; Core Collection for College Libraries.
Awards: Faculty research grant, Delaware State Coll., 1959; AAUW Nat. Short Story Award, 1961; faculty research grant, Fisk Univ., 1970.
Publications: Contributed articles to journals and books, and short stories to magazines, newspapers, and anthologies. Author, A Love So Bold (in preparation); editor, Living Black American Authors: A Biographical Directory (with Sue P. Chandler).
Mailing Address: 1809 Morena St., Apt. G-4, Nashville, Tenn. 37208.

SIMMONS, GLORIA M., Librarian
Born: Atlanta, Ga., Mar. 7, 1932.
Education: A.B., Bennett Coll., 1952-55; M.S.L.S., Atlanta Univ., 1955-57.
Family: m. Henry E.; Children, Goddess Yhrette, Giselle Yhronne.
Professional Experience: Asst., readers' advisory service, Atlanta Univ., 1957-58; asst. libn., Morris Brown Coll., Feb. 1958 - Aug. 1959; asst. libn., Wilberforce Univ., 1959-60; curriculum libn., Wilberforce State Coll., 1961-64; head libn., Kendall Coll., 1964-67; reference libn., Loop Coll., Chicago, 1967-.
Memberships: ALA; Ill. Lib. Assn.; Black Merit Academy.
Awards: Carnegie Fellowship, Atlanta Univ.
Publications: Editor, Black Culture Anthology (in press).
Mailing Address: 6900 South Constance, Chicago, Ill. 60649.

SIMMONS, HENRY EUGENE, Educator
Born: Pittsburgh, Pa., May 27, 1929.
Education: Morris Brown Coll; Miami Univ.; Univ. of Chicago.
Family: m. Gloria Mitchell; children, Goddess, Gisele.
Professional Experience: Dir., athletic publicity, Morris
    Brown Coll., 1951-52; dir., Student Union and instr.
    history, Wilberforce Univ., 1959-60; dir., News Bureau,
    Central State Univ., 1960-64; assoc. faculty, Indiana
    Univ., Northwest, 1965-67; dir., Oral history research,
    Chicago State Coll., 1967-68; asst. prof. history, Chicago
    City Coll., 1968-69; chmn., Black Studies Program,
    Indiana Univ., Northwest, 1969-; vis. lectr., Southwest
    Coll., Kendal Coll., DePaul Univ., Roosevelt Univ.; cons.,
    Evanston Pub. Schs.; Inner-City Studies Program, North-
    east State Coll.; Black Studies Program, Chicago State
    Coll.; Skokie-Niles Afro-American Studies Workshop;
    Black Studies Program Planning Com., Owensboro, Ky.
Memberships: Including Am. Historical Assn.; ASNLH; Am.
    Academy of Political and Social Sciences; Southern His-
    torical Assn.; Black Studies Roundtable; Civil War
    Roundtable; Institute of the Black World; Nat. Assn. of
    Afro-American Educators; Chicago Historical Soc.;
    Black Merit Academy; Organization of Am. Historians;
    Kappa Alpha Psi.
Awards: Including Status Achievement Award, 1968, Morris
    Brown Coll.; Achievement Award, Beta Delta Chapter,
    Kappa Alpha Psi; Man of the Year, Chicago Heights
    Alumni, Kappa Alpha Psi; Sports Writer of the Year,
    Morris Brown Coll.
Publications: A Concise Encyclopedia of the Civil War, 1965;
    The Black Compendium, 1970.
Mailing Address: 7959 South Jeffery Blvd., Chicago, Ill.
    60617.

SKINNER, TOM
Publications: Black and Free, 1968; How Black Is the Gospel?
    1970; Words of Revolution, 1970.

SMALL, ROBERT VAN DYKE, Educator
Born: Abbeville, Ala., Nov. 29, 1924.
Education: B.A., Morehouse Coll., 1949; M.A., Atlanta Univ.,
    1950; Rutgers Univ., 1963; hon. doctorate, Am. Bible
    Inst., 1969; staff sergeant and instr., U.S. Army, 1943-
    45; research asst., Atlanta Univ., 1950-51; psychology
    practice, Federal government, 1965-68; asst. prof.
    psychology, Mercer Coll., Trenton, N.J., 1969-; psycho-
    logical cons. to Fed. govt.
Memberships: AAUP; AMORL Order, N.Y. Psychological
    Corp.; N.J. Ed. Assn.

Awards: Literary Guild.
Publications: Contributed to professional journals. Author,
Legal Slaughter of Peace, 1953; The Victims, A Psy-
chological Treatise, 1968.
Mailing Address: 680 Summer Ave., Newark, N.J. 07104.

SMITH, ARTHUR LEE, JR., Educator
Born: Valdosta, Ga., Aug. 14, 1942.
Education: A.A., Southwestern Christian, 1960-62; B.A., Okla-
homa Christian, 1962-64; M.A., Pepperdine Coll., 1965;
Ph.D., Univ. of Calif., Los Angeles, 1966-68.
Family: m. Jean.
Professional Experience: Instr., San Fernando Valley State
Coll., Feb. - June 1968; asst. prof., Purdue Univ., 1969;
asst. prof., Univ. of Calif., Los Angeles, 1969-; com-
munication cons. to universities and pub. schs; LA pro-
bation dept.; editor, Journal of Black Studies; contribut-
ing editor, Encore; guest editor, The Speech Teacher.
Memberships: Internat. Communication Assn.; Speech Commu-
nication Assn.
Awards: Christian Ed. Guild Writer's Award, 1966.
Publications: Contributed to journals. Author, The Break of
Dawn, 1964; Rhetoric of Black Revolution, 1969; Rhetoric
of Revolution, 1970; The Voice of Black Rhetoric: Selec-
tions, 1972.
Mailing Address: Dept. of Speech, UCLA, Los Angeles, Calif.
90024.

SMITH, JESSIE CARNEY, Librarian
Born: Greensboro, North Carolina.
Education: B.S., North Carolina A & T Univ., 1946-50; M.A.,
Michigan State Univ., 1955-56; A.M., George Peabody
Coll., 1956-57; Ph.D., Univ. of Illinois, 1960-64.
Family: s. Frederick D. Smith, Jr.
Professional Experience: Head cataloger and instr., Tennes-
see State Univ., 1957-60; teaching asst., Univ. of Illinois,
1961-63; coordinator of library service and asst. prof.,
Tennessee State Univ., 1963-65; librn. and prof. library
science, Fisk Univ., 1965-; lectr., part-time, George
Peabody Coll., 1969-; assoc. prof. and cons., part-time,
Alabama A & M Univ., 1971-.
Memberships: Numerous professional organizations, including
ALA; TLA; AAUP; Martin Luther King, Jr. Memorial
Center, Advisory Council of the Library Documentation
Project; African Studies Assn.; NAACP; Beta Phi Mu;
Pi Gamma Mu.

Publications: Contributed to professional journals. Author,
Libraries in Research Collections in Traditionally
Black Colleges: A Survey (in process).
Mailing Address: Fisk University Library, Nashville, Tenn.
37203.

SMITH, L. SHELBERT, Educator
Born: Springfield, Ill, Aug. 26, 1922.
Education: B.S., Roosevelt Univ., 1947-51; M.S., Ph.D.,
Illinois Inst. of Technology, 1953-56.
Family: m. Frances Beal; children, Tamara Frances, Lynn
Shelbert.
Professional Experience: Project leader, Quaker Oats Re-
search Lab., 1947-56; group leader, Stepan Chemical
Co., 1956-57; prof. chemistry, Central State Univ.,
1957-69; assoc. sec., AAUP, 1969-71.
Memberships: Am. Chemical Soc.; Am. Assn. for Advance-
ment of Science; Sigma Xi, Phi Lambda Upsilon; Beta
Kappa Chi; Coblente Soc.; Nat. Inst. of Science; AAUP;
ACLU; Human Relations Commn., Yellow Springs,
Ohio.
Awards: Quaker Oats Research Paper Award.
Publications: Contributed to journals. Author, Experimental
Chemistry, 1964.
Mailing Address: 9703 Woodland Dr., Silver Spring, Md.
20910.

SMITH, WILLIAM GARDNER, Journalist
Born: Philadelphia, Pa., 1927.
Education: Temple Univ.
Family: m.; c.
Professional Experience: Reporter, Afro-American and Pitts-
burg Courier newspapers; dir., Ghana Inst. of Journalism;
news editor, English Language Services, Agence France-
Presse (French News Agency).
Publications: Last of the Conquerors, 1948; Anger at Innocence,
1950; South Street, 1954; Stone Face, 1963; Return to
Black America, 1970.
Mailing Address: c/o Prentice-Hall, Inc., 70 Fifth Ave., New
York, N.Y. 10011.

SMYTHE, HUGH H., Educator
Born: Pittsburgh, Pa.
Education: B.A., Va. State Coll., 1936; M.S., Atlanta Univ.,
1937; Fisk Univ., 1938-39; Univ. of Chicago, 1940; Ph.D.,
Northwestern Univ., 1945; LL.D. (hon.) Va. State Coll.,
1968; special studies, industrial relations, Woodstock
Sch., Vermont, 1950; Columbia Univ., 1950-51.

Family: m. Mabel Hancock Murphy; d. Karen Pamela.
Professional Experience: Research adminstrv. asst., Am.
 Youth Commn. of Am. Council on Ed., Washington, D.C.,
 1937-38; research asst. and instr., Fisk Univ., 1938-39;
 research assoc., Atlanta Univ., 1942; asst. dir., research, Negro Land Grant Coll. Cooperative Social Studies project, 1944; prof. sociology, Morris Brown Univ.,
 1944; prof. sociology, Tennessee State A & I Univ., 1945-
 46; deputy dir., special research, NAACP, N.Y.C., 1947-
 49; dir., research, W.B. Graham & Assoc., N.Y.C., 1949-
 50; vis. prof. sociology and anthropology, Yamaguchi
 Nat. Univ., Japan, 1951-53; prof. sociology, Brooklyn
 Coll., 1953-61; dir. research, N.Y. State Senate Fi-
 nance Com. Evaluation project of the State Commn.
 Against Discrimination, 1956; N.Y. State Civil Service
 Commn. Panel of Examiners, 1961-65; senior advisor,
 economic and social affairs, U.S. Mission to the UN,
 1961-62; prof. sociology, Brooklyn Coll., 1962-65; Am-
 bassador to the Syrian Arab Republic, 1965-67; Am-
 bassador to Malta, Grand Canary, 1967-69; UN correspondent, Eastern World and Africa Trace and Development, London, 1964-; prof. sociology, Brooklyn Coll.,
 1969-.
Memberships: Including Assn. of Asian Studies; Japan Assn.;
 Am. Assoc. of Tchrs. of Chinese Language and Culture;
 AAUP; NAACP; Nat. Urban League; ACLU; Am. Foreign
 Service Assn.; Alpha Phi Alpha; editorial bds., Journal
 of Human Relations, 1954, Africa Today, 1955, Sociologi-
 cal Abstracts, 1956, Doubleday & Co. Zenith Books,
 1963-, Journal of Asian and African Studies, 1967.
Awards: Including Distinguished Alumni, Va. State Coll., 1957;
 Soc. for Distinguished Work in Social Science, 1967;
 Diploma of the Internat. Inst. JVEK, Germany, for con-
 tributions to Better Human Relations and World Peace,
 1968; Knight of the Grand Cross of the Royal Crown of
 Crete, 1968; Knight of Grand Cross of Sov. Military
 Order of St. Agatha, 1969.
Publications: Contributed over 150 articles to journals, 400
 book reviews, and 15 chapters to 11 books. Author,
 Land Grant Colleges Social Studies Project (with W.E.B.
 DuBois), 1944; New Nigerian Elite (with M.M. Smythe),
 1960; Educating the Culturally Disadvantaged Child (with
 L. Crow and W. Murray), 1966.
Mailing Address: 345 Eighth Ave., New York, N.Y. 10001.

SMYTHE, MABEL M., Educational consultant
Born: Montgomery, Ala., 1918; Spelman Coll., 1933-36; A.A.,
 Mount Holyoke, 1936-37; M.A., Northwestern Univ.,
 1939-40; Ph.D., Univ. of Wisconsin, 1940-42; New York
 Univ., 1949.

Family: m. Hugh H.; d. Karen Pamela.
Professional Experience: Tchr., Fort Valley N & I Inst., Fort
Valley, Ga.; 1937-39; asst. prof. and acting head, eco-
nomics and business adminstrn., Tennessee State Coll.,
1945-46; lectr. economics, Brooklyn Coll., 1946-47; vis.
prof. economics, Shiga Univ., Japan, 1951-53; senior
core tchr. Am. history and economics, New Lincoln Sch.,
N.Y.C., 1954-59; lectr. economics, Baruch Sch., CCNY,
Feb 1959 - June 1960; assoc. prof., summer workshop on
African political, social and economic affairs, Queens
Coll., 1962; cons., Encyclopaedia Britannica Educational
Corporation and Phelps-Stokes Fund, 1969-; advisory ed.,
Journal of Human Relations, 1951-65.
Memberships: Including Am. Academy of Political and Social
Science; AAUP; Academy of World Economics; Am. Eco-
nomic Assn.; Am. Soc. of African Culture; Assn. of So-
cial Science Tchrs. in Negro Colleges; Am. Assn. for
Labor Legislation; Assn. for Supr. and Curriculum De-
velopment.
Awards: Distinguished Service Award, The Links, Inc., greater
N.Y. chapter.
Publications: Contributed to journals, and co-authored film-
strip, "Profile of Nigeria." Author, The New Nigerian
Elite (with Hugh H. Smythe), 1960, 1962; Intensive Eng-
lish Conversation (with Alan B. Howes), 1953; Curriculum
for Understanding (ed. with Edgar S. Bley), 1965.
Mailing Address: 345 Eighth Ave., New York, N.Y. 10001.

SNOWDEN, FRANK M., JR., Educator
Born: York County, Va., July 17, 1911.
Education: A.B., Harvard Univ., 1932; A.M., ibid., 1933; Ph.D.,
ibid, 1944; LL.D. (hon.) Bard Coll., 1957.
Professional Experience: Instr. Latin, French and English,
Virginia State Coll., 1933-36; instr. classics, Spelman
Coll., Atlanta Univ., 1936-40; instr., Howard Univ.,
1940-42; asst. prof., ibid., 1942-44; assoc. prof., ibid.,
1944-45; prof. of classics, ibid., 1945-; dir., summer
sch., 1942-54; dir., Evening Sch. and Adult Ed., 1942-48;
chmn., Humanities Program, 1950-51; dean, Coll. of
Liberal Arts, Howard Univ., Oct. 1956 - Sept. 1968;
lectr. International Information Adminstr., Dept of
State, Feb. - June 1953; lectr., university, governmental
circles, Bombay, New Delhi, Lucknow, Calcutta and
Madras areas, July-Aug. 1957; Cultural Attaché, American Embassy, Rome, Oct. 1954 - Oct. 1956.
Memberships: Including Am. Philological Assn., Archaeological Inst. of Am.; Classical Soc. of Am. Academy in
Rome; Vergilian Soc. of Am.; vice pres., Washington
Soc. of Archaeological Inst. of Am., 1968.

Awards: Fulbright research scholar, Italy, 1949-50; recipient
of Medaglia d'Oro, Italian Government, for special work
in the field of Italian culture and ed., 1958; recipient,
Am. Council of Learned Societies Fellowship, Sept. 1962 -
Aug. 1963.
Publications: Contributed numerous articles to professional
journals. Author, Blacks in Antiquity: Ethiopians in the
Greco-Roman Experience, 1970.
Mailing Address: Dept. of Classics, Howard University, Wash-
ington, D.C. 20001.

SOUTHERN, EILEEN JACKSON, Educator
Born: Minneapolis, Minn., Feb. 19, 1920.
Education: B.A., Univ. of Chicago, 1936-40; M.A., Univ. of
Chicago, 1940-41; Julliard; Chicago Musical Coll.; Ph.D.,
New York Univ., 1952-61.
Family: m. Joseph; children, April Southern Reilly, Edward
Joseph.
Professional Experience: Instr., Prairie View Coll., 1941-42;
asst. prof., Southern Univ., 1943-45, 1949-51; asst.
prof., Claflin Univ., 1947-49; tchr. music, pub. schs.,
N.Y.C., 1954-60; assoc. prof. music, City Univ. of N.Y.,
1960-; concert pianist.
Memberships: YWCA; NAACP; AKA.
Awards: Sojourner Truth, Queens Branch, N.Y., Negro Busi-
ness and Professional Women's Club, Inc.; Professional
Achievement Award, Univ. of Chicago, 1971.
Publications: Contributed to journals and books. Author, The
Buxheum Organ Book, 1963; The Music of Black Ameri-
cans: A History, 1970; Readings in Black American
Music, 1972; Anonymous Chansons in Two Manuscripts
at El Escorial (in process).
Mailing Address: 115-05 179 St., St. Albans, N.Y. 11434.

SPELLMAN, A. B.
Publications: Black Music: Four Lives, 1970.

STAPLES, ROBERT, Educator
Born: Roanoke, Va., June 28, 1942.
Education: A.A., Los Angeles Valley, 1958-60; A.B., Calif.
State Univ., 1960-63; M.A., ibid., 1963-65; Ph.D., Univ.
of Minnesota, 1965-71.
Professional Experience: Assoc. prof. sociology, Bethune-
Cookman Coll., 1967-68; asst. prof., Calif. State Univ.,
Hayward Calif., 1968-70; asst. prof. sociology, Fisk
Univ., 1970-71; assoc. prof. sociology, Howard Univ.,
1971-73; assoc. prof. sociology, Univ. of Calif., 1973-.

Memberships: Nat. Council of Family Relations; Pacific So-
ciological Assn.; Congress of Pan-African Peoples.
Publications: Contributed over 70 articles to professional
journals. Editor, The Black Family: Essays and
Studies, 1971; The Black Woman in America, 1973.
Mailing Address: 1222 Clayton St., Apt. 9, San Francisco,
Calif. 94114.

STARKE, CATHERINE J.
Publications: Portraiture in American Fiction: Stock Characters, Archetypes and Individuals, 1971.

STEPHANY (Fuller)
Publications: Morning Deep, 1969.

STEPTOE, JOHN LEWIS, Author
Born: Brooklyn, N.Y., Sept. 14, 1950.
Education: High Sch. of Art and Design.
Family: Children, Bioella, Javaka.
Professional Experience: Arts and culture dept., paintings
dept., Haryou, 1965-69.
Awards: ALA Notable Children's Book, Stevie, 1969; gold
medal, Soc. of Illustrators, Stevie, 1969; award, Black
Child Development Inst., 1973; lib. dedicated in his
name, Quincy St., Brooklyn, 1970.
Publications: Stevie, 1969; Uptown, 1970; Train Ride, 1971;
Birthday, 1972.
Mailing Address: 66 Grove St., Peterboro, N.H. 03458.

STEWART, PORTER ELLIS, Author
Born: Florence, Ala., Aug. 3, 1944.
Education: Tennessee State Univ., 1965-66.
Family: m. Dorothy Granberry.
Memberships: Omega Psi Phi.
Awards: Gwendolyn Brooks Award, Fisk University's Writer's
Conf., 1968.
Publications: Contributed poems to Flame magazine. Author,
Passing By, 1970.
Mailing Address: Route 1, Box 255, Hampton, Conn. 06247.

STONE, CHUCK, Educational director
Born: St. Louis, Mo., July 21, 1924.
Education: A.B., Wesleyan Conn. Univ., 1946-48; M.A., Univ.
of Chicago, 1948-50.
Family: m. Louise Davis; children, Krishna, Allegra, Charles
III.

Professional Experience: Air force navigator, W.W. II, 1943-
45; regional rep., World Politics and Am. Foreign
Policy, Adult Ed. Discussion Programs, 1952-56; overseas rep., CARE, Egypt, Gaza, India, 1956-57; editor,
New York Age, 1958-60; assoc. dir., Am. Com. on Africa,
N.Y.C., 1960; White House corr. and editor, Washington
Afro-American newspaper, 1960-63; instr. (part-time),
journalism, Columbia Coll., Chicago, 1963-64; editor-
in-chief, Chicago Daily Defender, 1963-64; special asst.
to Rep. Adam Clayton Powell, chmn., Ed. and Labor
Com., U.S. House of Representatives, 1965-67; editorial
research specialist to Rep. Robert N.C. Nix, chmn.,
Subcommittee on Postal Operations, U.S. House of Representatives, 1968; John T. Dorrance Vis. Prof., government, Trinity Coll., Hartford, Conn., 1969; dir.,Ed. Opportunities Projects, Ed. Testing Service, Princeton, N.J.;
contributing editor, the Black Scholar; chmn., Nat. Conf.
on Black Power.
Memberships: Fellow and founding member, The Black Acad-
emy of Arts and Letters; council mem., Nat. Conf. of
Black Political Scientists.
Awards: 1st prize, Best Column of the Year, NNPA, 1960;
Journalist of the Year, Capital Press Club, Washington,
D.C., 1961; Annual Distinguished Citizen's Award,
Frontiers Internat., Inc., D.C., 1963; Outstanding Citizen
of the Year, CORE, Chicago, 1964; Award of Merit for
Journalism, Alpha Phi Alpha, Chicago, 1965; Politician-
in-Residence, Morgan State Coll., 1969.
Publications: Tell It Like It Is, 1968; Black Political Power
in America, 1968; King Strut, 1970.
Mailing Address: 225 Cornwall Ave., Trenton, N.J. 08618.

STRICKLAND, ARVARH E., Educator
Born: Hattiesburg, Miss., July 6, 1930.
Education: B.A., Tougaloo Coll., 1951; M.A. (ed.), Univ. of Ill.,
1953; M.A. (history) ibid., 1960; Ph.D., ibid., 1962.
Family: m. Willie Pearl; children, Duane Arvarh, Bruce El-
more.
Professional Experience: Instr., Tuskegee Inst., 1955-56;
prin., 1956-57; supr. of schs., Madison County, Miss.,
1957-59; research asst., Univ. of Ill., summer 1962;
asst. prof., 1962-65; assoc. prof., Chicago State Coll.,
1965-68; vis. lectr., Univ. of Ill., summer 1967; prof.,
Chicago State Coll., 1968-69; prof., Univ. of Missouri,
1969-; special field, the Negro in Am. history.
Memberships: Including AAUP; Com. on Ed. Institutions,
Ill. State Historical Soc., 1965; vice pres. (hon.), ibid.,
1966-67; Bd. of Dirs., ibid., 1967.

Awards: Kappa Delta Pi, ed., 1953; Woodrow Wilson Fellow, history, 1959-60; Univ. Fellow, history, 1960-61; Phi Alpha Theta, history, 1960; Kendric C. Babcock Fellow, history, Univ. of Ill., 1961-62; Distinguished Service Award, Ill. State Historical Soc., 1967.
Publications: Contributed articles and book reviews to journals. Author, History of the Chicago Urban League, 1966.
Mailing Address: 4100 Defoe Dr., Columbia, Mo. 65201.

TARRY, ELLEN
Publications: Janie Bell, 1940; Hezekiah Horton, 1942; My Dog Rinty (with Marie H. Ets), 1946; Young Jim: The Early Years of James Weldon Johnson, 1967; Third Door, 1971.

TATE, MERZE, Educator
Born: Blanchard, Mich.
Education: B.A., Western Mich. Univ., 1921-23, 1926-27; M.A., Columbia Univ., 1932; B.Litt., Oxford Univ., 1935; Ph.D., Radcliffe Coll., 1941; D.Litt. (hon.), Western Mich. Univ.; D. Laws (hon.), Morgan State Coll.
Professional Experience: Prof. hist. and dean of women, Barber Scotia Coll., 1935-36; chmn., social science div., 1936-41; prof. political science and dean of women, Morgan State Coll., 1941-42; prof. hist., Howard Univ., 1942-; vis. prof., Wayne State Univ., summer 1953; vis. prof., Western Mich. Univ., summer 1955; holder of GS-18, U.S. Civil Service rating historian in three areas of history; Fulbright lectr., India, 1950-51; assigned to Tagore's World Univ.; lectr., eleven universities.
Memberships: AAUW; Am. Historical Assn.; Internat. Platform Assn.; Radcliffe Club, Washington, D.C.; Phi Beta Kappa; Pi Gamma Mu; Phi Delta Kappa; writers' club, Washington, D.C.; Phi Alpha Theta; Nat. Bd., Radcliffe Coll.
Awards: Third Alpha Kappa Alpha foreign fellowship, first Am. black woman to matriculate at Oxford Univ., and first Am. Black to receive a higher research degree; Nat. Urban League Outstanding Achievement Award, 1948; $100 award for most scholarly contribution to the Pacific Historical Review, for article, "Great Britain and the Sovereignty of Hawaii," 1962; Radcliffe Coll. Alumnae Assn., graduate chapter medal Distinguished Professional Service, 1953; Most Distinguished Citizen, Isabella County, Mich., 1969; Most Distinguished Alumnae, Western Mich. Univ., 1970.

Publications: Contributed 25 articles to journals. Author, The Disarmaments Illusion: The Movement for a Limitation of Armaments, 1948; The United States and the Hawaiian Kingdom, 1965; Hawaii: Reciprocity or Annexation, 1968.
Mailing Address: 1314 Perry St., N.E., Washington, D.C. 20017.

TEAGUE, BOB
Publications: Letters to a Black Boy, 1968; Adam in Blunderland, 1971.

THIBODEAUX, MARY RODGERS
Publications: A Black Nun Looks at Black Power, 1972; A Struggle in Black and White, 1972.

THOMAS, JESSIE O.
Publications: My Story in Black and White, 1967.

THOMAS, LORENZO, U.S. Navy
Born: Republic of Panama, 1944.
Education: B.A., Queens Coll., 1967.
Professional Experience: Ref. asst, Pratt Inst. Lib., 1967-68; U.S. Navy, 1968-.
Awards: John Golden Award in creative writing; Dwight Durling prize in poetry, 1963; Poetry Foundation grant, 1967.
Publications: Author of poetry included in Liberator, A Journal of Poetry, Art and Literature, Umbra, and the anthology, Black Fire, 1969.
Mailing Address: 161-21 119 Dr., Jamaica, N.Y. 11434.

THOMAS, ROSCOE A., Teacher
Born: Washington, D.C., Dec. 4, 1928.
Education: B.A., Catholic Univ., 1951-54; M.A., ibid., 1954-55; Ph.D., ibid., 1959-66.
Family: m. Margie Loretta; s. Roscoe Eugene.
Professional Experience: Tchr. Latin, Spanish, English, pub. schs., Washington, D.C., 1959-61; tchr., English, Spanish, French, pub. schs., Washington, D.C., 1962-65.
Memberships: Sigma Beta Kappa.
Awards: Smith-Mundt Ed. Grant to Tunis, Tunisia, 1961-62.
Publications: Author, Precious Poverty, 1969.
Mailing Address: 2518 Lyons St., S.E., Hillcrest Hgts., Md. 20031.

THOMPSON, DONNIS H., Educator
Born: Chicago, Ill., April 1, 1937.
Education: B.S., George Williams Coll., 1955; M.A., ibid.,
1959; Ed.D., Colorado State Coll., 1967.
Professional Experience: Tchr. and dept. chmn., Hyde Park
High Sch.; dir., Pearl Harbor Day Camp, June-Aug.
1963; head women's track coach, Univ. of Hawaii, 1961-
64; tchr. researcher, Evergreen High Sch., Jefferson
County, Colo.; asst. prof., Univ. of Hawaii; research,
workshops, speaking engagements; editor DGWS Track
and Field Guide, 1970-72; cons., Hawaii State Girl's
Athletics.
Memberships: Coll. rep., Hawaii State DGWS, 1968; Mayor's
Physical Fitness Council, 1968; chmn., Hawaii's
Women's Track and Field Com., 1968-69; pres., SWD
AAHPER Professional Ed. Com., 1968-70; AAU Nat.
vice chmn., Women's Track and Field, 1968.
Awards: Distinguished Service Award for the Hawaii AAU,
1963; AKA Outstanding Woman of the Year, 1967.
Publications: Contributed to athletic journals. Author, Track
and Field for Women, 1969.
Mailing Address: 1333 Lower Campus Rd., Honolulu, Hawaii.
96822.

THOMPSON, ERA BELL, Author, Editor.
Born: Des Moines, Iowa.
Education: B.A., Morningside Coll., 1933; Medill Sch. of
Journalism; hon. doctorates, Morningside Coll., 1965,
and Univ. of North Dakota, 1969.
Professional Experience: interviewer five years, Ill. and
U.S. Employment Services, Chicago; assoc. ed., Ebony,
four years; co-managing editor, 1951-64; book reviewer,
Chicago and N.Y. papers; internat. editor, Johnson Pub-
lishing Co., 1964-.
Memberships: Bd. of dir., Chicago Metropolitan YWCA,
1945-47; Friends of Chicago Public Library, 1959-60;
Hull House, 1960-64; Soc. of Midland Authors, 1961-;
Urban League; NAACP; Chicago Press Club; North Cen-
tral Region Manpower Advisory Com.; Chicago Council
on Foreign Relations.
Awards: Iota Phi Lambda Outstanding Woman of the Year,
1965; fellowship, Bread Loaf Writers Conf., 1949; New-
berry fellowship; Patron's Saints Award, 1968 for
American Daughter.
Publications: American Daughter, 1946; Africa, Land of My
Father, 1954; White on Black (co-editor), 1963.
Mailing Address: Ebony, 820 South Michigan Ave., Chicago,
Ill. 60605.

THOMPSON, JAMES W., Author
Born: Detroit, Mich., Dec. 21, 1935.
Education: Northeastern High Sch., 1951-53; Univ. of Detroit,
1959-60; Wayne State Univ., 1960-62; New York Univ.,
1965.
Publications: Contributed to journals. Editor, America Sings,
1961; Beyond the Blues, 1962; Sixes and Sevens, 1962;
Ik Ben de Nievwe Neger, 1965. Author, First Fire, 1970.
Mailing Address: 27 First Ave., New York, N.Y. 10003.

THOMPSON, JULIUS ERIC, Graduate student
Born: Vicksburg, Miss., July 15, 1946.
Education: B.S., Alcorn A and M Coll., 1965-69; Columbia
Univ., summer 1967; Yale Univ., summer 1968; Prince-
ton Univ., 1969.
Professional Experience: Asst. to dormitory dir., Alcorn
Coll., June 1965 - Nov. 1966.
Memberships: Alpha Kappa Mu Honor Society; Alpha Phi
Alpha.
Awards: Danforth Fellow, 1969; Princeton Univ. Fellow,
1969.
Publications: Contributed poetry to magazines. Author,
Hopes Tied Up in Promises, 1970.
Mailing Address: 2719 Graduate College, Princeton, N.J.
08540.

THORNHILL, LIONEL OSCAR
Born: British Guiana, S.A., Feb. 1, 1897.
Education: Regent St. R.C. High Sch., British Guiana; Morris
High Sch., Bronx, N.Y.
Family: m. Edith Caroline; children, Shirley May (deceased),
Oscar Fitzgerald, Lyra Maguerite (Mrs. Lyra T. Mc-
Gugins), Lloyd Egerton.
Professional Experience: Printer, the Daily Argosy, the Daily
Chronicle General Printers, British Guiana; janitor;
printer, William Allen & Co., N.Y.C., 1923-34; dining
car waiter, Pa. Railroad, now ret.
Awards: Pa. Railroad Honor Roll.
Publications: Author, The Huge Steel Bolt, 1966.
Mailing Address: 748 East 223 St., Bronx, N.Y. 10466.

THORPE, EARL E., Educator
Born: Durham, N.C., Nov. 9, 1924.
Education: A.B., North Carolina Coll., 1948; M.A., ibid.,
1949; Ph.D., Ohio State Univ., 1953.
Family: m. Martha Vivian Branch; children, 2.

Professional Experience: U.S. Army, World War II, 3 years;
  instr. history, Stowe Tchrs. Coll., St. Louis, Mo., 1951;
  prof. history, Alabama A & M Coll., 1952-55; assoc.
  prof. history, Southern Univ., Baton Rouge, La., 1955-
  62; prof. history and chmn., dept. of history and social
  science, 1962-; vis. prof. Afro-American Studies, Howard
  Univ., 1971.
Memberships: Omega Psi Phi; Phi Alpha Theta; Pi Gamma Mu;
  Organization of Am. Historians; Soc. for the Study of
  Southern Lit.; Am. Historical Assn.; Assn. of Social and
  Behavioral Scientists; ASNLH.
Publications: Contributed twenty-five articles to scholarly
  journals. Author, Negro Historians in the United States,
  1958 (reissued, 1971); Black Historians: A Critique,
  1971; The Desertion of Man: A Critique of Philosophy of
  History, 1958; The Mind of the Negro: An Intellectual
  History of Afro-Americans, 1961, 1970; Eros and Free-
  dom in Southern Life and Thought, 1967; The Central
  Theme of Black History, 1969; The Old South: A Psychohistory, 1972.
Mailing Address: Dept. of History, North Carolina Central College, Durham, N.C.

THURMAN, HOWARD, Theologian
Born: Daytona Beach, Fla., Nov. 18, 1900.
Education: A.B., Morehouse Coll., 1919-23; B.D., Colgate-
  Rochester Theological Seminary, 1923; D.D., Wesleyan
  Coll., Conn., 1946; D.D. (hon.), Morehouse Coll., 1935;
  D.D. (hon.), Howard Univ.; D.D. (hon.), Lincoln Univ.,
  Pa.; D.D. (hon.), Wesleyan Univ., Conn.; D.D. (hon.),
  Oberlin Coll.; H.H.D. (hon.), Ohio Wesleyan, 1954;
  Litt.D. (hon.), Tuskegee Inst., 1954; LL.D. (hon.), Allen
  Univ., 1954; L.D. (hon.), Washington Univ., Mo., 1955;
  L.H.D. (hon.), Va. State Coll.; L.H.D. (hon.), Florida
  Normal Coll., 1961; D.D. (hon.), Boston Univ., 1967.
Family: m. Sue E. Bailey; children, Olive Thurman Wong,
  Anne Thurman Chiarenza.
Professional Experience: Pastor, Mt. Zion Baptist Church,
  Oberlin, Ohio, 1926-28; dir., religious life and prof.
  religion, Morehouse Coll., Spelman Coll., 1929-32;
  dean, Rankin Chapel and prof. theology, Howard Univ.,
  1932-44; guest prof., Sch. of Religion, Univ. of Iowa,
  1948; organizer and minister, Church for the Fellowship
  of All Peoples, San Francisco, Calif. (under Dr. Thurman's leadership this was the first church completely
  integrated in leadership and membership in American
  Life), 1944-53; dean of Marsh Chapel, Boston Univ.,
  1953-65; vis. prof., Univ. of Ibadan, West Africa, 1963;
  dean emeritus, Marsh Chapel, 1965-; vis. prof. religion,

Earlham Coll., Richmond, Ind., 1966; vis. prof., Presbyterian Theological Seminary, Louisville, Ky., 1967; lectr., U.S. and foreign countries.
Memberships: Am. Academy of Arts and Science; Nat. Council of Religion in Higher Ed.; Author's Guild; NAACP; Calif. Writers Club; Harold Brunn Soc. for Medical Research; Northern Calif. Service League; Martin Luther King Memorial Center, Atlanta.
Awards: Phi Beta Kappa; Gutenberg Award, Chicago Bible Soc.
Publications: The Negro Spiritual Speaks of Life and Death, 1947; Jesus and the Disinherited, 1949; Deep Is the Hunger, 1951; Meditations of the Heart, 1953; The Creative Encounter, 1954; Deep River, 1955, 1969; The Growing Edge, 1956; Footprints of a Dream, 1959; The Inward Journey, 1961; Temptations of Jesus, 1962; Disciples of the Spirit, 1963; The Luminous Darkness, 1965; The Centering Moment, 1969.
Mailing Address: 2020 Stockton St., San Francisco, Calif. 94133.

TOPPIN, EDGAR ALLAN, Educator
Born: New York, N.Y., Jan. 22, 1928.
Education: B.A., Howard Univ., 1945-49; M.A., ibid., 1949-50; Ph.D., Northwestern Univ., 1950-52, 1955.
Family: m. Antionette Lomax; children, Edgar Allan, Jr., Avis Ann Lillian, Antionette Louise.
Professional Experience: Instr. history, Alabama State Coll., 1954-55; chmn., division of social sciences, Fayetteville State Coll., 1955-59; asst. prof. history, Univ. of Akron, 1959-63; assoc. prof. history, Univ. of Akron, 1963-64; vis. prof., North Carolina Coll., summer 1959, summer 1963; vis. prof., Western Reserve Univ., summer 1962; vis prof., Univ. of Cincinnati, summer 1964; vis. prof., San Francisco State Coll., summer 1969; prof. history, Virginia State Coll., 1964-; lectr., CBS-TV "Black Heritage" series.
Memberships: Exec. council, ASNLH; Bd. of Dir., Southern Fellowship Fund.
Awards: $40,000 grant from Old Dominion Foundation to produce own ed. television course, "Americans from Africa: A History," WCVE-TV, Richmond, Va.; award equivalent to "Emmy" in ed. television from the Inst. for Ed. by Radio-TV, Ohio State Univ., for "New Militancy and Black Power," Feb. 1970; Hearst Foundation Fellowship, 1950-51, 1952-53; Northwestern Univ. Fellowship, 1951-52; Whitney Foundation Opportunity Fellowship, 1953-54.

Publications: Contributed to journals. Author, Pioneers and
Patriots: Six Negroes in the Revolutionary Era (with
Labinia Dobler), 1965; A Mark Well Made: Negro Con-
tribution to American Culture, 1967; Blacks in America:
Then and Now, 1969; Unfinished March: Reconstruction
to World War I (with Carol Drisk), 1969; Biographical
History of Blacks in America, 1971.
Mailing Address: 20411 Williams St., Ettrick, Va. 23803.

TUCKER, STERLING
Publications: Beyond the Burning: Life and Death of the Ghetto,
1968; Black Reflections on White Power, 1969; For
Blacks Only, 1971.

TURNER, DARWIN T., Educator
Born: Cincinnati, Ohio, May 7, 1931.
Education: B.A., Univ. of Cincinnati, 1944-47; M.A., ibid.,
1947-49; Ph.D., Univ. of Chicago, 1956.
Family: m. Maggie Jean Lewis; children, Pamela, Darwin
Keith, Rachon.
Professional Experience: Asst. prof. English, Clark Coll.,
1949-51; asst. prof. English, Morgan State Coll., 1952-
57; prof. English and chmn. of dept., Florida A & M
Univ., 1957-59; prof. English and chmn. of dept., North
Carolina A & T State Univ., 1957-66; prof. English and
dean, graduate sch., North Carolina A & T State Univ.,
1966-70; adjunct prof. English, Univ. of Michigan, Jan. -
May 1970; prof. English, Univ. of Michigan, 1970-71;
vis. prof., Univ. of Hawaii, summer 1971; vis. prof.
English, Univ. of Iowa, 1970-; cons., institutes in humanities, English, Afro-American studies, teaching of
disadvantaged; consultant and reader, HEW, NDEA
inst. in English, title III proposals; lectr.
Memberships: numerous organizations, including sec., CLA,
1958-63; pres., CLA, 1963-65; pres. Piedmont Affiliate,
NCTE, 1963-65; pres., North Carolina-Virginia Coll.
Eng. Assn., 1964-65; chmn., Com. on Literature of
Minority Groups; Graduate Record Exam. Bd., 1969-;
editorial bds., CLA Journal, Coll. Compostion and
Communication.
Awards: Study grant, Am. Council of Learned Societies,
1965, research in writings of Jean Toomer; fellowship,
North Carolina - Duke Univs. co-operative program,
research in Afro-American literature; CLA award,
creative scholarship, 1971.
Publications: Contributed numerous articles to journals and
anthologies. Author, Katharsis, 1964; Frank Yerby,
the Golden Debunker, (in press); editor, Images of the
Negro in America, 1965; Black American Literature:

Essays, 1969; Black American Literature: Fiction,
1969; Black American Literature: Poetry, 1969; Black
American Literature: Essays, Fiction, Poetry, and
Drama, 1970; Black Drama in America: An Anthology,
1971; co-editor, Voices from the Black Experience:
African and Afro-American, 1972; co-author, The Teach-
ing of Literature by Afro-Americans, Theory and Prac-
tice, 1970; compiler, Afro-American Writers, 1970;
In a Minor Chord: Three Afro-American Writers and
Their Search for Identity, 1971.
Mailing Address: 2910 Chesterfield St., Ann Arbor, Mich.
48104.

TURNER, MAE CAESAR
Born: Ennis, Tex., 1889.
Education: B.S., Langston Univ.
Publications: Author, Memory Lane in My Southern World,
1948; Uncle Ezra Holds Prayer Meeting in the White
House, 1970.
Mailing Address: 43 G. St., Ardmore, Okla. 73401.

TURNER, MARY G.
Born: Washington, D.C., Oct. 14, 1917.
Education: B.S., Miner Teachers Coll., 1938; M.A., New York
Univ., 1956; Washington, D.C. Teachers Coll., 1947-63;
American Univ., 1960; Wayne State, 1967.
Family: m. Fletcher W. (deceased); d. Jean-Louise Landry.
Professional Experience: Tchr., S.E. Settlement House, Wash-
ington, D.C., 1938-39; tchr., pub. schs., Washington,
D.C., 1942-63.
Memberships: NEA; DCEA; NAPSAE; DCAPSAE; IRA; NCTE;
DCCTE; Basic Education Council; Community Sch. Assn.
Publications: Author, We Too Belong, 1969.
Mailing Address: 4005 20 St., N.E., Washington, D.C. 20018.

TYMS, JAMES D., Educator
Born: Aberdeen, Miss., Jan. 2, 1905.
Education: B.A., Lincoln Univ., 1934; B.D., Howard Univ.,
1937; M.A., ibid., 1938; Ph.D., Boston Univ., 1942.
Family: m. Brittie A.
Professional Experience: Pastor, New Hope Baptist Church,
Winchester, Mass., 1940-42; tchr., Morehouse Coll.,
1942-47; prof., Howard Univ., 1947-.
Memberships: Religious Ed. Assn.; Seminary Prof. in the
Practical Fields.
Awards: General Ed. Fellowship, 1945-46; Fulbright Senior
Research Scholar, Gold Coast, West Africa, 1956-5 /.

Publications: Contributed to journals. Author, The Rise of
Religious Education Among Negro Baptists, 1965.
Mailing Address: 1729 Varnum St., N.W., Washington, D.C.
20011.

VAN DYKE, HENRY, Author
Born: Allegan, Mich., Oct. 30, 1928.
Education: B.A., M.A., Univ. of Mich., 1950-54.
Professional Experience: Assoc. editor, Univ. of Mich., engi-
neering research, 1956-58; coor., Crowell-Collier-
Macmillan, 1959-67.
Awards: Avery Hopwood.
Publications: Ladies of the Rachmaninoff Eyes, 1965; Blood of
Strawberries, 1969.
Mailing Address: 64 St. Mark's Pl., New York, N.Y. 10003.

VAN DYKE, RICHARD L.
Publications: White-Collar Blacks, A Breakthrough (with
John S. Morgan), 1970.

VAN PEEBLES, MELVIN
Publications: Le Chinois du XIV, 1966; La Fête à Harlem,
1967; A Bear for the FBI, 1968.

VERNON, ROBERT
Publications: The Black Ghetto, 1969, 1964.

VINCENT, THEODORE G.
Publications: Black Power and the Garvey Movement, 1971.

VIVIAN, C. T., Clergyman
Born: Boone County, Mo., July 31, 1924.
Education: B.S., Western Ill. Univ.; B.Th., Am. Baptist Theo-
logical Seminary, 1959; Scarrit Sch. of Religion.
Family: m. Octavia; children, Alvier Denise, Cordy Jr., Kira,
Mark, Anita Charrise, Albert.
Professional Experience: Editor, Sunday Sch. Publ. Bd., Nat.
Baptist Convention, 1955-60; pastor, First Community
Church, Nashville, 1955-61; pastor, Community Church,
Chattanooga, Tenn., 1961-63; exec. staff, Dr. Martin
Luther King, 1963-67; Urban Training Center, 1967-69;
campus minister, Shaw Univ., 1969-; founder, Laymens
Magazine for the Sunday Sch. Publ. Bd.
Memberships: SCLC.

Awards: Key to City, hometown, Mocomb, Ill., 1971; numerous
civil rights, civic and cultural awards.
Publications: Contributed numerous articles to journals and
books. Author, Black Power and American Myth, 1970.
Mailing Address: Shaw University, Raleigh, N.C. 27602.

VIVIAN, OCTAVIA, Author
Born: South Bend, Ind., Feb. 23, 1928.
Education: B.A., Eastern Univ., 1950; Univ. of Dayton, 1951-
52.
Family: m. C.T. Vivian; children, Alvier Denise, Cordy Jr.,
Kira, Mark, Anita Charrise, Albert.
Professional Experience: Interviewer, Metropolitan Housing
Authority, Dayton, Ohio, 1951-52; girls' and women's
work supervisor, Carver Community Center, Peoria,
Ill., 1952-55; welfare worker, Hamit City, Chattanooga,
Tenn., 1962-63; coordinator, Decade of Black History,
Loop College, Chicago, Ill., 1970; feature editor, Pontiac
Challenger, Negro weekly, at age of 14; operated South-
ern Mediator's Journal, Little Rock, Ark., summer
1945 at age of 17; weekly columnist, "Ooops My
Thoughts," Michigan Chronical newspaper, Detroit,
while undergraduate, 1946-50.
Memberships: Alpha Kappa Alpha; Southern Christian Leader-
ship Conf. Com. on American/Vietnam Children.
Awards: Key to the City, Pontiac, Mich., 1972; Silver Cup
Award, Women's Civic Clubs, Chicago, Ill., 1971.
Publications: Contributed to magazines. Author, Coretta:
The Story of Mrs. Martin Luther King, Jr., 1970.
Mailing Address: 314 East Cabarrus, Raleigh, N.C. 27601.

WALKER, ALICE (Mrs. Melvyn Rosenman Leventhal), Author
Born: Eatonton, Ga., Feb. 9, 1944.
Education: Spelman Coll., 1961-63; B.A., Sarah Lawrence
Coll., 1963-66.
Family: m. Melvyn Rosenman Leventhal; d. Rebecca Grant.
Professional Experience: Caseworker, welfare dept., N.Y.C.,
Feb.-June 1966; voter registration, Miss., June-Sept
1966; cons., black studies, Friends of the Children of
Miss., 1967-68; writer-in-residence and tchr. of black
studies, Jackson State Coll., 1968-69; writer-in-resi-
dence, Tougaloo Coll., 1969-70.
Awards: Charles Merrill Writing Fellowship, 1967-68; Nat.
Foundation for the Arts Award in fiction, 1969-70.
Publications: Contributed to journals. Author, Once, 1968;
The Third Life of Grange Copeland, 1970.
Mailing Address: 1443 Rockdale, Jackson, Miss. 39213.

WALKER, MARGARET A., Educator, Author
Born: Birmingham, Ala., July 7, 1915.
Education: A.B., Northwestern Univ., 1935; M.A., Univ. of
Iowa, 1940; Ph.D., ibid., 1965.
Family: m. Firnist James Alexander; children, Marion
Elizabeth, Firnist James, Jr., Sigismund Walker, Marga-
ret Elvira.
Professional Experience: Prof. English, Livingstone Coll.,
Salisbury, N.C., 1941-42, 1945-46; prof. English, West
Va. State Coll., Institute, West Va., 1942-43; prof.
English, Jackson State Coll., Jackson, Miss., 1949-;
graduate asst., Rhetoric Program, Univ. of Iowa, 1962-
64.
Memberships: NCTE; MLA; Poetry Soc. of Am.; AAUP; NEA;
AKA.
Awards: Yale Award for Younger Poets, 1942; Rosenwald
Fellowship for Creative Writing, 1944; Ford Fellow,
Yale Univ., 1954; Houghton Mifflin Literary Fellowship,
1966.
Publications: Contributed poems to magazines and anthologies.
Author, For My People, 1942; Jubilee, 1966; Prophets
for a New Day, 1970; How I Wrote Jubilee, 1971.
Mailing Address: Department of English, Jackson State Col-
lege, Jackson, Miss. 39217.

WALTON, HANES, JR., Educator
Born: Augusta, Ga., Sept. 25, 1942.
Education: A.B., Morehouse Coll., 1959-63; M.A., Atlanta
Univ., 1963-64; Ph.D., Howard Univ., 1964-67.
Professional Experience: Instr., Atlanta Univ., summer
1966; assoc. prof., Savannah State Coll., 1967-.
Memberships: Am. Political Science Assn.; Nat. Conf. of
Black Political Scientists; Academy of Political and
Social Science; Kappa Alpha Psi; Pi Sigma Alpha.
Awards: Kappa Alpha Psi Scholarship and Achievement
Award: Social Science Council Research Fellowship.
Publications: Contributed 21 articles to journals and maga-
zines. Author, The Negro in Third Party Politics,
1969; Black Political Parties, 1970; The Political
Philosophy of Martin Luther King, Jr., 1970.
Mailing Address: Box 208, Savannah State College, Savannah,
Ga. 31404.

WALTON, ORTIZ MONTAIGNE, Educator, Composer
Education: B.A., Univ. of Hartford; B.S., Roosevelt Univ.;
M.A., Univ. of California, Berkeley; Ph.D., ibid.
Professional Experience: Tchr. sociology of Afro-American
music, Ethnic Studies, lectr., and performer, Ellington
Symposium, Univ. of Calif., Berkeley; tchr., Mission

Sch. of Music, San Francisco; tchr., East Bay Music
Center; Richmond and Boston Conservatory of Music;
master classes in the art of double bass performance;
solo bassist, Cairo, U.A.R. Symphony Orchestra; first
black and youngest to join Boston Symphony Orchestra;
asst. principal, Buffalo Philharmonic; member of Hartford, Conn. and Springfield, Mass. symphony orchestras;
principal bassist, Nat. Orchestra Assn., N.Y.C.
Memberships: Am. Sociological Assn.; Nat. Assn. of Afro-
American Musicians.
Awards: Including graduate div. dissertation grant, 1972;
Ford Foundation grant, dissertation writing in Ethnic
Studies, 1971-72; Nat. Inst. of Mental Health Trainee-
ship, 1968-71; Inst. of Community and Race Relations
grant, 1971.
Publications: Contributed articles to anthologies and journals.
Musical compositions "Night Letter to Duke," an un-
accompanied double bass sonata; songs with lyrics by
Ishmael Reed, recorded by Black Box, 1972, including
"The Wardrobe Master of Paradise," "Betty's Ball
Blues," " The Black Cock," "Mojo Queen of the
Feathery Plumes." Author, Coronation of the King:
Contributions by Duke Ellington to Black Culture, 1969;
Music: Black, White and Blue, 1972.
Mailing Address: 1129 Bancroft Way, Berkeley, Calif. 94702.

WAMBLE, THELMA, Medical social cons.
Born: Fort Smith, Ark., Jan. 9, 1916.
Education: A.B., Ark. State Coll., 1932-35; New York Univ.,
1940-41; M.A., Atlanta Univ., 1946-48.
Professional Experience: Field tchr. supr., Jewish Memorial
Hospital, N.Y.C., 1948-53; medical social cons., Health
Dept., N.Y.C., 1953-57; medical social work supr., Los
Angeles County, 1957-60; medical social cons., Los
Angeles County, 1960-.
Memberships: Nat. Assoc. of Social Workers.
Awards: Calif. Negro Authors Guild.
Publications: All in the Family, 1953; Knight of Courage, 1964;
Look Over My Shoulder, 1969.
Mailing Address: 4319 Santo Tomas Dr., Los Angeles, Calif.
90008.

WARD, DOUGLAS TURNER, Playwright, Actor
Born: Burnside, La.
Professional Experience: Paul Mann's Actors' Workshop,
N.Y.C.; journalist, N.Y.C., 1948-51; acting debut, off-
Broadway, The Iceman Cometh, Circle in the Square;
featured in Lost in the Stars; leading role in ten-month
national tour of A Raisin in the Sun; other roles, includ-

ing One Flew Over the Cuckoo's Nest, The Blacks, Blood
Knot, and Coriolanus, N.Y. Shakespeare Festival; TV
shows, East Side, West Side, The Edge of Night, and co-
star, Look Up and Live, CBS; assisted in establishing
Negro Ensemble Co.; first one-act plays produced,
Happy Ending and Day of Absence, fourteen months run,
St. Marks Playhouse, N.Y.C., Nov. 1965 - Nov. 1966.
Awards: Vernon Rice Drama Award for writing, and Obie
Award for acting (plays, Happy Ending and Day of Ab-
sence).
Publications: Two Plays, 1972.
Mailing Address: c/o Third Press, 444 Central Park West,
Suite 1-B, New York, N.Y. 10025.

WARREN, ALYCE (Mrs. Michael P. Pringle), Teacher
Born: Sampson County, N.C., 1940.
Education: B.A., Johnson C. Smith Univ., 1960.
Family: m. Capt. Michael P. Pringle.
Professional Experience: Tchr., N.C., Washington, D.C., and
Fla., 1960-69; lib. asst., Lib. of Congress, 1967-68;
reading specialist, pub. schs., Key West, Fla., 1968-69;
tchr., Korea, 1969-70.
Publications: Author, Into These Depths, 1968.
Mailing Address: 518 McRoy, Clinton, N.C. 28328.

WASHINGTON, JOSEPH REED, JR., Educator, Theologian
Born: Iowa City, Iowa, Oct. 30, 1930.
Education: Madison Central High, 1944-48; B.A., Univ. of
Wisconsin; B.D., Andover Newton Theological Sch.,
1954-57; Th.D., Boston Univ., 1958-61; D.D. (hon.), Univ.
of Vermont, 1969.
Family: m. Sophia Holland; children, Bryan Reed, David
Eugene.
Professional Experience: 1st lt., U.S. Army, 1952-54; assoc.
minister, Congregational West Newfield, Me.; minister,
Methodist Newfield, Me., 1956-57; assoc. Baptist minis-
ter, Brookline, Mass., 1957-58; assoc. Protestant Chap-
lain, Boston Univ., 1958-61; asst. prof. religion and
chaplain, Dillard Univ., 1961-63; asst. prof. religion and
chaplain, Dickinson Coll., 1963-66; assoc. prof. religion
and chaplain, Alburn Coll., 1966-69; prof. religion and
chaplain, Beloit Coll., 1969-70; prof. religion, Univ. of
Va., 1970-.
Memberships: Am. Academy of Religion; Am. Soc. of Christian
Ethics.
Publications: Contributed numerous articles to journals.
Author, The Politics of God, 1967; Black and White Power
Subreption, 1969; Marriage in Black and White, 1970.
Mailing Address: University of Virginia, Charlottesville, Va.
22901.

WASHINGTON, RAYMOND, Writer
Born: New Orleans, La., April 21, 1942.
Education: B.S., Southern Univ., New Orleans, 1971.
Family: m. Brenda; children, Damian, Ramona, Keisha.
Professional Experience: U.S. Navy, 1961-63; asst. lab. tech.,
    Tulane Univ., 1964-68; lab. tech., Tulane Med. Sch.,
    1968-69.
Awards: First prize winner in the Anthology of College Students
    Poetry Contest.
Publications: Contributed to journals. Author, Visions from
    the Ghetto, 1969.
Mailing Address: 3111 Rose Lane, New Orleans, La. 70114.

WEATHERLY, TOM
Publications: Maumau American Cantos, 1969; Natural Pro-
    cess, (with Ted Wilentz), 1971; Thumbprint, 1972.

WEAVER, FRANK B., School superintendent
Born: Tarboro, N.C., Aug. 16, 1927.
Education: B.S., Fayetteville State Univ., 1948; M.A., Colum-
    bia Univ., 1952; Ed. D., Pennsylvania State Univ., 1962.
Family: m. Queen L.; s. Frank Cornell.
Professional Experience: Tchr., Warren County Schs., 1948-
    50; prin., Edgecombe County Schs., 1950-62; state supr.,
    N.C. State Bd. of Ed., 1962-70; asst. dir., ibid., 1967-70;
    asst. supt., Durham City Schs., 1970-.
Memberships: Phi Delta Kappa; Omega Psi Phi; Bd. of Trust-
    ees, St. Augustine Coll.; Assn. of Governing Bds. of
    Univs. and Colls.
Awards: Plaques for meritorious service.
Publications: Practical Help for Meeting Needs of Slow Learn-
    ers, 1967.
Mailing Address: 900 Delanry Dr., Raleigh, N.C. 27610.

WEBB, MARGOT S., Teacher
Born: New York, N.Y., Mar. 18, 1914.
Education: B.A., Hunter Coll., 1940; M.A., Teachers Coll.,
    Columbia, 1948; post-graduate work, ibid.; Univ. of
    Ghana, 1969; m. William (deceased); children, Mrs.
    Marjorie Roachford, Mrs. Danielle Hesselman.
Professional Experience: Professional dancer; tchr., Bd. of
    Community Ed., N.Y.C., 1944-56; tchr., jr. high sch.,
    upper grades, Bd. of Ed., N.Y.C., 1944-70; columnist,
    L. I. Weekly Voice, "Afro-American Dimension."
Memberships: ASNLH; NAACP; Phi Delta Kappa; Caritas
    Guild, I.I.; Am. Heritage Soc.; Suffolk Afro-Am.
    Cooperative Lib.; African Am. Tchrs. Assn.

Awards: Council on Interracial Books for Children, Letters
from Uncle David: Underground Hero, 1970; Mary
McLeod Bethune Award, 1970.
Publications: Author, The Afro-American and U.S. Industry,
1969; Pioneers in Blues and Jazz, 1971.
Mailing Address: 11 Bayview Ave., West Amityville, N.Y.
11701.

WESLEY, CHARLES HARRIS, Organization executive (ret.),
Historian
Born: Louisville, Ky., Dec. 2, 1891.
Education: B.A., Fisk Univ., 1911; M.A., Yale, 1913; Ph.D.,
Harvard, 1925; D.D., Wilberforce Univ., 1938; LL.D.
(hon.), Allen Univ., 1932; LL.D. (hon.), Va. State Coll.,
1943; LL.D. (hon.), Morris Brown Univ., 1944; LL.D.
(hon.), Paul Quinn Coll.; LL.D. (hon.), Campbell Coll.,
1946; LL.D. (hon.), Morgan State Coll., 1961; LL.D.
(hon.), Univ. Cincinnati, 1964; LL.D. (hon.), Tuskegee
Inst., 1968; LL.D. (hon.), Howard Univ., 1970; LL.D.
(hon.), Western Univ., 1946; Ed.D. (hon.), Berea Univ.,
1971.
Family: m. Louise Johnson; children, Louise Johnson, Charlotte Harris.
Professional Experience: Instr. history, 1913-18; asst. prof.,
1918-19; assoc. prof., 1919-20; prof. and head, dept.
of history, 1921-42; dir., summer school, 1937; acting
dean, Coll. Liberal Arts, 1937-38; dean, Grad. Sch.,
Howard Univ., 1938-42; pres., Wilberforce Univ., 1942-
47; pres., Central State Coll., 1942-65; exec. dir.,
ASNLH, 1965-72.
Memberships: Alpha Phi Alpha, general pres., 1931-40, his-
torian, 1942-; grand prior, United Supreme Council,
Ancient Accepted Scottish Rite of Freemasony, Southern
Jurisdiction, U.S.A., Prince Hall Affiliation.
Awards: Founders Award, Alpha Phi Alpha Fraternity; Gold
Medal Award, United Supreme Council, Ancient Accepted
Scottish Rite of Freemasony, 33rd degree; Amistad
Award, American Missionary Association; Frontiers
Award; Certificate for Distinguished Service, The Links,
Inc.; Phi Beta Kappa; Recognition Award, American
Federation of Teachers.
Publications: Contributed numerous articles to journals, and
author of monographs. Author, most recent publica-
tions, History of the Prince Hall Grand Lodge of Free
and Accepted Masons of the State of Ohio, 1849-1960,
1961; Ohio Negroes in the Civil War, 1962; Neglected
History, 1965; History of Sigma Pi Phi, 1969.
Mailing Address: 1824 Taylor St. N.W., Washington, D.C.
20011.

WESLEY, RICHARD ERROL, Editor, Playwright
Born: Newark, N.J., July 11, 1945.
Education: B.F.A., Howard Univ., 1963-67.
Professional Experience: Passenger agent, United Air Lines,
Nov. 1967 - Sept. 1969; managing editor, Black Theatre.
Memberships: New Lafayette Theatre in Harlem.
Awards: Special playwriting, Samuel French Publishing Co.,
1965.
Publications: Contributed to journals. Author, plays: Put My
Dignity on 307, presented on WRC-TV's "Operation
Awareness," May 1967; The Streetcorner, produced at
Black Arts/West, Seattle, Wash., 1970; Headline News,
Black Theatre workshop, Harlem, 1970; Knock, Knock,
Who Dat, Theatre Black, Univ. of the Streets, N.Y.C.,
1970; Getting It Together, Theatre Black, Bed-Stuy Thea-
tre, Brooklyn, N.Y., 1971; Black Terror, W.A.S.T.S.A.,
Howard Univ., Washington, D.C., 1971.
Mailing Address: 96 Congress St., Newark, N.J. 07105.

WEST, DOROTHY
Publications: Living is Easy, 1948.

WHITE, EDGAR, B., Playwright
Born: British West Indies, April 4, 1947.
Education: B.A., New York Univ., 1968; Yale Univ.
Professional Experience: Orderly, Harlem Hospital.
Publications: Contributed to magazines and The Yardbird
Reader #1. Author, Underground: Four Plays, 1971;
Crucificado, 1971; Sati: The Rastifarian, 1973; Omar at
Christmas, 1973.
Mailing Address: 230 East 4 St., New York, N.Y. 10009.

WHITE, JOSEPH, Columnist, Radio announcer
Born: Philadelphia, Pa., Dec. 2, 1933.
Education: Southside High Sch., 1948-52.
Professional Experience: Assoc. dir., pub. information, United
Comm. Corp., Antipoverty Program, 1965-67; dir., pub.
information, Total Employment and Manpower Progress,
1967-68; newspaper columnist, Newark News, 1967-;
radio announcer, WNJR, Newark, 1969-.
Memberships: Pres., Local Antipoverty Neighborhood Bd.
Awards: John Hay Whitney Fellowship, 1963-64; N.Y. Council
of Arts Grant, 1969.
Publications: Author of short stories in the Liberator; plays,
Old Judge Mose Is Dead, TDR magazine; The Leader in
anthology, Black Fire.
Mailing Address: 74 Barclay St., Newark, N.J. 07103.

WIDEMAN, JOHN E., Writer, Educator
Born: Washington, D.C., June 14, 1941.
Education: B.A., Univ. of Pennsylvania, 1959-63; B. Phil., New
    Coll., Oxford, 1963-66.
Family: m. Judith Ann Goldman; children, Daniel Jerome,
    Jacob Edgar.
Professional Experience: Tchr. American lit., Howard Univ.,
    summer 1965; assoc. prof. English and dir., Afro-
    American Studies Program, Univ. of Pennsylvania,
    Sept. 1967-; TV book reviews.
Memberships: Rhodes Scholars Selection Com. (Penn.), Middle
    Atlantic States Finals; bd. of dirs., Am. Assn. of Rhodes-
    Scholars; Admissions Com., Univ. of Pennsylvania; Nat.
    Humanities Faculty.
Awards: Ben Franklin Scholar, Univ. of Pennsylvania, 1959-63;
    Rhodes Scholar, New Coll., Oxford, 1963-66; Kent Fel-
    lowship, Creative Writing, Univ. of Iowa, 1966-67;
    Thouron Fellowship, Creative Writing Prize.
Publications: Contributed to magazines and journals. Author,
    A Glance Away, 1967; Hurry Home, 1970; The Lynchers,
    1973.
Mailing Address: 4247 Regent Square, Philadelphia, Pa. 19104.

WIGGINS, JEFFERSON, Teacher
Born: Dothan, Ala., Feb. 22, 1929.
Education: B.A., Tennessee State Univ., 1946-48; Trenton
    State Coll., 1955; Jersey City State Coll., 1967-69.
Professional Experience: Capt., U.S. Army, 1942-46; 1950-
    54; tchr. dir. of student personnel, Southeast Ala. High
    Sch., 1948-50; correction officer, Dept. of Institutions
    and Agencies, N.J., 1955-57; tchr., pub. schs., Newark,
    N.J., 1960-66; dir., tutorial services, 1967; dir., Timothy
    J. Still Program, Upsala Coll.; community programs
    coordinator, East Orange, N.J., 1968-69; tchr., pub.
    schs., Newark, N.J., 1969-70.
Memberships: Alpha Phi Alpha; NAACP; CORE.
Publications: White Cross, Black Crucifixion, 1970.
Mailing Address: 376 William St., East Orange, N.J. 07018.

WILKINSON, DORIS Y., Educator
Born: Lexington, Ky., June 13, 1938.
Education: B.A., Univ. of Kentucky, 1954-58; M.A., Case
    Western Reserve Univ., 1959-60; Ph.D., ibid., 1963-66.
Professional Experience: Instr. sociology, Kent State Univ.,
    Kent, Ohio, 1961-63; asst. dir., Intergroup Relations
    Workshop, Case Western Reserve Univ., Cleveland,
    Ohio, summers 1963, 1965, 1966; instr. sociology, Car-
    negie Mellon Univ., Pittsburgh, Pa., 1966-67; asst.
    prof., Univ. of Kentucky, Lexington, Ky., 1967-70; cons.,

Nat. Commn. on the Causes and Prevention of Crime,
1968-69; assoc. prof., Macalester Coll., St. Paul, Minn.,
1970-.
Memberships: AAUP; Am. Sociol. Soc.; Ohio Valley Sociol.
Soc.
Awards: Woodrow Wilson Fellow, 1959-61; Delta Tau Kappa;
Outstanding Woman Faculty Member at Univ. of Kentucky,
1969.
Publications: Contributed to journals. Author, Workbook for
Introductory Sociology, 1968; editor, Black Revolt: The
Strategies of Protest, 1969.
Mailing Address: 61 Inner Dr., St. Paul, Minn. 55116.

WILLIAMS, DANIEL T., Archivist
Born: Miami, Fla., Sept. 20, 1937.
Education: B.S., West Va. State Coll., 1956; M.S.L.S., Univ.
of Ill.; certificate, archival adminstrn., American Univ.
Nat. Archives; Univ. of Chicago; Univ. of Mich.
Professional Experience: Serials libn., 1957-66; dir., pro-
fessional libraries and special collections, 1966-68;
archivist, Tuskegee Inst., 1968-.
Memberships: SAA; ASNLH; ALA; SLA; Special Libraries
Assn.; Alpha Phi Alpha; Alpha Phi Omega; Alabama
Council on Human Relations; Southern Regional Council;
Sigma Delta Pi.
Publications: Contributed to journals. Author, Eight Negro
Bibliographies, 1970.
Mailing Address: Tuskegee Institute, Tuskegee, Alabama
36088.

WILLIAMS, ETHEL L., Librarian
Born: Baltimore, Md., July 13, 1909.
Education: A.B., Howard Univ., 1930; B.S., Columbia Univ.;
Howard Univ., 1945.
Family: m. Louis J.; d., Carole Juanita (Mrs. George Jones).
Professional Experience: Searcher, Lib. of Congress; libn.,
1937-40; Sch. of Religion, Howard Univ., 1940-.
Memberships: NAACP; Am. Theological Lib. Assn.; D.C.
Lib. Assn.; Urban League.
Awards: Editor, A Biographical Directory of Negro Ministers,
1965, 1970; editor, A Cumulative Bibliography on Afro-
American Religion, 1970.
Mailing Address: Howard University, School of Religion Li-
brary, Washington, D.C. 20001.

WILLIAMS, G. BERNELL, Teacher (ret.)
Born: Bedford, Mich., Oct. 2, 1893.
Education: B.A., Mich. State, 1941.

Professional Experience: Health educator, insurance salesman,
supervisor, Boys Training School, Lansing, Mich.; sub-
stitute high sch. tchr., Lansing Sch. District.
Publications: Look Not Upon Me Because I Am Black, 1970.
Mailing Address: c/o Carlton Press, 84 Fifth Avenue, New
York, N.Y. 10011.

WILLIAMS, JAMYE COLEMAN, Educator
Born: Louisville, Ky., Dec. 15, 1918.
Education: B.A., Wilberforce Univ., 1934-38; M.A., Fisk Univ.,
1938-39; Ph.D., Ohio State Univ., 1953-59.
Family: m. McDonald; d. Donna Williams Selby.
Professional Experience: Instr. English, Edward Waters Coll.,
1939-40; asst. prof. English, Shorter Coll., 1940-42;
assoc. prof. English, Morris Brown Coll., 1956-58; prof.
speech, Tenn. State Univ., 1959-.
Memberships: Speech Assn. of Am.; Kappa Delta Pi; Nat. Col-
legiate Honors Council; AAUP; Am. Women in Radio and
Television; League of Women Voters; NAACP; Pi Kappa
Delta Forensic Soc.; Delta Sigma Theta; Links Inc.; Tenn.
Council on Human Relations; Tenn. Voters Council.
Awards: Tchr. of the Year, 1968, Tenn. State Univ.
Publications: Contributed to journals. Co-editor, The Negro
Speaks, 1970.
Mailing Address: Box 626, Tennessee State University, Nash-
ville, Tenn. 37203.

WILLIAMS, JOHN A., Author
Born: Jackson, Miss., Dec. 5, 1925.
Education: A.B., Syracuse Univ., 1946-50; ibid., 1950-51.
Family: m. Lorrain Issac; children, Gregory D., Dennis
A., Adam J.
Professional Experience: U.S. Navy, World War II; pub.
relations, Doug Johnson Associates, Syracuse, N.Y.,
1952-54; Arthur P. Jacobs Co.; CBS radio-TV special
events, Hollywood-New York, 1954-55; publicity dir.,
Comet Press Books, New York, 1955-56; editor and
pub.,Negro Market Newsletter, New York, 1956-57;
asst. to pub., Abelard-Schuman, New York, 1957-58;
dir. of information, American Com. on Africa, 1958;
European corr., Ebony, Jet, 1958-59; special events
announcer, WOV, New York, 1959; corr., Forum Service
News, Africa, 1964; corr., Newsweek, Africa, 1964-65;
lectr. writing, City Coll. of N.Y., 1968; lectr. Afro-
American lit., Coll. of the Virgin Islands, summer
1968; special assignments, reporter, script writer,
narrator, The History of the Negro People: Omowale-
the Child Returns Home, Nigeria, 1965; co-producer
and narrator, The Creative Person: Henry Roth, Spain,
1966; interviewer and panelist,Newsfront, Nat. Ed. Television, 1968.

Publications: Numerous magazine articles. Author, novels,
The Angry Ones, 1960; Night Song, 1961; Sissie, 1963;
The Man Who Cried I Am, 1967; Sons of Darkness,
Sons of Light, 1969; non-fiction, Africa, Her History,
Lands and People, 1963; The Protectors, 1964; This
Is My Country Too, 1965; The Most Native of Sons,
1970; The King God Didn't Save, 1970; editor, The Angry
Black, 1962; Beyond the Angry Black, 1967.
Mailing Address: 35 West 92 St., New York, N.Y. 10025.

WILLIAMS, McDONALD, Educator
Born: Pittsburgh, Pa., Nov. 13, 1917.
Education: A.B., Univ. of Pittsburgh, 1939; Litt. M., ibid.,
1942; Ph.D., Ohio State Univ., 1954.
Family: m. Jamye Coleman; d. Donna Williams Selby.
Professional Experience: Prof. English, Wilberforce Univ.,
1942-56; prof. English, Morris Brown Coll., 1956-58;
prof. English, Tennessee State Univ., 1958-.
Memberships: MLA; NCTE; NAACP; AAUP; NCHC; CCCC;
Alpha Phi Alpha.
Awards: Graduate asst., dept. of English, Ohio State Univ.,
1947-50.
Publications: Contributed to professional journals. Editor,
The Negro Speaks (with Jayme C. Williams), 1970.
Mailing Address: 20011 Jordan Dr., Nashville, Tenn. 37218.

WILLIAMS, SHERLEY ANNE
Publications: Give Birth to Brightness: A Thematic Study in
Neo-Black Literature, 1972.

WILLIE, CHARLES V., Educator
Born: Dallas, Tex., Oct. 8, 1927.
Education: A.B., Morehouse Coll., 1944-48; M.A., Atlanta
Univ., 1948-49; Ph.D., Syracuse Univ., 1949-57; L.H.D.
(hon.), Berkeley Divinity Sch., Yale Univ., 1972.
Family: m. Mary Sue Conklin; children, Sarah, Susannah,
Martin Charles, James Theodore.
Professional Experience: Instr., dept. of preventive medicine,
State Univ. of N.Y., 1955-60; vis. lectr., dept. of psy-
chiatry, Harvard Medical Sch., 1966-67; instr., asst.
prof., assoc. prof., prof., dept. of sociology, Syracuse
Univ., 1952-; chmn., dept. of sociology, Syracuse Univ.,
1967-71; vice pres., student affairs, Syracuse Univ.,
1972-; research dir., Washington, D.C., 1962-64.
Awards: Phi Beta Kappa, Morehouse, 1972.

Publications: Contributed to journals. Author, Church Action
in the World, 1969; The Family Life of Black People,
1970; Black Students at White Colleges, 1972; Racism
and Mental Health, 1973.
Mailing Address: Office of Student Affairs, Steele Hall, Syracuse University, Syracuse, N.Y.

WILLIS, JOHN RALPH, Educator
Born: Loraine, Ohio, Aug. 1, 1938.
Education: B.A., Univ. of Arizona; Ph.D., Univ. of London, Sch.
of Oriental and African Studies.
Professional Experience: Lectr. African history and Islamic
studies, Centre of West African Studies, Univ. of Bir-
mingham, United Kingdom, 1965-69; vis. prof. African
history, Univ. of Wisconsin, Madison, Wis.; prof. African
history, Univ. of Calif., Berkeley.
Memberships: Assn. of Marshall Scholars and Alumni.
Awards: Woodrow Wilson Fellow; John Hay Whitney Opportu-
nity Fellow; Marshall Scholar, Univ. of London.
Publications: Contributed to journals. Editor, Studies on the
History of Islam in West Africa, The Cultivators of
Islam, Vol. I.
Mailing Address: Dept. of History, University of California,
Berkeley, Calif. 94720.

WINDSOR, RUDOLPH R., Recreational therapist
Born: Long Branch, N.J., Mar. 28, 1935.
Education: Gratz Coll., 1963-67; Community Coll., 1967.
Family: m. Mary Ellen; children, Johnaton, Machshon, David,
Joel.
Professional Experience: Psychiatric technician, Veterans
Adminstn., 1958-60; psychiatric technician, Eastern Pa.
Psychiatric Institute, 1960-67; recreational therapist,
Hahnemann Community Mental Health Center, 1967-70.
Memberships: Aloth Emeth Israel; pres., The Federation of
the Black Israelites.
Publications: From Babylon to Timbuktu, 1969.
Mailing Address: 5111 Marion St., Philadelphia, Pa. 19144.

WINSTON, ERIC V.A., Administrative assistant, Urban Af-
fairs.
Born: Savannah, Ga., April 16, 1942.
Education: B.A., Morehouse Coll., 1959-64; M.S.L.S., Atlanta
Univ., 1964-65; Mich. State Univ., 1970-.
Professional Experience: Adult services libn., Brooklyn Pub.
Lib., 1965-66; U.S. Army, Vietnam, 1966-68; libn., U.S.
Military Academy, West Point, N.Y.; adminstrv. asst.
to the dir., Center for Urban Affairs, Michigan State
Univ., East Lansing.

Awards: U.S. Army Commendation Medal.
Publications: Editor, Directory of Urban Affairs Information and Research Centers, 1970; Library Service to the Disadvantaged, 1971.
Mailing Address: 5947 Bois Ile Dr., #51, Haslett, Mich. 48840.

WOFFORD, CHLOE ANTHONY, see MORRISON, TONI

WOOD, JOHANNA B. SMITH, Librarian, Educator
Born: Washington, D.C., Jan. 14, 1927.
Education: B.A. Fisk Univ., 1948; M.S.L.S., Case Western Reserve Univ., 1949; Univ. of Maryland.
Family: 2nd m. John Roland Wood; children, 1st m., Lynda Yvonne Morris, David Keith Morris.
Professional Experience: Readers advisor, Pub. Lib., Washington, D.C. 1949-53; adult asst., Detroit Public Lib., 1954-56; tchr. and libn., Crosman Elementary Sch., Detroit, Mich., 1957-60; libn., Ballow Senior High Sch., 1960-65; asst dir., sch. libraries, Washington, D.C., 1965-; vis. instr., District of Columbia Tchrs., spring 1973.
Memberships: ALA; Am. Assoc. Sch. Lib. (nat. com. treatment of minorities), 1968-70; Assn. Sch. Libns. (pres. 1963-65); D.C. lib. Assn. (membership com., 1966-69); Delta Kappa Gamma (chapter corresponding secretary, 1970-72).
Publications: Contributed to professional journals.
Mailing Address: Dept. of Libraries, Public Schools of the District of Columbia, Presidential Bldg. 609, 415 - 12 St. N.W., Washington, D.C. 20004.

WORTHY, WILLIAM
Publications: Black Power and the World Revolution, 1972.

WRIGHT, CHARLES
Publications: The Messenger, 1963; The Wig, A Mirror Image, 1963.

WRIGHT, DALE, SR., Press officer
Born: Pa.; July 19, 1925.
Education: B.A., Ohio State Univ., 1950.
Family: m. Dolores V. Grigsley; children, Dale, Jr., Kimberly Elaine.
Professional Experience: Reporter-editor, N.Y. Amsterdam News, 1950-52; assoc. editor, Ebony Magazine, 1952-59; staff writer, N.Y. World-Telegram & Sun, 1959-62; senior staff, NYS, Division for Human Rights, 1962-63;

public affairs officer, U.S., OEO, Washington, D.C., 1963-64; news editor, NBC News, Washington, D.C., 1964-65; press officer, N.Y.S. Narcotic Addiction Control Commn., 1966-; adjunct prof. journalism, Columbia Univ., summer 1969.
Memberships: Sigma Delta Chi; Bd. of Dir., USO, NYC; N.Y. Reporters Assn.; Public Relations Officer Soc.; Am. Newspaper Guild; Am. Writer's Guild.
Awards: Newspaper Guild of N.Y. Page One Prize for Crusading Journalism; Citizens Budget Commn. Press Medal; Pulitzer Prize Nominee for Nat. Reporting; Heywood Broun Memorial Award of Am. Newspaper Guild; Community Relations Award; N.Y.C. Patrolmen's Benevolent Assn.; Paul Tobenkin Memorial Award for best newswriting in the U.S. on racial intolerance and bigotry; Soc. of the Silurians Award for best pub. service newswriting in metropolitan N.Y. area.
Publications: Author, They Harvest Despair: The Migrant Farm Worker, 1965.
Mailing Address: 555 Kappock St., Riverdale, N.Y. 10463.

WRIGHT, JAY
Publications: Death as History, 1967; Homecoming Singer, 1971.

WRIGHT, NATHAN, JR., Educator, Clergyman
Born: Shreveport, La., 1923.
Education: B.D., Episcopal Theological Seminary; S.T.M., Harvard Univ.; Ed. M., State Tchrs. Coll., Boston; Ed.D., Harvard Graduate Sch. of Ed.
Family: m. Barbara Taylor; children.
Professional Experience: Rector, St. Cyprian's Episcopal Church; protestant chaplain, L.I. Hospital, Boston; exec. dir., Dept. of Urban Work, Episcopal Diocese, Newark, N.J.; chmn., Dept. of Afro-American Studies and prof. Urban Affairs, State Univ. of N.Y., Albany-; chmn., Nat. and Internat. Conferences on Black Power, 1967, 1968; cons., Compensatory Ed., staff asst., Mass. Ed. Comm.
Publications: Author, Black Power and Urban Unrest: The Creative Possibilities, 1967; Let's Face Racism, 1970; Let's Work Together, 1968; Ready to Riot, 1968; editor, What Black Educators Are Saying, 1970; editor, What Black Politicians Are Saying, 1972.
Mailing Address: Dept. of Afro-American Studies, State University of New York, Albany, N.Y. 12203.

WRIGHT, SARAH E. (Mrs. Joseph G. Kaye), Author
Born: Maryland.
Education: Howard Univ.; Cheyney State Tchrs. Coll.; Univ. of Pennsylvania; New School for Social Research.

Family: m. Joseph G. Kaye.
Memberships: Harlem Writers' Guild; Author's Guild of
    America; Authors' League.
Awards: N.Y. Times Outstanding Book Award, 1969; Read-
    ability Award in the State of Maryland.
Publications: Contributed to journals. Author, This Child'
    Gonna Live.
Mailing Address: 780 West End Ave., New York, N.Y. 10025.

YERBY, FRANK, Author
Born: Augusta, Ga., Sept. 5, 1916.
Education: A.B., Paine Coll., 1937; M.A., Fisk Univ., 1938;
    Univ. of Chicago.
Family: 2nd m. Bianquita Calle-Perez; children, Jacques
    Loring, Nikki Ethylyn, Faune Ellena, Jan Keith.
Professional Experience: Tchr., Florida A & M Coll., 1939-
    40; tchr., Southern Univ., 1940-41; war work, Ford
    Motor Co., Dearborn, Mich., 1942-44; Rangel Aircraft,
    Jamaica, N.Y., 1944-45.
Awards: O'Henry Memorial Award, 1944, for best short story.
Publications: Numerous books, including latest publications,
    An Odor of Sanctity, 1965; Goat Song, 1967; Judas, My
    Brother, 1968; Speak Now, 1969; The Dahomean, 1971.
Mailing Address: William Morris Agency, 1350 Ave. of Ameri-
    cas, New York, N.Y. 10020.

YETTE, SAMUEL F.
Publications: Choice: The Issue of Black Survival in America,
    1971.

YOUNG, AL, Educator, Author
Born: Ocean Springs, Miss., May 31, 1939.
Education: Univ. of Michigan, 1957-61; B.A., Univ. of Calif.,
    1968-69.
Family: m. Arlin Young; s. Michael James.
Professional Experience: Free-lance musician, 1958-64; disk
    jockey, radio station KJAZ, San Francisco, Calif., 1961-
    64; linguistic cons., Neighborhood Youth Corps, Berke-
    ley, Calif., 1967-69; Edward H. Jones Lectr. in Creative
    Writing, Stanford Univ., Stanford, Calif., 1969-; lectr.,
    including M.I.T., Rhode Island Sch. of Design, Univ. of
    Calif., Berkeley, Mills Coll., Univ. of New Mexico, Acad-
    emy of Am. Poets.
Memberships: AAUP; ACLU; Writer's Guild of America, West;
    Authors Guild; Authors League.
Awards: Wallace E. Stegner Creative Writing Fellowship,
    1966-67; Joseph Henry Jackson Award, 1969; Nat. Arts
    Council Awards, 1968, 1969; Calif. Assoc. of Tchrs. of
    English Special Award, 1973.

Publications: Contributed numerous works of fiction, poetry, articles, reviews to magazines, journals and anthologies. Author, Dancing, 1969; Snakes, 1970; The Song Turning Back Into Itself, 1971; Who is Angelina? (in press); Geography of the Near Past (in press).
Mailing Address: Creative Writing Center, Stanford University, Stanford, Calif. 94305.

YOUNG, ANDREW STURGEON NASH, (A.S. "Doc" Young), Author, Editor
Born: Oct. 29, 1924; B.S., Hampton Inst.
Professional Experience: Advertising manager and sports editor, Los Angeles Sentinel, 1944-46; sports editor, Cleveland Call-Post, 1947-48; dept. coordinator, writer department, editor, Los Angeles Sentinel, 1949-51; sports editor, Ebony, Jet, Hue magazines; managing editor, Jet, Tan, Copper magazines; dept. head, story and feature writer, Jet, Ebony, Hue, Tan, Copper and Negro Digest, 1951-58; asst. pub., Los Angeles Sentinel, 1963-66; sports editor, N.Y. Amsterdam News, 1965-66; editor, Los Angeles Sentinel, 1967-68; daily and weekly newspaper columnist, newspaper and magazine feature writer, 1968-70; exec. editor, Los Angeles Sentinel, 1970-; black pioneer, Hollywood studio publicist, 1957; sports commentator, Negro baseball, Cleveland, 1948; writer, radio commercials, 1950; numerous radio and TV appearances; edited and produced twenty special editions of newspapers.
Memberships: NAACP; Los Angeles Urban League; Nat. Sports Writers Assn.; Publicists Guild, Hollywood motion picture industry; adv. bd., Black Economic Union; Greater Los Angeles Press Club; Men of Tomorrow.
Awards: Including Los Angeles Urban League "Ghetto Award"; Best Columnist, NNPA; President's Anniversary Sports Award, NNPA, 1970; ALA Award for Negro Firsts in Sports, 1963.
Publications: Great Negro Baseball Stars, 1953; Negro Firsts in Sports, 1963; Sonny Liston: The Champ Nobody Wanted, 1963; Black Champions of the Gridiron: Leroy Keyes and O.J. Simpson, 1969; The Mets From Mobil: Tommie Agee and Cleon Jones, 1970; Black Athletes in the New Golden Age of Sports, 1970.
Mailing Address: 1800 North Highland Ave., Suite 616, Hollywood, Calif. 90028.

A List of Black Publishers

Afro-Am Publishing Company
1727 South Indiana Ave.
Chicago, Ill. 60616

Associated Publishers
1407 14 St., N.W.
Washington, D.C. 20005

Black Academy Press
135 University Ave.
Buffalo, N.Y. 14214

Black Star Publishers
8824 Finkle St.
Detroit, Mich.

Blyden Press
Box 621
Manhattanville Station
New York, N.Y.

Broadside Press
12651 Old Mill Pl.
Detroit, Mich. 48238

Buckingham Learning Corporation
76 Madison Ave.
New York, N.Y. 10016

Drum and Spear Press
1902 Belmont Rd., N.W.
Washington, D.C. 20009

DuSable Museum of African-
American History Press
3806 South Michigan Ave.
Chicago, Ill. 60653

East African Literature Bu-
reau
Headquarters of the Bureau
East African Community
Nairobi, Kenya

East African Publishing House
Uniafric House
Koinage St.
P.O. Box 30571
Nairobi, Kenya

Emerson Hall Publishers, Inc.
209 West 97 St.
New York, N.Y. 10025

Free Black Press
c/o DuSable Museum
3806 South Michigan Ave.
Chicago, Ill. 60653

Johnson Publishing Company,
Inc.
820 South Michigan Ave.
Chicago, Ill. 60616

New Beacon Books Ltd.
2 Albert Rd.
London, N4 3RW
United Kingdom
(Specializes in Caribbean writ-
ing. Distributes in England,
Europe, and the West In-
dies)

New Dimensions Publishing
Company
151 West 25 St.
New York, N.Y. 10001

New Pyramid Productions, Inc.
Box 835
Chester, Pa. 19016

Pan African Center for Education Materials, Inc.
Box 1632
Durham, N.C. 27702

The Third Press
444 Central Park West
Suite 1-B
New York, N.Y. 10025

Third World Press
7850 South Ellis Ave.
Chicago, Ill. 60619

Title Index

All books cited under authors' listings in the Biographies section are listed alphabetically by title in this index. Each title is followed by author's name and bibliographic information for its latest available edition. Thus, publication dates given here may differ from those in the biographical listings, which usually refer to a title's first publication. Bibliographic data is as complete as possible; for some titles that were privately published, full bibliographic data was unobtainable.

New York: Harcourt Brace Jovanovich.

The Afro-American: Selected Documents. Bracey, J.H., Jr. ed. (with August Meier and Elliott Rudwick). 1972. Boston: Allyn & Bacon.

Afro-American Writers. Turner, D.T., ed. 1970. New York: Appleton-Century Crofts.

Afro-American Writings: An Anthology of Prose and Poetry. Collier, E., ed. (with Richard A. Long). 1972. New York: New York University Press.

Afro-American Writing: An Anthology of Prose and Poetry. Long, R.A., ed. (with Eugenia Collier). 1972. New York: New York University Press.

Afro U.S.A.: A Reference Work on the Black Experience. Kaiser, E., ed. 1971. New York: The Bellwether Co.

Afrodisia. Joans, T. 1971. New York: Hill & Wang.

Ain't No Ambulances for No Nigguhs Tonight. Crouch, S. (with Julius Lester). 1972. New York: Richard W. Baron.

Airline Stewardess Handbook. Linde, S.M. 1968. New York: Crown Publishers, Inc.

All in the Family. Wamble, T. 1953. New York: New Voices.

An All-Negro Ticket in Baltimore. Fleming, G.J. 1960. New York: Holt, Rinehart & Winston.

All-Night Visitors. Major, C. 1969. New York: Grove Press.

Alpha, the Myths of Creation. Long, C.H. 1969. New York: Macmillan & Co.

The Amen Corner. Baldwin, J. 1968. New York: Dial Press.

America, Red, White, Black and Yellow. Fauset, A.H. (with Nella B. Bright). 1969. Philadelphia: Franklin Publishing Co.

America Sings. Thompson, J.W., ed. 1961. National Poetry Association.

American Daughter. Thompson, E.B. 1946. Chicago: University of Chicago Press.

The American Negro. Clemons, L. 1965. New York: McGraw-Hill.

American Negro Folklore. Brewer, J.M. 1968. Chicago: Quadrangle Books.

American Negro Short Stories. Clarke, J.H., ed. 1966. New York: Hill & Wang.

The American Revolution: Pages from a Negro Worker's Notebook. Boggs, J. 1963. New York: Monthly Review Press.

American Society and Black Revolution. Hercules, F. 1972. New York: Harcourt Brace Jovanovich.

The American Tradition of Violence. Pinkney, A. 1971. New York: Random House.

Analytical Study of Afro-American Culture. Neal, L., ed. 1972. New York: Random House.

Anchor Man. Jackson, J. 1947. New York: Dell Press.

And Then We Heard the Thunder. Killens, J.O. 1963. New York: Alfred G. Knopf.

Anger at Innocence. Smith, W.G. 1950. New York: Farrar, Straus & Young.

Angles. Cornish, S.J. 1971. Beanbag Press.

The Angry Black. Williams, J.A., ed. 1962. New York: Lancer Books.

The Angry Ones. Williams, J.A. 1960. Washington, D.C.: Ace Books.

Annie Allen. Brooks, G. 1949. New York: Harper & Row.

Anonymous Chansons in Two Manuscripts at El Escorial. Southern, E.J. Rome: The American Institute of Musicology.

Another Country. Baldwin, J. 1962. New York: Dial Press.

Another Kind of Rain. Barrax, G.W. 1970. Pittsburgh: University of Pittsburgh Press.

Anthology of the American Negro in the Theatre: A Critical Approach. Patterson, L., ed. 1968. New York: Publishers Co.

Apropos of Africa: Sentiments of Negro American Leaders on Africa from the 1800's to the 1950's. Hill, A.C., ed. 1969. New York: Humanities Press.

Apropos of Africa: Sentiments of Negro American Leaders on Africa from the 1800's to the 1950's. Kilson, M.L., ed. (with Adelaide C. Hill). 1969. New York: Humanities Press.

Arthur Ashe, Tennis Champion. Robinson, L. 1970. Garden City, N.Y.: Doubleday & Co.

Ask the Prophets. Cleveland, E.E. 1970. Washington, D.C.: Review and Herald Publishing Association.

At That Moment. Patterson, R.R. 1970. Detroit: Broadside Press.

The Aura and the Umbra. Addison, L. 1970. Detroit: Broadside Press.

The Autobiographical Writings of Booker T. Washington. Blassingame, J.W. (with Louis Harlan). 1972. Urbana, Ill.: University of Illinois Press.

The Autobiography of Malcolm X. Haley, A. 1965. New York: Grove Press.

Autobiography of Miss Jane Pittman. Gaines, E.J. 1971. New York: Dial Press.

Baba and the Flea. Scott, G.V. 1973. Philadelphia: J.B. Lippincott Co.

Babel-17. Delany, S.R. 1966. New York: Ace Books.

The Back Door. Royster, P.M. 1971. Chicago: Third World Press.

The Ballad of Beta-2. Delany, S.R. 1965. New York: Ace Books.

A Ballad of Remembrance. Hayden, R.E. 1963. London: Paul Breman Ltd.

Basic Statistics. Blackwell, D. 1969. New York: McGraw-Hill.

The Beach Umbrella. Colter, C. 1970. Iowa City, Iowa: University of Iowa Press.

The Bean Eaters. Brooks, G. 1960. New York: Harper & Row.

A Bear for the FBI. Van Peebles, M. 1968. New York: Trident Press.

Beetlecreek. Demby, W. 1950. New York: Holt, Rinehart & Winston.

Before the Darkness Covers
Us. Jackson, C.O. 1970.
Jericho, N.Y.: Exposition
Press.

Before the Mayflower. Bennett, L. 1969. Chicago:
Johnson Publishing Co.

Belly Song and Other Poems.
Knight, E. 1972. Detroit:
Broadside Press.

Beyond the Angry Black. Wil-
liams, J.A., ed. 1967.
New York: Cooper Square
Publishers.

Beyond the Blues. Thompson,
J.W., ed. 1962. London:
Hand and Flower Press.

Beyond the Burning: Life and
Death of the Ghetto.
Tucker, S. 1968. New
York: Association Press.

A Bibliographical Handbook on
the Life and Literary Ca-
reer of Langston Hughes.
Barksdale, R.K., ed. 1973.
Chicago: American Library
Assn.

A Bibliography of Black American Literature, 1746-1971.
Gant, L. 1972. Washing-
ton, D.C.: African Bibliographic Center.

Bibliography of Negro History
and Culture for Young
Readers. Jackson, M.M.,
Jr. (with others). 1969.
Pittsburgh, Pa.: University
of Pittsburgh Press.

The Big Black Fire. DeCoy,
R.H. 1969. Los Angeles:
Holloway House.

The Big Ditch: Story of the
Suez Canal. Linde, S.M.
1966. Burlington, Iowa:
National Research Bureau.

Bio-Bibliography of Countee
P. Cullen, 1903-1946.
Perry, M. 1970. West-
port, Conn.: Negro Uni-
versities Press.

A Biographical Directory of
Negro Ministers. Williams,
E.L., ed. 1965. Metuchen,
N.J.: Scarecrow Press.

A Biographical History of
Blacks in America. Toppin,
E.A. 1971. New York:
David McKay Co.

Birthday. Steptoe, J. 1972.
New York: Holt, Rinehart
& Winston.

A Birthday Present for
Katheryn Kenyatta. Rus-
sell, C.L. 1970. New
York: McGraw-Hill.

Black Abolitionists. Quarles,
B.A. 1969. Fair Lawn,
N.J.: Oxford University
Press.

Black Activism in the United
States. Brisbane, R.H.
(in press). Valley Forge,
Pa.: Judson Press.

The Black Aesthetic. Gayle,
A., Jr. 1971. Garden City,
N.Y.: Doubleday & Co.

Black Africa on the Move.
Lacy, L.A. 1969. New
York: Franklin Watts.

The Black Almanac. Hornsby,
A., ed. 1972. New York:
Richard W. Baron Co.

Black America and the World
Revolution. Lightfoot, C.M.
1970. New York: New Out-
look Publishers.

The Black American: A Documentary History. Quarles,
B.A. (with Leslie H. Fishel,
Jr.). 1970. New York: William Morrow.

Black American Literature:
Essays. Turner, D.T., ed.
1969. Columbus, Ohio:
Charles Merrill Publishing
Co.

Black American Literature:
Essays, Fiction, Poetry, and
Drama. Turner, D.T., ed.

1970. Columbus, Ohio:
Charles Merrill Publishing
Co.

Black American Literature:
Fiction. Turner, D.T., ed.
1969. Columbus, Ohio:
Charles Merrill Publishing
Co.

Black American Literature:
Poetry. Turner, D.T., ed.
1969. Columbus, Ohio:
Charles Merrill Publishing
Co.

The Black Americans. Lincoln,
C.E. 1969. New York: Ban-
tam Press.

Black Americans. Pinkney,
A. 1969. Englewood Cliffs,
N.J.: Prentice-Hall.

Black and Free. Skinner, T.
1968. Grand Rapids, Mich.:
Zondervan Publishing
House.

Black and White. Rutherford,
T. n.d. Detroit: Broadside
Press.

Black and White Nations.
Bryant, L.A. 1966. Crown
Bryant Publishing Co.

Black and White Power Subreption. Washington, J.R., Jr.
1969. Boston: Beacon
Press.

The Black Anglo Saxons.
Hare, N. 1970. New York:
Macmillan Co.

Black Arts: An Anthology of
Black Creations. Alhamisi,
A.A., ed. (with Harum
Kofi Wangara). 1969.
Detroit: Black Arts Publica-
tions.

Black Athletes in the New
Golden Age of Sports.
Young, A.S.N. (in process).

Black Awakening in Capitalist
America. Allen, R.L. 1969.
Garden City, N.Y.: Double-
day & Co.

Black Awareness: A Theology
of Hope. Jones, M.J. 1971.
Nashville, Tenn.: Abingdon
Press.

The Black Book. Ofari, E.
1969. Radical Education
Project.

Black Britannia: A History of
Blacks in Britain. Scobie,
E. 1972. Chicago: John-
son Publishing Co.

Black Business Enterprise:
Historical and Contempo-
rary Perspectives. Bailey,
R.W., ed. 1971. New York:
Basic Books.

Black Champions of the Gridiron: Leroy Keyes and O.J.
Simpson. Young, A.S.N.
1969. New York: Harcourt,
Brace & World.

The Black College: A Strategy
for Achieving Relevancy.
Le Melle, T.J. 1969. New
York: Praeger Publishers.

The Black Compendium.
Simmons, H.E. (in pro-
cess).

Black Crusaders in History,
Congress and Government.
Harris, J.H. 1972. Wash-
ington, D.C.: Associated
Publishers.

Black Culture. Simmons, G.M.,
ed. 1971. New York: Holt,
Rinehart & Winston.

Black Drama in America: An
Anthology. Turner, D.T.,
ed. 1971. New York: Faw-
cett World Library.

Black Drama Anthology. King,
W., Jr. (with Ron Milner).
1972. New York: Columbia
University Press.

Black Drama: The Story of the
American Negro in the The-
ater. Mitchell, L. 1970.
New York: Hawthorn Books.

The Black Experience in Children's Books. Baker, A.

1971. New York: New York Public Library.

Black Expression: Essays by and about Black Americans in the Creative Arts. Gayle, A., Jr. 1969. New York: Weybright and Talley.

Black Faces in High Places. Edmonds, H.G. 1971. New York: Harcourt Brace Jovanovich.

Black Families in White America. Billingsley, A. 1968. Englewood Cliffs, N.J.: Prentice-Hall.

The Black Family: Essays and Studies. Staples, R., ed. 1971. Belmont, Calif.: Wadsworth Publishing Co.

Black Feeling, Black Talk. Giovanni, N. 1968. Detroit: Broadside Press.

Black Feeling, Black Talk-Black Judgement. Giovanni, N. 1970. New York: William Morrow.

Black Fire. Neal, L., ed. (with Leroi Jones). 1971. New York: William Morrow.

Black Flowers. Monroe, R. 1970. Secaucus, N.J.: Lyle Stuart.

Black Folktales. Lester, J. 1969. New York: Richard W. Baron.

The Black Ghetto. Vernon, R. 1964, 1969. New York: Merit Publishers.

Black Gods of the Metropolis: Negro Religious Cults of the Urban North. Fauset, A.H. 1970. New York: Octagon Books.

The Black Hebrews. Jenkins, C. 1969. Detroit: Balar Publishers and Printers.

Black Historians: A Critique. Thorpe, E.E. 1971. New York: William Morrow.

Black History. Hodges, N.E. 1971. New York: Simon & Schuster.

Black Is a Panther Caged. Fabio, S.W.

Black Judgement. Giovanni, N. 1969. Detroit: Broadside Press.

The Black Librarian in America. Josey, E.J., ed. 1970. Metuchen, N.J.: Scarecrow Press.

Black Literature. Goddard, N.G. (in process). New York: McGraw-Hill.

Black Love, Black Hope. Long, D. 1971. Detroit: Broadside Press.

Black Madonna. Lawrence, H. n.d. Detroit: Broadside Press.

Black Magic Poetry. Baraka, I.A. (Le Roi Jones). 1969. Indianapolis, Ind.: Bobbs-Merrill.

The Black Man and the Promise of America. Nelson, S. (with Lettie J. Austin and Lewis H. Fenderson). 1970. Chicago: Scott-Foresman and Co.

The Black Man in the United States and the Promise of America. Austin, L.J. 1970. Chicago: Scott-Foresman & Co.

Black Man in the White House. Morrow, E.F. 1963. New York: Coward-McCann.

Black Man Listen. Marvin X. 1969. Detroit: Broadside Press.

Black Man's America. Booker, S.S. 1964. Englewood Cliffs, N.J.: Prentice-Hall.

Black Man's Burden. Killens, J.O. 1970. New York: Simon & Schuster.

Black Men in Chains. Nichols, C.H. 1970. Westport Conn.: Lawrence Hill.

Black Velvet. Hoagland, E. n.d. Detroit: Broadside Press.

Black Voices from Prison. Knight, E. 1969. New York: Pathfinder Press.

The Black Wine. Bennett, H. 1968. Garden City, N.Y.: Doubleday & Co.

The Black Woman. Bambara, T.C. 1970. New York: New American Library.

Black Woman. Higgins, C. 1970. New York: McCall Publishing Co.

The Black Woman in America. Staples, R. 1973. Chicago: Nelson-Hall Co.

Black Worker in the Deep South. Hudson, H. 1972. New York: International Publishers Co.

Black Writers of America: A Comprehensive Anthology. Barksdale, R.K., ed. (with Kenneth Kennamon). 1972. New York: Macmillan Co.

Blackness and the Adventure of Western Culture. Kent, G.E. 1972. Chicago: Third World Press.

Blacks in America: Then and Now. Toppin, E.A. 1969. Boston: Christian Science Publishing Society.

Blacks in Antiquity: Ethiopians in the Greco-Roman Experience. Snowden, F.M., Jr. 1970. Cambridge, Mass.: Harvard University Press.

Blackspirits. King, W., Jr. 1972. New York: Random House.

Blind Man with a Pistol. Himes, C. 1969. New York: William Morrow.

Blood of Strawberries. Van Dyke, H. 1969. New York: Farrar, Straus & Giroux.

Blood on the Forge. Attaway, W. 1941. Garden City, N.Y.: Doubleday & Co.

Bloodline. Gaines, E.J. 1968. New York: Dial Press.

Blues for an African Princess. Greenlee, S. 1970. Chicago: Third World Press.

Blues for Mama. Raven, J. n.d. Detroit: Broadside Press.

Blues for Mr. Charlie. Baldwin, J. 1964. New York: Dial Press.

Blueschild Baby. Cain, G. 1971. New York: McGraw-Hill.

The Bluest Eye. Morrison, T. 1970. New York: Holt, Rinehart & Winston.

Bondage, Freedom and Beyond. Gayle, A., Jr. 1971. Garden City, N.Y.: Doubleday & Co.

Book of Numbers. Pharr, R.D. 1969. Garden City, N.Y.: Doubleday & Co.

Booker T. Washington, Educator. Graham, S.L. 1955. New York: Julian Messner.

Books for Occupational Education Programs: A List for Community Colleges, Technical Institutes and Vocational Schools. Mapp, E.C. 1971. New York: R.R. Bowker.

Born Black. Parks, G.A.B. 1971. Philadelphia: J.B. Lippincott Co.

Born to Rebel. Mays, B.E. 1970. New York: Charles Scribner's Sons.

Boss Cat. Hunter, K. 1971. New York: Charles Scribner's Sons.

Brass Horses. Danner, M., ed. 1968. Richmond, Va.: Virginia Union University.

The Break of Dawn. Smith,
A.L., Jr. 1964. Philadel-
phia: Dorrance & Co.
Breaking the Chains of Bond-
age. Hodges, N.E. 1972.
New York: Simon & Schus-
ter.
A Bridge to Saying It Well.
Collier, E. (et al). 1970.
Washington, D.C.: Norvec
Co.
Bronzeville Boys and Girls.
Brooks, G. 1956. New
York: Harper & Row.
Brooklyn Story. Mathis, S.B.
1970. New York: Hill &
Wang.
Brown Girl, Brownstones.
Marshall, P. 1959. New
York: Random House.
Brown Rabbit. Morse, E.F.
1967. Chicago: Follett Pub-
lishing Co.
The Brown Thrush: An Anthol-
ogy of Verse by Negro Col-
lege Students. Gloster,
H.M., co-ed. 1935. Clare-
mont, Calif.: Lawson-Rob-
erts Publishing Co.
Bubbles. Greenfield, E. 1972.
Washington, D.C.: Drum &
Spear Press.
The Buxheum Organ Book.
Southern, E.J. 1963.
Brooklyn, N.Y.

Cables to Rage. Lorde, A.
1970. London: Paul Brenan.
Call Me Charlie. Jackson, J.
1945. New York: Harper &
Row.
Call of the Wild. Halliburton,
W.J., ed. Jack London.
1968. New York: McGraw-
Hill.
Calypso Song Book. Attaway,
W. 1957. New York: Mc-
Graw-Hill.
Captives of the Flame. Delany,
S.R. 1963. New York:
Ace Books.

Casebook #1: Uncle Spike, the
Negro History Detective.
Harris, M. 1967. Detroit:
Negro History Associates.
Cast the First Stone. Himes,
C. 1972. New York: New
American Library.
The Catacombs. Demby, W.
1965. New York: Pantheon
Books.
Catalogue of Books in the
Moorland Foundation Col-
lection. Porter, D.B., ed.
1939. Washington, D.C.:
Howard University Li-
brary.
Catalogue of the African Col-
lection at Howard Univer-
sity. Porter, D.B., ed.
1958. Washington, D.C.:
Howard University Press.
Catching the Editor's Eye.
Murphy, B. 1947. (pam-
phlet).
Catherine Carmier. Gaines,
E.J. 1964. New York:
Atheneum.
Cavalcade: Negro American
Writers from 1760 to the
Present. Davis, A.P., ed.
(with Saunders Redding).
1971. Boston: Houghton
Mifflin.
Celebration. Rivers, C.
1969. New York: Herder
& Herder, Inc.
The Centering Moment. Thur-
man, H. 1969. New York:
Harper & Row.
The Central Theme of Black
History. Thorpe, E.E.
1969. Durham, N.C.:
Printed by Seeman Print-
ery.
The Challenge of Blackness.
Bennett, L. 1972. Chi-
cago: Johnson Publishing
Co.
Charley Starts from Scratch.
Jackson, J. 1968. New
York: Dell Press.

Cheer the Lonesome Traveller. Lacy, L.A. 1970. New York: Dial Press.

Chicory: Young Voices from the Black Ghetto. Cornish, S.J., ed. (with W. Lucian). 1969. New York: Association Press.

Children of Bondage. Davis, A. (with John Dollard). 1940. Washington, D.C.: American Council on Education.

Children of the Storm. Billingsley, A. (with Jeanne Giovannoni). 1972. New York: Harcourt Brace Jovanovich.

A Choice of Weapons. Parks, G.A.B. 1966. New York: Harper & Row.

Choice: The Issue of Black Survival in America. Yette, S.F. 1971. New York: G.P.Putnam's Sons.

The Chosen Place, the Timeless People. Marshall, P. 1969. New York: Harcourt, Brace & World.

Christmas Gif'. Rollins, C. 1964. Chicago: Follett Publishing Co.

Church Action in the World. Willie, C.V. 1969. New York: Morehouse Barlow.

Churches and Voluntary Associations among Negroes in Chicago. Drake, S.C. 1940. Chicago: Works Projects Administration.

Cities Burning. Randall, D.F. 1968. New York: Broadside Press.

City of a Thousand Suns. Delany, S.R. 1965. New York: Ace Books.

Claude McKay: The Black Poet at War. Gayle, A., Jr. 1972. Detroit: Broadside Press.

Cold Black Preach. DeCoy, R.H. 1971. Los Angeles: Holloway House.

College Education as Personal Development. Noble, J. (with Margaret Barrow Fisher). 1960. Englewood Cliffs, N.J.: Prentice-Hall.

College Reading Skills. Austin, L.J. 1966. New York: Alfred G. Knopf.

Coming Home. Davis, G. 1972. New York: Random House.

Coming of Age in Mississippi. Moody, A. 1968. New York: Dial Press.

Coming Together: White Hate, Black Power and Sexual Hangups. Hernton, C.C. 1971. New York: Random House.

The Committed: White Activists in the Civil Rights Movement. Pinkney, A. 1968. New Haven, Conn.

Common Folk in an Uncommon Cause. Poinsett, A. 1972. Chicago: Liberty Baptist Church.

The Common People's Manifesto of World War II. Christian, M.B. 1948. New Orleans: Les Cemelles Society of Arts and Letters.

Comparative and International Librarianship: Essays on Themes and Problems. Jackson, M.M., Sr. 1970. Westport, Conn.: Greenwood Press.

A Comparative Study of Faith and Reason in Pascal, Bergson and James. Roberts, J.D., Sr. 1962. Santa Barbara, Calif.: Christopher Books.

Comparison of Two Methods of Teaching Remedial English to College Freshmen. Le Melle, T.J. 1963.

Louisiana: Grambling College, by Office of Education, Department of Health, Education and Welfare, U.S. Government.

Compensatory Education for the Disadvantaged: Programs and Practices— Preschool through College. Gordon, E.W. (Doxey A. Wilkerson). 1966. New York: College Entrance Examination.

The Complete Allergy Guide. Linde, S.M. 1971. New York: Simon & Schuster.

Concise Encyclopedia of the Civil War. Simmons, H.E. 1967. Cranbury, N.J.: A.S. Barnes.

Confrontation: Black and Whité. Bennett, L. 1965. Chicago: Johnson Publishing Co.

A Contemporary Approach to Nongraded Education. Lewis, J. 1969. West Nyack, N.Y.

Contemporary Black Leaders. Fax, E.C. 1970. New York: Dodd, Mead & Co.

Coretta: The Story of Mrs. Martin Luther King, Jr. Vivian, O. 1970. Philadelphia: Fortress Press.

Coronation of the King: Contributions by Duke Ellington to Black Culture. Walton, O.M. 1969. Berkeley, Calif.: University of California Press.

Cosmetic Surgery: What It Can Do for You. Linde, S.M. 1971. New York: Award Books.

The Cotillion. Killens, J.O. 1971. New York: Trident Press.

Cotton Comes to Harlem. Himes, C. 1970. New York: Dell Press.

Count on Me. Carter, M.K. 1970. New York: American Book Co.

Countee Cullen and the Negro Renaissance. Ferguson, B.E. 1966. New York: Dodd, Mead & Co.

Country Cousin. Kirkpatrick, O.A. 1941. Gleane Co., Ltd.

Craters of the Spirit: Studies in the Modern Novel. Scott, N.A., Jr. 1968. Cleveland: Corpus Books.

The Creative Encounter. Thurman, H. 1954. New York: Harper & Row.

The Crisis of the Negro Intellectual. Cruse, H.W. 1967. New York: William Morrow.

Crucificado. White, E.

Crusade for Justice: The Autobiography of Ida B. Wells. Duster, A.M.B., ed. 1970. Chicago: University of Chicago Press.

Cry Baby (City Limits Series). Halliburton, W.J. 1968. New York: McGraw-Hill.

The Cry for Freedom. Hale, F.W., Jr. 1970. New York: A.S. Barnes & Co.

Cry Like a Man. Mason, B.J. (in press).

A Cumulative Bibliography on Afro-American Religion. Williams, E.L., ed. 1970. Metuchen, N.J.: Scarecrow Press.

Curling. Boles, R. 1968. Boston: Houghton Mifflin.

Current Problems and Issues in Special Education. Jones, R.L., ed. 1971. Boston: Houghton Mifflin.

Curriculum for Understanding. Smythe, M.M., ed. (with Edgar S. Bley). 1965. Valley Stream, N.Y.: Union Free School District.

Daddy Was a Number Runner.
Meriwether, L.M. 1971.
Englewood Cliffs, N.J.:
Prentice-Hall.
The Dahomean. Yerby, F.
1972. New York: Dell
Press.
Damn Reading: A Case
Against Literacy. Hall,
J.C., Jr. 1969. New York:
Vantage Press.
The Dancers. Myers, W.D.
1972. New York: Parents
Magazine Press.
Dancers on the Shore. Kelley,
W.M. 1964. Garden City,
N.Y.: Doubleday & Co.
Dancing. Young, A. 1969.
New York: Corinth Books.
Danger Song. Rollins, B.
1967. Garden City, N.Y.:
Doubleday & Co.
Dark Ghetto. Clark, K.B.
1965. New York: Harper
& Row.
The Dark Messenger. Cooper,
C. 1962. Evanston, Ill.:
Regency Books, Inc.
Dark Symphony: Negro Litera-
ture in America. Emanuel,
J.A., ed. (with Theodore L.
Gross). 1968. New York:
Free Press.
Dark Waters. Gamble, Q.V.G.
1969. New Orleans: Free
Southern Theatre.
Davis-Eells Test of General
Intelligence. Davis, A.
(with Kenneth Eells). 1953.
Yonkers, N.Y.: World Book
Co.
Dear John, Dear Coltrane.
Harper, M.S. 1970. Pitts-
burgh, Pa.: University of
Pittsburgh Press.
Death as History. Wright, J.
1967. Millbrook, N.Y.:
Kriya Press.
The Death of White Sociology.
Ladner, J.A., ed. (in press).
New York: Random House.

Deep Is the Hunger. Thurman,
H. 1951. New York: Harper
& Row.
Deep River. Thurman, H.
1955. New York: Harper &
Row.
Deep South: A Social Anthropo-
logical Study of Caste and
Class. Davis, A. 1941.
Chicago: University of Chi-
cago Press.
Dem. Kelley, W.M.
Desegregation of Schools in
Missouri, 1954-1959.
Greene, L.J. n.d. Ther-
mofared by U.S. Commis-
sion of Civil Rights.
The Desertion of Man: A
Critique of Philosophy of
History. Thorpe, E.E.
1958. Baton Rouge, La.:
Orlieb Press.
Destination: Ashes. Jordan,
N. 1971. Chicago: Third
World Press.
Diary of a Harlem School-
teacher. Haskins, J.
1970. New York: Grove
Press.
Dices on Black Bones. Miller,
A.D. 1970. Boston: Hough-
ton Mifflin.
Dick Gregory's Political
Primer. J. R. McGraw.
1972. New York: Harper
& Row.
Dictionary of Afro-American
Slang. Major, C. 1970.
New York: International
Publishers.
Did You Feed My Cow? Bur-
roughs, M.T.G. 1969. Chi-
cago: Follett Publishing Co.
Die Nigger Die. Brown, H.R.
1970. New York: Dial
Press.
A Different Drummer. Kelley,
W.M. 1962. Garden City,
N.Y.: Doubleday & Co.

Differentiating the Teaching Staff. Lewis, J. 1971. West Nyack, N.Y.

Directory of Black Historians (in process). Harris, J.H. 1973. Washington, D.C.: Howard University Press.

A Directory of College and University Libraries in New York State. Josey, E. J. 1967. New York: State Education Department.

A Directory of Reference and Research Library Resources Systems. Josey, E.J., ed. 1969. New York: State Education Department.

Directory of Urban Affairs Information and Research Centers. Winston, E.V.A., ed. 1970. Metuchen, N.J.: Scarecrow Press.

The Disarmaments Illusion: The Movement for a Limitation of Armaments. Tate, M. 1942. New York: Macmillan Co.

Disaster and Organizational Changes. Anderson, W.A. 1969. Columbus, Ohio: Ohio State University Press.

Disciples of the Spirit. Thurman, H. 1963. New York: Harper & Row.

Disturbed About Man. Mays, B.E. 1969. Richmond, Va.: John Knox Press.

Do You See My Love for You Growing? Coombs, O. 1972. New York: Dodd, Mead & Co.

Dr. George Washington Carver, Scientist. Graham, S.L. (with George Lipscombe). 1944. New York: Julian Messner.

Documents on the Black Experience. Harding, V., ed. (with Wilfred Cartey and Hoyt Fuller). (in preparation).

Does the Secret Mind Whisper? Kaufman, B.G. 1960. San Francisco: City Lights.

Dog Ghosts and Other Texas Negro Folk Tales. Brewer, J.M. 1958. Austin, Tex.: University of Texas Press.

Don't Cry, Scream. Lee, D.L. 1969. Detroit: Broadside Press.

Don't Ride the Bus on Monday: The Rosa Parks Story. Meriwether, L.M. 1973. Englewood Cliffs, N.J.: Prentice-Hall.

Down the Line. Rustin, B. 1971. New York: Quadrangle Press.

The Dragon Takes a Wife. Myers, W.D. 1972. New York: Bobbs-Merrill.

Drive Suite. Carrington, H. 1970. Detroit: Broadside Press.

A Drop of Patience. Kelley, W.M. 1965. Garden City, N.Y.: Doubleday & Co.

The Drugstore Cat. Petry, A. 1949. New York: Thomas Y. Crowell.

Dry Victories. Jordan, J. 1972. New York: Holt, Rinehart & Winston.

Dunfords Travels Everywheres. Kelley, W.M. 1970. Garden City, N.Y.: Doubleday & Co.

Eagle in the Air. Robinson, R. 1969. New York: Crown Publishers.

Early Black American Poets. Robinson, W.H. 1969. Dubuque, Iowa: William Brown & Co.

Early Black American Prose (1734-1930). Robinson, W.H. 1970. Dubuque, Iowa: William Brown & Co.

Eastern Religions in the Electric Age. Coombs, O. (with

John H. Garebedian). 1972.
New York: Grosset & Dunlap.

Eat of Me, I Am the Savior.
Kemp, A. 1972. New York:
William Morrow.

Ebony Brass. Johnson, J.J.
1967. New York: William-
Frederick Press.

Ebony Rhythm. Murphy, B.,
ed. 1948. New York: Exposition Press.

Ed and Ted. Robinson, F.
1965. Jericho, N.Y.: Exposition Press.

Educating the Culturally Disadvantaged. Murray, W.I.
(with Crow and Smythe).
1966. New York: David
McKay Co.

Educating the Culturally Disadvantaged Child. Smythe,
H.H. (with L. Crow & W.
Murray). 1966. New York:
David McKay Co.

Education in Haiti. Cook, M.
1948. Washington, D.C.:
Federal Security Agency,
Office of Education.

EECCHHOOEESS. Pritchard,
N.H., II. 1971. New York:
New York University
Press.

Effective Expression. Hurst,
C.G., Jr. 1966. Columbus,
Ohio: Charles E. Merrill
Books.

Eight Negro Bibliographies.
Williams, D.T. 1970. New
York: Kraus Reprint.

The Einstein Intersection.
Delany, S.R. 1967. New
York: Ace Books.

Eldridge Cleaver. Cleaver, E.
1967. New York: Random
House.

Elfenbein Zahne (Ivory Tusks).
Allen, S. (Paul Vesy). 1956.
Heidelberg, Germany: W.
Rothe.

The Emancipation Proclamation. Franklin, J.H. 1963.
Garden City, N.Y.: Doubleday & Co.

Emergency Family First Aid
Guide. Linde, S.M. 1971.
New York: Cooper Publishing Co.

Empire Star. Delany, S.R.
1966. New York: Ace Books.

Ernest Hemingway. Scott,
N.A., Jr. 1965. Grand
Rapids, Mich: Erdmans.

Eros and Freedom in Southern Life and Thought.
Thorpe, E.E. 1967. Durham, N.C.: Seeman Printery.

Essays in Comparative and
International Librarianship: Essays on Themes and
Problems, 1970. Jackson,
M.M.N., Jr. 1970. Westport,
Conn.: Greenwood Press.

Every Man Heart Lay Down.
Graham, L. 1970. New
York: Thomas Y. Crowell.

Everywhere Is Yours. Cobb,
C. 1971. Chicago: Third
World Press.

Experimental Biochemistry
for Medical Science Students. Moses, H.A. 1970.
Ann Arbor, Mich.: Edwards
Brothers.

Experimental Chemistry.
Smith, L.S. 1964. Minneapolis, Minn.: Burgess
Publishing Co.

The Fall of the Towers.
Delany, S.R. 1972. New
York: Ace Books.

The Family Life of Black
People. Willie, C.V. 1970.
Columbus, Ohio: Charles
Merrill & Co.

Famous Negro American Series. Green, R.L., ed. 1970. Milwaukee, Wis.: Franklin Press.

Famous Negro Entertainers. Rollins, C. 1967. New York: Dodd, Mead & Co.

Famous Negro Poets. Rollins, C. 1965. New York: Dodd, Mead & Co.

Father of the Man. Davis, A. (with Robert J. Havighurst). 1947. Boston: Houghton Mifflin.

Festivals and Funerals. Cortez, J. 1971.

Fight on: Resistance to the African Slave Trade. Gant, L. (in press). Garden City, N.Y.: Doubleday & Co.

The Fire Next Time. Baldwin, J. 1963. New York: Dial Press.

The Fires That Burn in Heaven. Major, C. 1954. Coercion Press.

The First Cities. Lorde, A. 1968. New York: Poets Press.

First Fire. Thompson, J.W. 1970. London: Paul Breman Ltd.

Five French Negro Authors. Cook, M. 1943. Washington, D.C.: Associated Publishers.

Five Plays. Bullins, E. 1969. Indianapolis, Ind.: Bobbs-Merrill.

The Flagellants. Polite, C.H. 1967. New York: Farrar, Straus & Giroux.

The Flame in the Icebox. Morrison, C.T. 1968. Jericho, N.Y.: Exposition Press.

Folklore of Nova Scotia. Fauset, A.H. 1931. Millwood, N.Y.: Kraus Reprint.

The Folklore of the North Carolina Negro. Brewer, J.M. 1965. Chicago: Quadrangle Books.

Footfalls, They Speak of Dawns. LaGrone, C.O.

Footprints of a Dream. Thurman, H. 1959. New York: Harper & Row.

For Blacks Only. Tucker, S. 1971. Grand Rapids, Mich.: Eerdmans.

For Freedom: A Biographical Story of the American Negro. Fauset, A.H. 1927. Philadelphia: Franklin Publishing Co.

For Malcolm. Randall, D.F. (with Margaret J. Burroughs). 1967. Detroit: Broadside Press.

For My People. Walker, M.A. 1942. New Haven, Conn.: Yale University Press.

Four Black Revolutionary Plays. Baraka, I.A. (Le Roi Jones). 1969. Indianapolis, Ind.: Bobbs-Merrill.

The Fourteenth Cadillac. Jackson, J. 1972. Garden City, N.Y.: Doubleday & Co.

Frank Yerby, the Golden Debunker. Turner, D.T. (in press). Chicago: Third World Press.

Frederick Douglass. Quarles, B.A. 1948. Washington, D.C.: Associated Publishers.

Free at Last. Cleveland, E.E. 1970. Washington, D.C.: Review and Herald Publishing Association.

The Freedom Ship of Robert Small. Meriwether, L.M. 1971. Englewood Cliffs, N.J.: Prentice-Hall.

The Free-Lance Pallbearers. Reed, I. 1967. Garden City, N.Y.: 1967.

Free Southern Theater. Dent, T. (with Richard Schechner). 1969. New York: Bobbs-Merrill.

Friends Together: Ned and Ed. Robinson, F. 1967. Jericho, N.Y.: Exposition Press.

From Africa to the United States and Then. Goode, K. 1969. Glenview, Ill.: Scott, Foresman Co.

From Babylon to Timbuktu. Windsor, R.R. 1969. Jericho, N.Y.: Exposition Press.

From Puritanism to Platonism in Seventeenth Century England. Roberts, J.D., Sr. 1968. The Hague, Netherlands: Martinus Nijhoff.

From Slavery to Freedom: A History of American Negroes. Franklin, J.H. 1967. New York: Random House.

From the Back of the Bus. Gregory, D. 1964. New York: E.P.Dutton & Co.

From the Roots: Short Stories by Black Americans. James, C.L., ed. 1970. New York: Dodd, Mead & Co.

From the Windows of My Mind. Sharp, S. 1970.

Gamal Abdel Nasser: Son of the Nile. Graham, S.L. 1972. New York: Third Press.

Garvey: Story of a Pioneer Black Nationalist. Fax, E.C. 1972. New York: Dodd, Mead & Co.

The Garveys: The Human Side of Two Black Nationalists. Hodges, N.E. (in press). New York: Praeger Publishers.

Gemini. Giovanni, N. 1972. New York: Bobbs-Merrill.

Generations. Cornish, S.J. 1971. Boston: Beacon Press.

Geography of the Near Past. Young, A. (in process).

George W. Cable. Butcher, P. 1962. New York: Twayne Publishers.

George W. Cable: The Northampton Years. Butcher, P. 1959. New York: Columbia University Press.

Get Caught: A Photographic Essay. Patterson, R.R. 1964. New York: Verge Publications.

Ghetto Rebellion to Black Liberation. Lightfoot, C.M. 1968. New York: International Publishing Co.

Ghetto Sketches. Hawkins, O. 1972. Los Angeles: Holloway House.

Ghetto Waif. Felton, B. n.d. Detroit: Broadside Press.

Giant in the Earth. Boddie, C.E. 1944. Berne, Ind.: Berne Witness Co.

Giovanni's Room. Baldwin, J. 1956. New York: Dial Press.

Give Birth to Brightness: A Thematic Study in Neo-Black Literature. Williams, S.A. 1972. New York: Dial Press.

A Glance Away. Wideman, J.E. 1967. New York: Harcourt, Brace & World.

Go South to Sorrow. Rowan, C.T. 1957. New York: Random House.

Go Tell It on the Mountain. Baldwin, J. 1953. New York: Dial Press.

Goat Song. Yerby, F. 1967. New York: Dial Press.

God Bless the Child. Hunter, K. 1964. New York: Charles Scribner's Sons.

God in the Inner City. O'Donnell, L. 1970. New York: Exposition Press.

God's Bad Boys. Boddie, C.E. 1972. Valley Forge, Pa.: Judson Press.

Goin Down Slow. Rollins, B. (in press). New York: Doubleday & Co.

Going to Meet the Man. Baldwin, J. 1965. New York: Dial Press.

The Golden Lynx. Baker, A. 1960. Philadelphia: J.B. Lippincott Co.

The Golden Sardine. Kaufman, B.G. 1966. San Francisco: City Lights.

Gordon Parks: A Poet and His Camera. Parks, G.A.B. 1968. New York: Viking Press.

Gordon Parks: Whispers of Intimate Things. Parks, G.A.B. 1971. New York: Viking Press.

Gorilla, My Love. Bambara, T.C. 1972. New York: Random House.

Grains of Pepper. Haskett, E.R. 1967. New York: John Day Co.

The Grand Parade. Mayfield, J. 1967. New York: Vanguard Press.

Great Gitting up Morning: A Biography of Denmark Vesey. Killens, J.O. 1972. Garden City, N.Y.: Doubleday & Co.

Great Negro Baseball Stars. Young, A.S.N. 1953. New York: Barnes & Noble.

Great Negroes Past and Present. Adams, R., ed. 1963-1964. Chicago: Afro-American Publishers.

The Growing Edge. Thurman, H. 1956. New York: Harper & Row.

Guerilla Warfare. Alhamisi, A.A. 1970. Detroit: Broadside Press.

Guests in the Promised Land. Hunter, K. 1973. New York: Charles Scribner's Sons.

A Guide Through American Literature. Nichols, C.H. 1970. Dortmund, Lambert-Lensing Publishers.

A Guide to African Reference Books. Aman, M.M. (in press).

A Guide to Vocational Rehabilitation. Peters, J.S. 1967. New York: American Press.

Haitian American Anthology. Cook, M., ed. 1944. Port-au-Prince, Haiti: Imprimerie de l'état.

Half Black, Half Blacker. Plump, S.D. 1970. Chicago: Third World Press.

Harlem Renaissance. Huggins, N.I. 1971. New York: Oxford University Press.

Harriet Tubman: Conductor on the Underground Railroad. Petry, A. 1955. New York: Thomas Y. Crowell.

Hawaii: Reciprocity or Annexation. Tate, M. 1968. East Linsey, Mich.: Michigan State University Press.

Healing Intelligence. Edwards, H. 1971. New York: Taplinger Publishing Co.

Heart Attacks That Aren't. Linde, S.M. 1966. Burlington, Iowa: National Research Bureau.

The Heist (City Limits Series). Halliburton, W.J. 1968. New York: McGraw-Hill.

Heretofore. Atkins, R. 1968. London: Paul Breman Ltd.

The Hero and the Blues. Murray, A. 1973. Columbia, Mo.: University of Missouri Press.

Hezekiah Horton. Tarry, E. 1942. New York: Viking Press.

Hidden Lookout (Skyline Series). Brown, V.S. 1965. New York: McGraw-Hill.

High Ground. Christian, M.B. 1958. New Orleans: Southern Publishing Co.

The Hippodrome. Colter, C. 1973. Chicago: Swallow Press.

His Day Is Marching On: A Memoir of W.E.B. DuBois. Graham. S.L. 1971. Philadelphia: J.B. Lippincott Co.

History Is Your Own Heartbeat. Harper, M.S. 1971. Urbana, Ill.: University of Illinois Press.

The History of Religions: Essays in Understanding. Long, C.H., ed. (with Joseph Kilagawa). 1967. Chicago: University of Chicago Press.

History of Sigma Pi Phi. Wesley, C.H. 1969. Houston, Tex.: Foundation Publishers.

A History of the Black Novel (in process). Gayle, A., Jr.

History of the Chicago Urban League. Strickland, A.E. 1966. Urbana, Ill.: University of Illinois Press.

History of the Prince Hall Grand Lodge of Free and Accepted Masons of the State of Ohio, 1849-1960. Wesley, C.H. 1961. Washington, D.C.: Associated Publishers.

The Hit. Mayfield, J. 1957. New York: Vanguard Press.

Hog Butcher. Fair, R. 1966. New York: Harcourt, Brace & World.

Holy Ghosts. Alhamisi, A.A. 1972. Detroit: Broadside Press.

Homecoming. Sanchez, S. 1969. Detroit: Broadside Press.

Homecoming Singer. Wright, J. 1971. New York: Corinth Books.

Home Is Where the Soul Is. Eckels, J. (Askia Akhnaton). 1969. Detroit: Broadside Press.

Hoodoo Hollerin' Bebop Ghosts. Neal, L. 1971. New York: Random House.

Hopes Tied Up in Promises. Thompson, J.E. 1969. Philadelphia: Dorrance & Co.

Hot Day Hot Night. Himes, C. 1970. Garden City, N.Y.: Doubleday & Co.

The House on Corbett Street. Johnson, W.M. 1967. William-Frederick Press.

How Black Is the Gospel? Skinner, T. 1970. Philadelphia: J.B. Lippincott Co.

How I Wrote Jubilee. Walker, M.A. 1972. Chicago, Ill.: Third World Press.

How to Wear Colors with Emphasis on Dark Skin. Edwards, C.S. 1965. Minneapolis, Minn.: Burgess Publishing Co.

Howard Street. Heard, N.C. 1968. New York: Dial Press.

Hue and Cry. McPherson, J.A. 1969. Boston: Little, Brown & Co.

The Huge Steel Bolt. Thornhill, L.O. 1966. New York: Vantage Press.

Human Juices. Major, C.
1965. Coercion Press.
Hurry Home. Wideman, J.E.
1970. New York: Harcourt,
Brace & World.

I Always Wanted to Be Some-
body. Darden, A. 1958.
New York: Harper & Row.
I Am a Black Woman. Evans,
M. 1970. New York: Wil-
liam Morrow.
I Have a Dream: The Life and
Times of Martin Luther
King, Jr. Davis, L.G. 1969.
Salisbury, N.C.
I Heard a Young Man Saying.
Fields, J. n.d. Detroit:
Broadside Press.
I Know Why the Caged Bird
Sings. Angelou, M. 1969.
New York: Random House.
I Love Raps. Rogers, C.M.
1969. Chicago: Third World
Press.
I, Momolu. Graham, L. 1966.
New York: Thomas Y.
Crowell.
I Want a Black Doll. Hercules,
F. 1967. New York: Simon
& Schuster.
If He Hollers Let Him Go.
Himes, C. 1971. New York:
New American Library.
If Not Now, When: The Many
Meanings of Black Power.
Greenidge, E. 1969. New
York: Delacorte Press.
Ik Ben de Nievwe Neger.
Thompson, J.W., ed. 1965.
Holland: Bert Bakker.
Illustrated History of Black
Americans. Franklin, J.H.
1970. New York: Time-
Life.
Images of the Negro in Amer-
ica. Turner, D.T., ed.
1965. Boston: Heath & Co.
Impressions in Asphalt: Images
of Urban America. Collier,

E. (with Ruthe T. Sheffrey).
1969. New York: Charles
Scribner's Sons.
Impressions of African Art.
Danner, M. 1961. Detroit:
Broadside Press.
In a Minor Chord: Three Afro-
American Writers and Their
Search for Identity. Turner,
D.T. 1971. Carbondale,
Ill.: Southern Illinois Uni-
versity Press.
In Defense of the People's
Black and White History
and Culture. Kaiser, E.
1970. New York: Freedom-
ways Magazine.
In Essence: Epigrams and
Quotable Quotes in Race
Relations from the Writings
of Dr. Dan W. Dobson.
Pittman, S.N. 1968. New
York: Vantage Press.
In Love. Parks, G.A.B. 1971.
Philadelphia: J.B. Lippin-
cott Co.
In Search of America. Blas-
singame, J.W., ed. (with
David Fowler, Eugene Levy,
and Jacqueline Haywood).
1972. New York: Holt,
Rinehart & Winston.
In the Cage: Eyewitness Ac-
counts of the Freed Negro
in Southern Society, 1877-
1929. Hornsby, A., ed.
1971. Chicago: Quadran-
gle Books.
In the Mecca. Brooks, G.
1968. New York: Harper
& Row.
Intelligence and Cultural Differences. Davis, A. (with
Kenneth Eells, R.J. Havighurst, and Ralph Tyler).
1951. Chicago: University
of Chicago Press.
Intensive English Conversation. Smythe, M.M. (with
Alan B. Howes). 1953.
Tokyo: Kairyudo.

Legends of the Saints. Petry, A. 1970. New York: Thomas Y. Crowell.

The Legislation of Morality. Duster, T. 1969. New York: Free Press.

Les Danses D'Haiti. Dunham, K. 1950. Paris: Fasquelle Editeurs.

Let Me Breathe Thunder. Attaway, W. 1939. Garden City, N.Y.: Doubleday & Co.

Let's Face Racism. Wright, N., Jr. 1970. Appleton, Wis.: Nelson Publishing Co.

Let's Go Somewhere. Latimore, J. (Amini, Johari). n.d. Detroit: Broadside Press.

Let's Work Together. Wright, N., Jr. 1968. New York: Hawthorne Publishing Co.

Letter from a Wife. Reese, C. n.d. Detroit: Broadside Press.

Letters to a Black Boy. Teague, B. 1968. New York: Walker & Co.

Liberation and Reconciliation. Roberts, J.D., Sr. 1971. Philadelphia, Pa.: Westminister Press.

Library Service to the Disadvantaged. Winston, E.V.A., ed. 1971. Metuchen, N.J.: Scarecrow Press.

Life and Loves of Mister Jiveass Nigger. Brown, C. 1969. New York: Farrar, Straus & Giroux.

Like One of the Family: Conversations from a Domestic's Life. Childress, A. 1956. Brooklyn, N.Y.: Independence Publishers.

Lincoln and the Negro. Quarles, B.A. 1962. Fair Lawn, N.J.: Oxford University Press.

The Lion and the Archer. Hayden, R.E. (with Myron O'Higgins). 1948. Nashville, Tenn.: Hemphill Press.

The Lives of Great American Chiefs. Clarke, J.H. 1958. Pittsburgh: Pittsburgh Courier Publishing Co.

Living Black American Authors: A Biographical Directory. Shockley, A.A., ed. (with Sue P. Chandler). 1973. New York: R.R. Bowker.

Living is Easy. West, D. 1948. Boston: Houghton Mifflin.

Lonely Crusader. Himes, C. 1947. New York: Alfred Knopf.

The Lonesome Road. Redding, J.S. 1958. Garden City, N.Y.: Doubleday & Co.

Long Black Song: Essays in Black American Literature and Culture. Baker, H.A., Jr. 1972. Charlottesville, Va.: University Press of Virginia.

Long Day in November. Gaines, E.J. 1971. New York: Dial Press.

Long Journey Home: Stories from Black History. Lester, J. 1972. New York: Dial Press.

The Long Night. Mayfield, J. 1958. New York: Vanguard Press.

Long Shadow of Little Rock: A Memoir. Bates, D. 1962. New York: David McKay Co.

Long Struggle for Black Power. Peeks, E. 1971. New York: Charles Scribner's & Sons.

Look Not upon Me Because I am Black. Williams, G.B. 1970. New York: Carleton Press.

The Messenger. Wright, C. 1963. New York: Farrar, Straus & Giroux.

The Mets from Mobile: Tommie Agee and Cleon Jones. Young, A.S.N. 1970. New York: Harcourt, Brace & World.

Militant Black Writer in Africa and the United States. Cook, M. (with Stephen E. Henderson). 1969. Madison, Wiscon.: University of Wisconsin Press.

The Mind of the Negro: An Intellectual History of Afro-Americans. Thorpe, E.E. 1961. Westport, Conn.: Negro Universities Press.

Minorities and Majorities: A Syllabus of United States History for Secondary Schools. Halliburton, W.J., ed. (with William L. Katz). 1970. New York: Arno Press.

A Mirror a Soul. Fabio, S.W. 1969. San Francisco, Calif.: J. Richardson.

Miss Muriel and Other Stories. Petry, A. 1971. New York: Houghton Mifflin & Co.

The Modern Vision of Death. Scott, N.A., Jr. 1967. Richmond, Va.: John Knox Press.

Modern Woman's Medical Dictionary. Linde, S.M. 1968. New York: Bantam Books.

Moja Means One: The Swahilli Counting Book. Feelings, M. 1971. New York: Dial Press.

Mojo Hand. Phillips, J. 1966. New York: Trident Press.

More to Remember. Randall, D.F. 1970. Chicago: Third World Press.

The Morning Duke Ellington Praised the Lord. Dodson, O.V. (in process).

The Most Native of Sons. Williams, J.A. 1970. Garden City, N.Y.: Doubleday & Co.

Moving Deep. Stephany, (Fuller). n.d. Detroit: Broadside Press.

Multimedia Materials for Afro-American Studies. Johnson, H.A. 1971. New York: R.R. Bowker.

Music: Black, White and Blue. Walton, O.M. 1972. New York: William Morrow & Co.

The Music of Black Americans: A History. Southern, E.J. 1970. New York: W.W. Norton & Co.

Must Walls Divide? Harding, V. 1965. New York: Friendship Press.

My Blackness is the Beauty of This Land. Jeffers, L. 1970. Detroit: Broadside Press.

My Dog Rinty. Tarry, E. (with Marie H. Ets). 1946. New York: Viking Press.

My Face is Black. Lincoln, C.E. 1964. Boston: Beacon Press.

My House: Poems. Giovanni, N. 1972. New York: William Morrow.

My Life, My Country, My World: College Readings for Modern Living. Gloster, H.M., ed. 1952. New York: Prentice-Hall.

My Life with Martin Luther King, Jr. King, C.S. 1969. New York: Holt Rinehart & Winston.

My Main Mother. Beckham,
B.E. 1971. New York:
Walker and Co.

My Story in Black and White.
Thomas, J.O. 1967. Jeri-
cho, N.Y.: Exposition Press.

The Myth of Black Capitalism.
Ofari, E. 1970. New York:
Monthly Review Press.

Myths about Malcolm X: Two
Views. Cleage, A.B., Jr.
(with George Brietman)
1971. Pathfinder Press.

Myths and Symbols: Essays in
Honor of Mircea Eliade.
Long, C.H., ed. (with Joseph
Kilagawa). 1969. Chicago:
University of Chicago
Press.

The Nail and Maefictum. Atkins, R. 1971. Cleveland,
Ohio: Free Lance Press.

Naja the Snake and Mangus the
Mongoose. Kirkpatrick,
O.A. 1970. Garden City,
N.Y.: Doubleday & Co.

Naked Soul of Iceberg Slim.
Beck, R. (Iceberg Slim).
1971. Los Angeles: Hollo-
way House.

The Narrows. Petry, A. 1953.
Boston: Houghton Mifflin &
Co.

Natural Process. Weatherly,
T. (with Ted Wilentz). 1971.
New York: Hill & Wang.

Negative Capability: Studies in
the New Literature and the
Religious Situation. Scott,
N.A., Jr. 1969. New Haven,
Conn.: Yale University
Press.

Neglected History. Wesley,
C.H. 1965. Wilberforce,
Oh.: Central State College
Press.

Negrito: A Volume of Negro
Dialect Poems. Brewer,
J.M. 1933. San Antonio,
Tex.: Naylor Printing Co.

Negritude: Essays and Stories.
Long, R.A., ed. (with Albert
H. Berrian). 1967. Hamp-
ton, Va.: Hampton Institute
Press.

The Negro. Redding, J.S.
1967. Washington, D.C.:
Potomac Books.

The Negro Almanac. Kaiser,
E., ed. 1971. New York:
The Bellwether Co.

The Negro and Fusion Politics
in North Carolina. Ed-
monds, H.G. 1951. Chapel
Hill, N.C.: University of
North Carolina Press.

The Negro Caravan. Davis,
A.P., ed. (with Sterling
Brown and Ulysses Lee).
1969. New York: Arno
Press.

Negro Firsts in Sports.
Young, A.S.N. 1963. Chi-
cago: Johnson Publishing
Co.

Negro Folktales from Texas.
Brewer, J.M. 1942. St.
Louis: Webster Publish-
ing Co.

Negro Historians in the United
States. Thorpe, E.E.
1958. Baton Rouge, La.:
Fraternal Press.

A Negro History Tour of Manhattan. Harris, M. 1968.
Westport, Conn.: Green-
wood Publishing Corp.

The Negro in American Cities.
Porter, D.B., ed. 1967.
Washington, D.C.: Howard
University Press.

The Negro in American Culture. Butcher, M.J. 1956.
New York: Alfred Knopf.

The Negro in American Fic-
tion. Brown, S. 1937.
Washington, D.C.: The
Associates in Negro Folk
Education.

comp. 1969. New York: Bantam Books.

New York the Nine Million and Other Poems. Martin, H.W. 1969.

Nigger. Gregory, D. 1964. New York: E.P. Dutton & Co.

Nigger Bible. DeCoy, R.H. 1967. Los Angeles: Holloway House.

The Nigger Factory. Scott-Heron, G. 1972. New York: Dial Press.

Night Comes Softly: Anthology of Black Female Voices. Giovanni, N. 1970. New York: TomNik Publishers.

Night Song. Williams, J.A. 1961. New York: Farrar, Straus & Giroux.

Nineteen Necromancers from Now. Reed, I. 1970. Garden City, N.Y.: Doubleday & Co.

No Day of Triumph. Redding, J.S. 1942. New York: Harcourt Brace

No More Lies. Gregory, D. 1971. New York: Harper & Row.

No Name in the Street. Baldwin, J. 1972. New York: Dial Press.

No Place to Be Somebody: A Black Comedy in Three Acts. Gordone, C. 1969. New York: Bobbs-Merrill.

Nommo: A Modern Anthology of Black African and Black American Literature. Robinson, W.H. 1971. New York: Macmillan & Co.

North American Negro Poets: A Bibliographical Checklist of Their Writings, 1760-1944. Porter, D.B., ed. 1945. Hattiesburg, Miss.: The Book Farm.

North Town. Graham, L. 1965. New York: Thomas Y. Crowell.

Notes of a Native Son. Baldwin, J. 1955. Boston: Beacon Press.

Notes of a Processed Brother. Reeves, D. 1971. New York: Pantheon Books.

Nothing Personal. Baldwin, J. 1964. New York: Atheneum Publishers.

Nova. Delany, S.R. 1968. Garden City, N.Y.: Doubleday & Co.

Oak and Ivy: A Biography of Paul Laurence Dunbar. Gayle, A. 1971. Garden City, N.Y.: Doubleday & Co.

Objects. Atkins, R. 1963. Eureka, Calif.: Hearse Press.

Objects 2. Atkins, R. 1963. Cleveland, Ohio: Renegade Press.

An Odor of Sanctity. Yerby, F. 1965. New York: Dell Press.

Of Love and Dust. Gaines, E.J. 1967. New York: Dial Press.

Ohio Negroes in the Civil War. Wesley, C.H. 1962. Columbus, Oh.: Ohio State University Press.

Okelo and Akelo. Carter, M.K. 1967. Uganda: Longmans.

The Old South: A Psychohistory. Thorpe, E.E. 1972. Durham, N.C.: Seeman Printery.

Omar at Christmas. White, E. 1973. New York: Lothrop, Lee & Shepherd.

The Omni-Americans. Murray, A. 1970. New York: Outerbridge Lazard, Inc.

On Being Negro in America. Redding, J.S. 1952. Indianapolis, Ind.: Bobbs-Merrill.

On to Freedom. Carter, M.K. 1970. New York: Hill & Wang.

Once. Walker, A. 1968. New York: Harcourt Brace & World.

Once upon a Time. Baker, A., ed. 1964. New York: Library Association.

One and the Many. Madgett, N.L. 1956. Jericho, N.Y.: Exposition.

The Oratory of Negro Leaders: 1900-1968. Boulware, M.H. 1969. Westport, Conn.: Greenwood Publishing Corp.

Orthotherapy. Linde, S.M. (with Arthur Michele). 1971. New York: M. Evans Co.

Our Business in the Streets. Eckels, J. (Askia Akhnaton). 1971. Detroit: Broadside Press.

Out Jumped Abraham. Phillips, B.A.McK. 1967. New York: McGraw-Hill & Co.

The Outnumbered. Brooks, C.K. 1969. New York: Dell Press.

Pan-Africanism Reconsidered. Allen, S., co-ed. 1962. Berkeley, Calif.: University of California Press.

A Panther Is a Black Cat. Major, R. 1972. New York: William Morrow.

Paper Soul. Rodgers, C.M. 1968. Chicago: Third World Press.

Passing By. Stewart, P.E. 1970. Porter Stewart Publishers.

Pathways to the Houston Negro Market. Bullock, H.A. 1957. Ann Arbor, Mich.: J.W. Edwards.

Paul Robeson, Citizen of the World. Graham, S.L. 1946. New York: Julian Messner.

Pearl's Kitchen. Bailey, P.M. 1973. New York: Harcourt Brace Jovanovich.

The People One Knows. Boles, R. 1964. Boston: Houghton Mifflin.

Phenomena. Atkins, R. 1961. Wilberforce, Ohio: The Free Lance Poets and Prose Workship.

Picking up the Gun. Anthony, E. 1970. New York: Dial Press.

A Pictorial History of Black Soldiers in the U.S. in Peace and War. Johnson, J.J. 1970. Hampton, Va.

Pimp: Story of My Life. Beck, R. (Iceberg Slim). 1968. Los Angeles: Holloway House.

Pinktoes. Himes, C. 1967. New York: Dell Press.

Pioneers and Patriots: Six Negroes in the Revolutionary Era. Toppin, E.A. 1965. Garden City, N.Y.: Doubleday & Co.

Pioneers in Blues and Jazz. Webb, M.S. 1971. New York: Garrard Publishing Co.

Pioneers in Protest. Bennett, L. 1968. Chicago: Johnson Publishing Co.

Pisstained Stairs and the Monkey Man's Wares. Cortez, J. 1969. New York: Phrase Text.

The Pitiful and the Proud. Rowan, C.T. 1956. New York: Random House.

Poem Counterpoint. Randall, D.F. (with Margaret Danner). 1966. Detroit: Broadside Press.

cation, Department of Health, Education and Welfare.

Psychology of the Child in the Middle Class. Davis, A. 1960. Pittsburgh: University of Pittsburgh Press.

Psychovisualism. Atkins, R. 1956-1958. Cleveland, Ohio: Free Lance Press.

Quality of Hurt. Himes, C. 1972. Garden City, N.Y.: Doubleday & Co.

Quest for a Black Theology. Roberts, J.D., Sr., ed. (with James J. Gardner). 1971. Philadelphia: United Church Press.

Race Results, U.S.A. Fabio, S.W. 1966. Detroit: Broadside Press.

Racial Crisis in American Education. Green, R.L. 1969. Chicago: Follett Publishing Co.

Racism and Human Survival: The Lessons of Nazi Germany. Lightfoot, C.M. 1972. New York: International Publishers Co.

Racism and Mental Health. Willie, C.V. 1973. Pittsburgh: University of Pittsburgh Press.

Racism and the Class Struggle: Further Pages from a Black Worker's Notebook. Boggs, J. 1970. New York: Monthly Review Press.

Radioactivity in Man. Linde, S.M., ed. 1961. Springfield, Ill.: Charles C. Thomas Publishing Co.

Raindrops and Pebbles. Jones, R.L.L. 1957.

A Rap on Race. Baldwin, J. (with Margaret Mead). 1971. Philadelphia: J.B. Lippincott.

The Raw Pearl. Bailey, P.M. 1968. New York: Harcourt Brace and World.

Readings from Negro Authors, for Schools and Colleges. Cromwell, O., ed. (with Lorenzo Dow Turner & Eva B. Dykes). 1931. New York: Harcourt Brace and World.

Ready to Riot. Wright, N., Jr. 1968. New York: Holt, Rinehart & Winston.

Realities vs. Spirits. Johnson, A.L. (privately published).

Rebellion in Rhyme. Clarke, J.H. 1948. Prairie City, Ill.: Dicker Press.

Rebellion or Revolution. Cruse, H.W. 1968. New York: William Morrow.

Reconstruction after the Civil War. Franklin. J.H. 1961. Chicago: University of Chicago Press.

Recordings for Children. Baker, A., ed. 1964. New York: New York Library Assn.

Re:Creation. Giovanni, N. 1970. Detroit: Broadside Press.

Reference Library of Black America. Kaiser, E., ed. 1971. New York: The Bellwether Co.

Regroup. Danner, M., ed. 1969. Richmond, Va.: Virginia Union University.

Relationships Between Achievement in High School, College and Occupation: A Follow-up Study. Davis, A. 1963. Washington, D.C.: U.S. Office of Education.

A Relevant War Against Poverty. Clark, K.B. (with

Jeannette Hopkins). 1968. New York: Harper & Row.

The Republican Crisis: Race and Politics in America. Holden, M. 1970. San Francisco: Chandler Publishing Co.

Response of the Nervous System to Ionizing Radiation. Linde, S.M., ed. 1962. New York: Academic Press.

Restoration of Judah. Bryant, L.A. 1961. Crown Bryant Publishing Co.

Resurrection. Bryant, L.A. 1959. Crown Bryant Publishing Co.

Return to Black America. Smith, W.G. 1970. Englewood Cliffs, N.J.: Prentice-Hall.

Revolt of the Black Athlete. Edwards, H. 1970. New York: Free Press.

Revolutionary Notes. Lester, J. 1969. New York: Richard A. Baron.

Revolutionary Suicide. Newton, H. 1973. New York: Harcourt Brace Jovanovich.

Rhetoric of Black Revolution. Smith, A.L., Jr. 1970. Durham, N.C.: Moore Publishing Co.

Rhetoric of Revolution. Smith, A.L., Jr. 1969. Boston: Allyn & Bacon.

The Riddle of Snoring. Boulware, M.H. 1969. Mokelume Hill, Calif.: Health Research.

Riot. Brooks, G. 1969. Detroit: Broadside Press.

The Rise and Fall of a Proper Negro. Lacy, L.A. 1970. New York: Macmillan Co.

The Rise of Religious Education Among Negro Baptists. Tyms, J.D. 1965. Jericho, N.Y.: Exposition Press.

A River Divided. Odell, A.C. 1963. New York: Vantage Press.

River of Bones and Flesh and Blood. Redmond, E. 1972. East St. Louis, Ill.: Black River Press.

The River of Eros. Colter, C. 1972. Chicago: Swallow Press.

The Rocks Cry Out. Murphy, B. (with Nancy Arnez). 1969. Detroit: Broadside Press.

Role of Expectation of Blindness in an Oaxaca Village. Gwaitney, J.L. 1970. New York: Columbia University Press.

Room for Randy. Jackson, J. 1957. New York: Friendship Press.

St. Nigger. Cannon, C.E. 1972. Detroit: Broadside Press.

Sambos and Rebels: The Character of the Southern Slave. Blassingame, J.W. 1972. Washington, D.C.: Howard University Press.

Sammy's Baby. Mathis, S.B. 1970. New York: Hill & Wang.

Samuel Gompers. Mandel, B. 1963. Kent, Ohio: Kent State University Press.

Sati: The Rastifarian. White, E. 1973. New York: Lothrop, Lee & Shepherd.

The Scene. Cooper, C. 1960. New York: Crown Publishers.

The School in the Social Order: A Sociological Introduction to Educational Understanding. Bullock, H.A. (with Francesco Cordasco and

Solitudes Crowded with Loneliness. Kaufman, B.G. 1965. New York: New Directions.

Some Changes. Jordan, J. 1970. New York: Richard W. Baron.

Some Gold, A Little Ivory. Haskett, E.R. 1971. New York: John Day Co.

Some Things That Glitter (City Limits Series). Halliburton, W.J. 1969. New York: McGraw-Hill.

Somebody's Angel Child: The Story of Bessie Smith. Moore, C.L. 1970. New York: Thomas Y. Crowell.

Song for Nia. Long, D. 1971. Detroit: Broadside Press.

The Song Turning Back into Itself. Young, A. 1971. New York: Holt, Rinehart & Winston.

Songs of a Blackbird. Rogers, C.M. 1970. Chicago: Third World Press.

The Songs of our Years. Jackson, C.O. 1968. Jericho, N.Y.: Exposition Press.

Songs to a Phantom Nightingale. Madgett, N.L. 1941. New York: Fortuny's Publishers.

Sonny Liston: The Champ Nobody Wanted. Young, A.S.N. 1963. Chicago: Johnson Publishing Co.

Sons of Darkness, Sons of Light. Williams, J.A. 1969. Boston: Little Brown & Co.

The Soul Brothers and Sister Lou. Hunter, K. 1968. New York: Charles Scribner's Sons.

Soul Clap Hands and Sing. Marshall, P. 1961. New York: Atheneum Publishers.

Soul in Solitude. Lyons, W.T. 1970. Jericho, N.Y.: Exposition Press.

The Soul of Christmas. King, H.H. 1972. Chicago: Johnson Publications.

Soul on Ice. Cleaver, E. 1968. New York: McGraw-Hill.

Soulscript. Jordan, J. 1970. Garden City, N.Y.: Doubleday & Co.

The Sound of Soul. Garland, P.T. 1969. Chicago: H. Regnery Co.

Sounds of the Struggle. Lincoln, C.E. 1967. New York: William Morrow.

Source Readings in Black American Music (in process). Southern, E.J. 1971. New York: W.W. Norton & Co.

South of Freedom. Rowan, C.T. 1953. New York: Alfred Knopf.

South Street. Smith, W.G. 1954. New York: Farrar, Straus and Young.

South to a Very Old Place. Murray, A. 1972. New York: McGraw-Hill.

Southern Road. Brown, S. 1932. New York: Harcourt Brace & Co.

Southtown. Graham, L. 1958. Chicago: Follett Publishing Co.

Sparks from the Anvil. Cleveland, E.E. 1971. Washington, D.C.: Review and Herald Publishing Association.

Speak Now. Yerby, F. 1969. New York: Dial Press.

Spin a Soft Black Song: Poems for Children. Giovanni, N. 1971. New York: Hill & Wang.

The Spook Who Sat by the Door. Greenlee, S. 1969. London: Allison & Bushy Ltd.

The Squared Circle. Killebrow, C. n.d. Detroit: Broadside Press.

S.R.O. Pharr, R.D. 1971.
Garden City, N.Y.: Doubleday & Co.

Star by Star. Madgett, N.L.
1965. Detroit: Harlo Press.

Stevie. Steptoe, J.L. 1969.
New York: Harper & Row.

The Stone Face. Smith, W.G.
1963. New York: Farrar,
Straus.

The Story of Phyllis Wheatley.
Graham, S.L. 1949. New
York: Julian Messner.

The Story of Pocahantas.
Graham, S.L. 1954. New
York: Grosset & Dunlap.

Stranger and Alone. Redding,
J.S. 1950. New York: Har-
court Brace.

The Street. Petry, A. 1946.
Boston: Houghton Mifflin.

A Street in Bronzeville.
Brooks, G. 1945. New
York: Harper & Row.

A Struggle in Black and White.
Thibodeaux, M.R. 1972.
New York: Sheed & Ward.

Studies in Black and White.
Pinson, I.D. 1966. New
York: Vantage Press.

Studies on the History of
Islam in West Africa. Vol.
I. The Cultivators of Islam.
Willis, J.R., ed. (in press).
London: Frank Cass & Co.,
Ltd.

The Study of Race Among Na-
tions. Le Melle, T.J. 1970.
Lexington, Mass.: Heath
Lexington.

Sugarfields. Mahone, B. 1970.
Detroit: Broadside Press.

Suggestions for Instructors to
Accompany Contexts for
Composition. Royster, P.M.
1969. New York: Appleton-
Century Crofts.

A Survey of Texas Southern
University Library. Josey,
E.J. 1967. Houston, Tex.

Swallow the Lake. Major, C.
1970. Middletown, Conn.:
Wesleyan University Press.

System of Dante's Hell.
Baraka, I.A. (Le Roi Jones).
1965. New York: Grove
Press.

A Systems Approach to De-
veloping Behavioral Objec-
tives. Lewis, J. 1970.
Wyandanch, N.Y.

Tales and Short Stories for
Black Folks. Bambara,
T.C. 1971. Garden City,
N.Y.: Zenith.

Tales from Harlem. Clarke,
J.H., ed. 1970. New York:
New American Library.

Talking to Myself. Bailey,
P.M. 1971. New York:
Harcourt Brace Jovanovich.

The Talking Tree. Baker, A.
1955. Philadelphia: J.B.
Lippincott Co.

T.C. Terry Callier, True
Christian. Bradford, W.
n.d. Detroit: Broadside
Press.

Teachers Manual for Your
Life in a Big City. Baxter,
Z.L. 1967. New York:
McGraw-Hill.

Teaching Art in the Elementary
School, K-6 Grade. Brown,
V.S. (in process).

The Teaching of Literature by
Afro-Americans, Theory
and Practice. Turner, D.T.
(in press).

Teaching the Language Arts in
the Elementary School.
Murray, W.I. (with Crow
and Bloom). 1968. Dubuque,
Iowa: William C. Brown &
Co.

Teacup Full of Roses. Mathis,
S.B. 1972. New York:
Viking Press.

Timo the Draftsman. Hamer, M.J. 1968. New York: Mc-Graw-Hill.

Tituba of Salem Village. Petry, A. 1964. New York: Thomas Y. Crowell.

To Be a Slave. Lester, J. 1968. New York: Dial Press.

Today's Negro Voices. Murphy, B., ed. 1970. New York: Julian Messner.

To Die for the People. Newton, H. 1972. New York: Random House.

To Find an Image. Murray, J.P. 1973. New York: Bobbs-Merrill.

To Flower: Poems. Danner, M. 1963. Nashville, Tenn.: Hemphill Press.

"Together" Black Women. Reid, I.S. 1972. New York: Emerson Hall.

To Gwen With Love: A Tribute to Gwendolyn Brooks. Brown, P.L., ed. (et al). 1971. Chicago: Johnson Publishing Co.

To Make a Black Poet. Redding, J.S. 1942. Chapel Hill, N.C.: University of North Carolina Press.

Tomorrow's Tomorrow: The Black Woman. Ladner, J.A. 1971. Garden City, N.Y.: Doubleday & Co.

To Reach a Dream. Heard, N.C. 1970. New York: Dial Press.

Total Rehabilitation of Epileptics. Linde, S.M. 1962. Washington, D.C.: U.S. Government Printing Office.

A Touch of Innocence. Dunham, K. 1959. New York: Harcourt, Brace & Co.

The Towers of Toron. Delany, S.R. 1964. New York: Ace Books.

Track and Field for Girls and Women. Jackson, N.C. 1968. Minneapolis, Minn.: Burgess Publishing Co.

Track and Field for Women. Thompson, D.H. 1969. Boston: Allyn and Bacon.

The Tragedies in American Education. Lewis, J. 1970. Jericho, N.Y.: Exposition Press.

Train Ride. Steptoe, J.L. 1971. New York: Harper & Row.

Treasures of Life. Jones, R.L.L. 1945. Riesel, Tex.: Riesel Rustker.

The Treehouse and Other Poems. Emanuel, J.A. 1968. Detroit: Broadside Press.

Trial of God. Anderson, O. 1970. Jericho, N.Y.: Exposition Press.

Trick Baby. Beck, R. (Iceberg Slim). 1971. Los Angeles: Holloway House.

Trouble with Being a Mama. Rutland, E. Nashville: Abingdon Press.

Twentieth Century Interpretations of Native Son. Baker, H.A., Jr. 1972. Englewood Cliffs, N.J.: Prentice-Hall.

Twenty-six Ways of Looking at a Black Man and Other Poems. Patterson, R.R. 1969. New York: Award Books.

Two Black Poems. Johnson, A.L. (pamphlet).

Two Love Stories. Lester, J. 1972. New York: Dial Press.

Two Plays. Ward, D.T. 1972. New York: Third Press.

Unbought and Unbossed. Chisholm, S.A. 1970. Boston: Houghton Mifflin.

The Welfare Bitch. Pharr, R.D. 1973. Garden City, N.Y.: Doubleday & Co.

West Africa Vignettes. Fax, E.C. 1963. New York: American Society of African Culture.

What Black Educators Are Saying. Wright, N., Jr., ed. 1970. New York: Hawthorne Publishing Co.

What Black Librarians Are Saying. Josey, E.J. 1972. Metuchen, N.J.: Scarecrow Press.

What Black Politicians Are Saying. Wright, N., Jr., ed. 1972. New York: Hawthorne Books.

What Manner of Man. Bennett, L. 1964. Chicago: Johnson Publishing Co.

What Shall I Tell My Children, Who Are Black. Burroughs, M.T.G. 1970. Chicago: Follett Publishing Co.

What's Happening. Gregory, D. 1965. New York: E.P. Dutton & Co.

What We Must See: Young Black Storytellers, an Anthology. Coombs, O., ed. 1971. New York: Dodd, Mead & Co.

When Thy King Is a Boy. Roberson, E. 1970. Pittsburgh: University of Pittsburgh Press.

Where Continents Meet. Lambie, N. 1971. New York: John Day & Co.

Where Does the Day Go? Myers, W.D. 1969. New York: Parents Magazine Press.

Where the Hummingbird Flies. Hercules, F. 1961. New York: Harcourt, Brace & World.

Whip Me Whop Me Pudding. Burroughs, M.T.G. 1966. Chicago: Praga Press.

White-Collar Blacks, A Breakthrough. Van Dyke, R.L. (with John S. Morgan). 1970. American Management.

White Cross, Black Crucifixion. Wiggins, J. 1970. Jericho, N.Y.: Exposition Press.

White on Black. Thompson, E.B., ed. 1963. Chicago: Johnson Publishing Co.

White Papers for White Americans. Hernton, C.C. 1967. Garden City, N.Y.: Doubleday & Co.

Who Cares. Brown, V.S. 1965. New York: McGraw-Hill.

Who Cares. Phillips, B.A.McK. 1965. New York: McGraw-Hill.

Who Is Angelina? Young, A. (in process).

Who Look at Me. Jordan, J. 1969. New York: Thomas Y. Crowell.

Whose Town? Graham, L. 1965. New York: Thomas Y. Crowell.

Why Baltimore Failed to Elect a Black Mayor in 1971. Fleming, G.J. 1972. Washington, D.C.: Joint Center for Political Studies.

Why Blacks Kill Blacks. Poussiant, A.F. 1972. New York: Emerson Hall.

A Wife's Guide to Baseball. Gibson, C. 1970. New York: Viking Press.

The Wig, a Mirror Image. Wright, C. 1966. New York: Farrar, Straus & Giroux.

A Wilderness of Vines. Bennett, H. 1966. Garden City, N.Y.: Doubleday & Co.